Baseball's New Frontier

Baseball's New Frontier

A History of Expansion, 1961–1998

Fran Zimniuch

Foreword by Branch Rickey III

University of Nebraska Press | Lincoln and London

Library of Congress Cataloging-in-Publication Data
Zimniuch, Fran.
Baseball's new frontier: a history of expansion,
1961–1998 / Fran Zimniuch; foreword by Branch Rickey III.
p. cm.
Includes bibliographical references.
ISBN 978-0-8032-3994-4 (pbk.: alk. paper) 1. Baseball—
United States—History—20th century. 2. Major League Baseball
(Organization)—History—20th century. I. Title.
GV863.A1Z56 2013
796.357'64097309045—dc23   2012045110

Set in Adobe Garamond Pro by Laura Wellington.
Designed by Jesse Vadnais.

*This is for the true visionaries of the game,
who look and have looked with no limits.*

It is also for my sons, Brent and Kyle.

Contents

Foreword

The phrase "The Game of Baseball" has been a companion of mine since my birth. Over the years, as others have used it to reference some grander institution, it was never that for me. Rather, it always seemed more like referring to one's neighborhood, or discussing cousins in an extended family. Over the years I have seen that phrase mean different things. Television commentators and newspaper writers making critical reference can analyze it as a depersonalized thing, almost a monolithic institution. And in contrast, some people use the phrase with great deference, as if they were speaking of a revered cathedral.

Thankfully, for so many of us it instead conjures up a mental picture of the players, kids or professionals, out on the field of play, an elegant image with artistic and geometrical symmetries and embedded nostalgia to so many of our own previous experiences at the ballpark. What allure, what emotional associations this wonderful game truly has. The Game of Baseball, our wonderful sport.

Not quite so heartwarming is the more modified phrase "The Expansion of Major League Baseball," which is, for so many fans, as easily inelegant in symmetry and happily clouded in our memories. I think it true that the very adjective "expansion" when it precedes the word "team" immediately drags down the intrinsic value of the latter—whether by definition, or in the practical overview of most loyalists to the sport. Anyone who seriously delves into this topic of Major League Baseball expansion has the unquestionable advantage of access nowadays to an infinite reservoir of historical opinions, evaluations, press assessments, and scurrilous diatribes. How so, then, that I come to this topic with a relaxed sense of connection, and that I welcome the opportunity to give some preface to Fran Zimniuch's ample elaborations?

Expansion is a concept that in and of itself is filled with such boundless potential for doing good. In my earliest years as an amateur player, in the 1950s, with a fascination for all things interwoven in the play of the game, I was originally introduced to the concept by my grandfather. His was an inflexible belief in America's right to have Major League Baseball played beyond the existing sixteen teams, to include new franchises across and throughout our great nation. That the two existing Major Leagues back then, of eight teams each—that stretched only from the Atlantic to the Mississippi River and from our northern boundaries to no further south than the southern tip of Illinois—must be immediately broadened, was a position he ingrained in me and a topic that only needed the slightest common sense discussion to be firmly validated. From years before expansion eventually was implemented, I couldn't imagine anyone unable to accept the logic of it.

Of course, my grandfather throughout his long career in the sport, first as a player, then as a field manager, and a general manager in St. Louis, later as president and part owner of the Brooklyn Dodgers, and lastly as general manager of the Pittsburgh Pirates, had already enjoyed playing a role in changing the National Pastime in quite a number of fundamental ways. Signing Jackie Robinson to end the practice of excluding of African Americans will long linger as his most lauded impact, but there were so many others, including a huge structural influence in the formation of what has become known as the farm system, where each Major League team has a development program of graduated levels of affiliated Minor League teams.

I suspect my grandfather's own limitations as a player probably helped motivate him in his future roles. And his refusal to go into a ballpark on Sunday, honoring an early promise to his parents, provoked him, surely, into a legitimate sense of individuality. Combined with the fact he had also begun his career backed by a college degree when those credentials were scarce among Major League players and then supplementing his credentials with a law degree, these were forces that must have caused him to view his profession through somewhat distinctive lenses. He learned, early in life, to be unafraid of innovation, and, as I saw clearly as his grandson when I came to know him better, he had reached a point of being patient, if not generally tolerant of persons unwilling to accept clear reasoning, those too timid to be creative and too willing to be self-deceiving. But while he generally showed patience with such perspectives in public, I saw occasions he would privately unleash his intellectual contempt for that genre of baseball professionals who instinctively opposed many forms of progress, especially obvious and needed changes that could bring short-term and long-term benefits.

A slogan coined by Scottish philosopher Sir William Drummond, hand-lettered in oversized calligraphy and bordered by a handsome gold-leaf and painted floral trim, framed and behind glass, hung conspicuously on my grandfather's office wall. It read, "He that will not reason is a bigot, he that cannot reason is a fool and he that dares not reason is a slave." Knowing him throughout my youthful years, while living across a farm pasture from his house, I'd watch him mesmerize family, friends, and others at suppers, with perhaps eight, ten, or a dozen persons at a meal. Over that time, I never remember him to have referred to this slogan. He didn't need to. Its presence on his office wall spoke volumes to his inner commitments.

Having now strayed from my mission, let me get back on track. I said above that the word "expansion" drags down both the intrinsic and public value of the word "team," and I mean that specifically, and say it here, to provoke the reader into an appreciation of how flawed the implementation was of this stage in the history of baseball.

If, as historians now seem to insist, the effort to found a new third Major League, the Continental League, immediately forced expansion in order for the existing teams to protect the exclusivity of the National and American Leagues, then let's take a look at what was conceived in the heart of the radical effort that got blocked.

Quite simply, the Continental League would have added new teams across the United States, broadened the sixteen existing by adding another eight. Today, when there are thirty teams in Major League Baseball, it's hard to imagine that an increase from sixteen cities to twenty-four in three leagues was fought so furiously. The Continental League had no plan to compete against its sister leagues initially. The new eight clubs could have played independently and with very predictable parity in their level of play. Only after years and years of maturation of its own teams, its own development systems, its own scouting staffs, was it conceived that the Continental League would become a worthy rival to its more senior competitors. Only when the new league demonstrated that it had advanced adequately would these new teams make sense as competitors to the league's senior partners. This was the vision I learned as a grandson. It seemed such a desirable path, one that could be widely accepted if one was not enslaved to another concept.

As president of that envisioned new circuit, my grandfather quietly predicted to me that baseball would, of course, oppose the Continental League, that it would instead propose expanding its own ranks with expansion teams. That kind of "expansion" would line the existing teams' pockets with expansion monies but, as so many new team owners and so many new member cities learned afterward so harshly, would then deprive those new teams from receiving back in exchange real quality players and would doom these new teams to starting up with no reserves to draw from established Minor League development programs, and that all these steps would cause "expansion teams" to be cellar dwellers for long periods. More callous yet was that it would sentence the wonderful new fans in these markets to a long cycle of despair waiting for their local favorites to be really competitive for championship levels of success.

I was a youngster when hearing his forecast. He had the benefit of knowing the characters and reasoning capacities of the persons in charge, those who would be able to parade out star players and field managers for a cause célèbre and provoke Congress to legislate its bidding. Some of those were intent on making an industry out of the Game of Baseball, using ballparks to become their venues. Their general sense of treating their new expansion partners with any fairness regarding the play on the field was seemingly lacking. The incumbents dared not reason.

Years afterward, several Major League general managers and even a pair of team owners, as I came across them in random situations, lamented to me that they had fought the Continental League. "You know," they said in words that all approximately paralleled the following, "your grandfather had it right. How I wish we had not chosen that other option. The way we went about expansion was a terrible mistake."

I think the Game of Baseball has learned from this stage of its history and that there are many more forces inside the establishment endeavoring to protect and nurture the game rather than only exploit the business. It's a delicate balance, but what a wonderful challenge, indeed, a magnificent challenge—especially for those who can reason as to why they should care, must care.

Branch Rickey III

Acknowledgments

Writing a book is a lot like falling in love. The idea is like that first look that ignites a spark that makes it difficult to think about anything else. While going about a typical day, your mind continues to return to this new object of your affection. With every thought the possibilities become endless.

Any book idea is exciting and scary. Can I do this? Will I be able to sell the concept to publishing company that will share my commitment to the idea? But despite the questions and the doubt, you know deep down that the concept will fly. Someone will share at least enough of your excitement to help you make it happen. This will be the one book that will give you all of the satisfaction you yearn for but just can't quite achieve. It will finally include that perfect phrase or the one word you spend hours reaching balance, and that elusive connection to the subject matter that reflects your thoughts and feelings will be made. This is the book that will make you feel more complete and finally accomplished.

Yeah sure . . . then reality sets in.

An agreement with a publishing company is like winning the lottery. But writing the book can be a grind, needing the discipline to dedicate the time necessary to complete the task while still maintaining the excitement and vision that first struck you like a bolt of lightning. Research, writing, interviews and staying the course represents a strong jolt of reality.

By far the most creative part of any book project is coming up with a concept that you can convince a publishing company to partner with you. Like anyone else who has ever written a book will tell you, ideas are plentiful. But it's the ability to get someone else on board with the project that makes it tough. And thanks to significant changes in the book publishing industry, you often find yourself shooting at a moving target.

The publishing industry has changed over the past decade thanks in large part to the economic uncertainty in our society. Folks just aren't flocking to the bookstores the way they did in the past. That has a dramatic effect on publishing companies that trickles down to authors, who have a much more difficult time selling their ideas. Anybody can self-publish, but that's not *being* published.

Countless companies now have to adjust the offerings they bring to the market because of that increasingly difficult bottom line. When people don't have the money or even the time to read as much as they'd like to, stirring an interest in them is an elusive challenge. While thought-provoking concepts and books with interesting historical analyses can still be found, books dealing with big-name celebrities are a much easier sale. People love to learn about the famous few in our society. Big names sell. But not all of us are interested in reading about celebs, and very few of us are interested in researching and writing about them. Plus, the rich need to get richer so the financial reward of writing such a book goes to them. So our jobs just got tougher.

That being said, I thank my lucky stars for the kind, professional, supportive, and incredibly intelligent people at the University of Nebraska Press for the willingness to partner with me on *Baseball's*

New Frontier: A History of Expansion, 1961–1998. Rob Taylor was my point man, and he was the perfect person to deal with. Rob was like a good neighbor: there when you need him but never interfering or micromanaging. Much like that new relationship that endures some rough spots, writing a book can be a rocky and winding road that ends up taking you to places you didn't think you'd be visiting. Rob was always there with advice and confidence. And he also realized that much like speed limits on the interstate, deadlines are a good starting point. Thanks for your confidence, Rob. You made writing fun.

If you like baseball and have an interest in how the game got to where it is now, you may very well enjoy reading about expansion in baseball. If you're not into America's Game, you will more than likely have the opinion that "Man, this guy needs to get a life." But much as baseball makes life a little more fun for millions of us, expansion made that personal connection with the game available to millions of other fans. It also opened the door for thousands of players. Has the talent pool been thinned out by the process, or has expansion caused more youngsters to put their athletic attention into baseball? That's a debate that may never end.

From its roots in calming potential legal issues with baseball's antitrust exemption thanks to franchise shifts; to a true champion of the game on so many fronts, Branch Rickey; to his partner in the Continental League, William Shea; and finally, to the outpouring of millions of fans who wanted their own big league team, expansion was an inevitable force that was not about to be stopped or delayed any longer. Expansion is sort of like death and taxes, just a whole lot more enjoyable, except for the Seattle Pilots, of course.

But once you get the book deal you are looking for, the whole project can take over much of your life. You become infatuated with the idea. And as your work and dedication to the book grow, you begin to not only see the limitless possibilities, but also those familiar imperfections. While you love the research and the interviews and the prospective that has never really been put in such a manner, the roadblocks, the writer's blocks and finding that elusive perfect phrase can drive you nuts. That's where family and friends come into play, as you spend nearly all of your free time breathing life into your book.

My two sons, Brent and Kyle, always cut me some slack when I'm involved with a book. It affects their lives, but they realize and understand how important it is to me. You'd be surprised how many times they help me out with one of those words or phrases that I lose even more hair over. I'm also one of those people who believes that our animals are family members too. While at the end game of this manuscript, our family lost perhaps its nicest member, our dog Allie. She had graced us with her love and attention for seven years and we all miss her terribly.

I have a great support group of friends who are willing to listen to my countless array of new ideas that are no doubt going to put me on the best-seller list. My friends Lou and Marcia Chimenti always listen and give their support, as well as getting me out and about. John Warren has read over my book proposals with meticulous care and always takes an interest, offering his gut reaction based on decades of sports and life knowledge. And there are countless former colleagues, such as Christina Mitchell and Carole Fleck, who also offer their support and understanding.

My favorite place in the world is the beach. That's where my world works best. And it works perfectly there. Whether I'm searching for a book idea or in the midst of self-doubt over whether or not I can really pull a project off, one of the best things I can do is to bounce ideas off some good friends at DiOrios in Somers Point, New Jersey. Owner Denny DiOrio is a lifelong sports fan who is more than willing to talk and offer suggestions. And in addition to making the best Bloody Mary in the Garden State, Jim Driscoll has a great feel for sports in general and baseball in particular. Without these guys, my ideas would be much more limited. Although, I must admit that as hard as I tried, it was tough to work through Jim's latest book idea for me, "Babes, Booze, and Baseball." Maybe next time.

Another good buddy, Peter Coolbaugh, a baseball aficionado in the truest sense, helped with many aspects of the project, such as the title. He has been a true supporter and a good friend who is never too busy to offer suggestions and ideas. I only wish I didn't embarrass Peter and myself by my second-division finishes in his fantasy baseball league.

While I'm anything but starstruck, picking the brains of other authors, baseball executives, former players, and historians is just plain fun. Peter Golenbock, Dick Beverage, Bob McGee, Professor John Rossi, Tal Smith, Bill Giles, Hall of Famer Pat Gillick, Eli Grba, Steve Arlin, Bob Bruce, Carl Erskine, Jay Hook, Larry Colton, Dean Chance, Bill Stoneman, and others shared their knowledge and experience to give credibility to the effort. I can't say enough about Branch Rickey III, who shared his heartfelt feelings about the game of baseball, expansion, and his grandfather, Branch Rickey, who I consider the greatest innovator and the most influential person in the history of America's Game. Branch III's good friend Justice George Nicholson, Court of Appeals, Third Appellate District, State of California, who has a lifelong passion for baseball, was a great source of information and encouragement for me as well.

Two of the most enjoyable parts of my life are baseball and writing. Having the opportunity to write about baseball and put my words out there for public consumption and yes, even criticism, is a satisfying, interesting and very enjoyable process. Well, not so much the criticism part of the equation. How dare you not like my new love interest!

Here's to hoping that you enjoy *Baseball's New Frontier*. If you find it interesting and entertaining and learn something new about a phenomenon that began a generation ago, then I've succeeded and completed my task. And if it leaves you underwhelmed, at least know that it was an effort filled with a love of the game and a thirst for more knowledge about it.

Enjoy!

Baseball's New Frontier

Introduction

For just about a hundred years, the baseball universe was centered right near the border of Pennsylvania and Ohio. The eight National League teams and eight American League teams were located in and around the mid-Atlantic states, going only as far west as Chicago and St. Louis.

At the turn of the last century, it took nearly a day to travel from New York to those "far west" destinations via the railways. In those days, when baseball teams traveled, they did so almost exclusively by train and sometimes by bus. A travel day was just that, a day of travel. In today's game, for the most part, a travel day is basically a day off. While these long train sojourns served as a way for teammates to develop friendships and bond as a team, this kind of travel was certainly no walk in the park.

The first team to fly to another city was the Cincinnati Reds, who flew to Chicago on June 8, 1934, but it wasn't until the 1950s that air travel happened on a more regular basis. This certainly made travel between baseball venues an easier endeavor, making further western expansion a viable option. Baseball moved slowly in many areas, including travel, integration, and basic individual rights for its employees. America's Pastime has always seemed to lag behind the curve. But then it always seems to make up for lost time.

As the game progressed into the post–World War II era, American society was changing in many ways. Following the Second World War and the bloody Korean "conflict," the economies of the Western World boomed, leading to a consumer-led economy that appeared to have no bounds. In 1950 the average income in the United States was $3,210 per year. By 1959 it had jumped to $5,010, an increase of 64 percent. People were buying homes and the affordability of automatic transmissions in 1950 helped fuel an increase in automobile sales. While 60 percent of American families owned a car in 1950, a decade later that figure had risen to 77 percent.

The living habits of many were also changing. As more and more people purchased automobiles, there was an exodus from the cities to the suburbs. This suburbanization of society was associated with increased city crime rates and congestion, as well as pollution. For most, the American Dream now consisted of a home in the suburbs and a driving commute to work.

This car-centric society no doubt influenced the changing landscapes in major cities. While the population became stagnant in many big cities, such was not the case in Los Angeles. The tenth largest city in the country in the 1920s, LA was one of the few cities to enjoy continued growth. With a population of nearly 2 million by the end of the 1950s, the City of Angels trailed only New York, Chicago, and Philadelphia in population. Eight of the ten largest American cities in 1950 neither maintained nor increased the population of that year. The only exceptions were New York and Los Angeles.

There was an exodus to California, and there was also an exodus from the major cities across the country. In previous years it was easy to walk to the baseball park to see a game, or perhaps catch a bus or hop on a local train. But now people flocked to the suburbs and most owned cars. This suburban shift enabled teams to relocate and build stadiums out of the typical downtown areas, to the outskirts of a city where land was cheaper, parking was safer, and to a large degree, zoning laws were not as stringent.

Change was on the horizon and it would not be stopped. In 1955 the average distance between Major League ballparks was 469 miles. As a comparison, that average distance in 2005 was 1,155 miles. While today's game has spread out geographically, the 1950s saw a number of changes in the cities that sported big league teams. That comfortable, parochial feel of the game was gradually giving way to a more national presence. The exodus to the suburbs as well as some changing lifestyle choices saw long-time baseball teams in financial trouble with sagging attendance.

When the American League came into being in 1901, franchises were awarded to cities that already had National League teams, such as New York, Chicago, Boston, and Philadelphia, putting the teams in direct competition for audiences. Other franchises were awarded in cities that were part of the contraction of 1899, in which Cleveland and Washington DC lost their franchises. The United States and baseball were both changing with difficult decisions being made.

After suffering through difficult times on the field and at the gate, with the Red Sox gaining more popularity, the Boston Braves left Beantown in 1953 and became the Milwaukee Braves, in the home of what was their top farm team, the Brewers. A year later, the St. Louis Browns, not as successful as the National League Cardinals, moved to Baltimore to become the Orioles. And in 1955 the Philadelphia Athletics moved to Kansas City, becoming the westernmost city in Major League Baseball. Clearly, as time moved through the 1950s, baseball became increasingly open to the concept of shifting franchises and moving to the west.

If it ain't broke, don't fix it. But baseball attendance was on the wane. At the end of the Great Depression, baseball enjoyed a spike in attendance, and the same was the case in the era immediately after World War II, more than doubling the per-game average of the war years. But in the 1950s, the number of fans attending games began to drop. The average per-game attendance from 1946 to 1949 was 16,027. But in the following decade, attendance fell to an average of 13,366. In fact, even through the 1960s, the per-game average, at 14,047 for each game, was still below that of the late 1940s. It was not until 1978 that the per-game average surpassed that of the immediate postwar years.

Competition for the ever-increasing personal discretionary income moved forward. While baseball had its own internal struggles and issues, the successful growth of the National Football League and the upstart American Football League proved to be a guiding light for America's Pastime. The NFL, which was formed in 1933, enjoyed steady growth and a rapid increase in popularity. As early as 1946, football saw the value in a franchise on the West Coast when the Cleveland Rams moved to Los Angeles. Four years later, in 1950, the NFL expanded to San Francisco and embraced the 49ers. And when the AFL debuted in 1960, it included such teams as the Dallas Texans, Denver Broncos, Houston Oilers, Buffalo Bills, Los Angeles Chargers, and the Oakland Raiders.

To a large degree the NFL and AFL were true trailblazers in American sport, having the vision and the determination to take the game of football all across the country. While there was a comfort zone because of the loyal support that college football had garnered in all regions of the United States, there was no guarantee that such support would be enjoyed for the pro game.

But it was enjoyed and supported. Baseball had long-range aspirations to add more teams, but despite some concerns over attendance, the popularity of the game was undeniable.

The postwar era in America was a time of conformity, prosperity, and peace. People liked Ike and there was a genuine feeling of well-being in the country. People had more spending money and it was spent on homes, cars, television sets and numerous household appliances. But much like in baseball, there were some cracks in the pretty picture and a dangerous undertow lurking.

Led by Wisconsin senator Joseph McCarthy, thousands of Americans were accused of being communist sympathizers, or being actual communists, often with little regard for evidence. Individual liberties were at stake, and McCarthyism was one of the most polarizing elements of the era. Baseball was able to steer clear of this area, but it should be noted that from 1954 until 1959, the Cincinnati Reds officially changed the team name to the Cincinnati Redlegs, to avoid confusion and possible association with "reds," a moniker for communists.

At the same time, a number of social issues confronted America that were at some point mirrored by baseball. It took nearly a hundred years before Jackie Robinson broke the color barrier to become the first black professional player for the Brooklyn Dodgers in 1947. Racial discrimination and segregation became a lightning rod, eventually leading to demonstrations, violence, and calls for change. While Americans were able to enjoy various leisure activities as the use of television drastically increased, that venue for information and news also brought discrimination, violence, and the resulting demonstrations into every living room on a daily basis during the nightly news.

The skyline of America was gradually changing. As we will see time and again, societal changes would at some point be reflected in America's Game. One shifting domino would cause another to tumble.

Robinson's Brooklyn Dodgers had finally defeated the New York Yankees in the World Series in 1955. But the joy over that giant leap would soon be overcome by the harsh realities of the business side of baseball. The Dodgers needed a new stadium to replace Ebbets Field, which was increasingly in disarray and afforded only seven hundred parking spaces in a decaying area. The very things that drove residents out of the cities and into the suburbs were now keeping them from coming back to the city to enjoy baseball and threatening the health of a proud franchise. Dodgers owner Walter O'Malley wanted to keep his team in Brooklyn, but obtaining a site for a new ballpark would take several hundred acres. This was a difficult task in New York.

Buying the necessary land from individual landholders would have exceeded the team's financial means. At this stage, the only answer was either a gift of municipally owned land or the use of the city's power of eminent domain to obtain private property could make such a project even remotely feasible. At the same time the Dodgers hit a roadblock in New York, an attractive suitor presented an opportunity across the country in Los Angeles. That option appeared to be manna from heaven, since the city of New York would not gift land or use eminent domain to help the franchise develop a new stadium site.

"The city of New York refused to do either," wrote Benjamin G. Rader in his book *Baseball: A History of America's Game.*

> Even though the Dodgers promised to bear all the construction costs for a new stadium, Robert Moses, the powerful head of the city's public parks department, blocked O'Malley's efforts to acquire an ideal site at the Atlantic Avenue Railroad Terminal. Moses argued that the acquisition would erase $10 million from the city's tax rolls. Fortunately for Los Angeles, it already owned Chavez Ravine, a choice hilltop location overlooking the downtown area that the city had purchased for public housing.
>
> Seizing over a growing hostility in Southern California toward public housing and anxious to attract the Dodgers, city officials quickly decided that transferring the land to O'Malley for nominal considerations constituted a proper use of the land.

Walter O'Malley did not want to leave Brooklyn, at least not initially. In an effort to make his situation better, he commissioned Norman Bel Geddes to investigate renovating Ebbets Field. In addition, more than a decade before the birth of the Astrodome in Houston, O'Malley was quite serious about building a domed stadium in Brooklyn, which would have been designed by Buckminster Fuller.

The Dodgers were not the only team experiencing difficult times in New York. The Giants, too, were a suffering franchise. Their on-field exploits in the mid-1950s were unremarkable, and attendance dropped dramatically. In 1954, 1,115,067 fans flocked to see the Giants play. That mark shrunk to 824,112 the following year. The Polo Grounds had clearly seen better days, and the team's majority owner, Horace Stoneham, began to investigate moving the team. It was Stoneham's belief that playing night baseball in Harlem was not a successful recipe to attract fans from outside of the area.

Much like O'Malley, Stoneham investigated either renovating or replacing the Polo Grounds. In April of 1956, he expressed interest in a proposal made by Hulan Jack, the Manhattan Borough president. Jack floated an idea about building a triple-decker stadium on Manhattan's West Side, above the New York Central Railroad yards. The new stadium would also feature a subway station and parking for twenty thousand cars.

"As the Polo Grounds began to be viewed as an ancient, out-modeled relic, there was talk of a new ballpark for the Giants," wrote Peter Golenbock in his enjoyable book *Amazin': The Miraculous History of New York's Most Beloved Baseball Team.*

> On April 10, 1956, Stoneham announced he was "very interested" in a proposal made by Manhattan Borough President Hulan Jack for the construction of a new stadium on Manhattan's West Side. It was to be a triple-deckered arena seating 110,000 fans to be built above the tracks of the New York Central Railroad yards. There would be parking for twenty thousand cars and a subway station under the stadium. The cost would be $75 million.
>
> There was one catch: the city was not offering to pay for it. Stoneham had decided that Harlem was becoming too black for him to stay at his current location, that with the advent of night baseball he was concerned that his fans would think it was too dangerous to venture to upper Manhattan. Once he considered and rejected the notion of paying for this new stadium, he decided he had no choice but to leave New York. His first choice was Nordic Minnesota, the lilliest of lily-white suburbs.

The Giants' top farm team, the Minneapolis Millers, who played in Minneapolis–St. Paul, offered an attractive option for Stoneham, who seriously considered shifting his team there. While contemplating this move, San Francisco mayor George Christopher began negotiations with the Giants at the same time O'Malley was being courted by Los Angeles. A major hiccup in the Dodgers' grand scheme was that unless a second team relocated to the West Coast with them, Brooklyn would not be granted permission to move. At that point O'Malley approached Stoneham and pushed him to make the move. It certainly made sense on a couple of different levels. First, it would be much more attractive for visiting teams to play two teams in California rather than just one as far as cost effectiveness was concerned. And it would maintain the tremendous rivalry that the two teams enjoyed. While they would no longer be crosstown rivals, the cities of Los Angeles and San Francisco already had a natural rivalry in place.

There was also a successful track record of baseball in California. The Pacific Coast League had been in existence since 1903, with core teams that included the Hollywood Stars, Los Angeles Angels, Oakland Oaks, Portland Beavers, Sacramento Solons, San Francisco Seals, San Diego Padres, and Seattle Rainiers.

"The Pacific Coast League wanted to be recognized as a third Major League," said Dick Beverage, secretary-treasurer of the Professional Ballplayers of America and a PCL historian.

> That was really the thrust of expansion out here on the West Coast. The PCL operated independently for years. There were no farm teams, but some teams had gentlemen's agreements. Toward the end of the 1930s, the St. Louis Cardinals purchased the Sacramento franchise, which was a legit farm club. At that point, the Los Angeles Angels PCL team was owned by William Wrigley Jr., who was the major stockholder of the Chicago Cubs. In 1941 the Cubs purchased the Angels from the Santa Catalina Island Company along with all the contracts of the players, equipment, and the territorial rights to the Cubs.

So while the Pacific Coast League operated much like a Major League, the establishment was not about to open the door. A yearly occurrence saw the PCL commissioner Clarence Pants Rowland approach Major League Baseball about forming a third Major League. His league was frustrated with Major League teams taking its players. Early MLB commissioners Kenesaw Mountain Landis and Happy Chandler refused those overtures, and MLB hoped to do away with the Pacific Coast League, because it was viewed as a rival and partly because it was a natural area for eventual expansion.

"Year after year, the Coast League would make the same presentation to Major League Baseball," said Dick Beverage.

Postwar attendance was really high. The Los Angeles and San Francisco clubs in the Coast League were outdrawing some big league teams. That ended after 1949 with the advent of television.

Major League Baseball said that they [the PCL teams] didn't have big league parks. They said you have the population, but you don't have the parks. But the nation was just coming out of a war, and before that there was a Depression. If you granted the PCL Major League status those parks eventually would have been built. County Stadium in Milwaukee was the first new ballpark since probably Yankee Stadium in 1923.

If this league had been earmarked as a Major League, the parks would have been built out here. The role of the Pacific Coast League was to bring to the attention to the moguls of Major League Baseball that there was a lot of money to be made out here. People settled in droves. Citizens were clamoring for Major League Baseball, and the owners saw California as a fertile market that was untapped. They wanted to keep the area available to them. They needed a place for some clubs that were not doing well to go to.

The Pacific Coast League was the Major League for fans on the West Coast. It offered quality baseball and had entertained fans for generations. They knew the players and enjoyed rivalries with other teams. While there was newspaper coverage of the Major Leagues and weekly televised games, the PCL was king of the hill out west.

"I grew up in Los Angeles, and the Hollywood Stars were in the [Pacific] Coast League," said former pitcher Larry Colton, who was nominated for a Pulitzer Prize in Literature for his book *Counting Coup: A True Story of Basketball and Honor on the Little Big Horn.* "They were the Major Leagues for me. I followed the Major Leagues in the paper, and later they had the Game of the Week on TV. But the PCL was the Major Leagues to us on the West Coast. I knew every player on every team. My dad used to take me to games at Gilmore Field. Later in my pro career, I played in the PCL in San Diego and was the Opening Day pitcher at San Diego Stadium. I threw the very first pitch in that stadium."

The baseball world often is affected by events in the real world. That truth had occurred repeatedly during the history of the game. But one of the most interesting examples is one of the least known. Every baseball fan in Brooklyn and Los Angeles is familiar with the City of Angels wooing the Dodgers out west in the 1950s. But in an interesting sideline, had a tragic occurrence not happened on December 7, 1941, when the Japanese attacked Pearl Harbor, it could very well be that the Brooklyn Dodgers would still be a National League club and that the New York Mets would never have been conceived.

"During the first week of December, the St. Louis Browns were moving toward the baseball winter meetings, which were to be held on December 8, 1941," said Dick Beverage. "Donald Barnes, the owner of the Browns, was going to move his team to Los Angeles. The Browns were to have two-week home stands. So the Yankees would play one week in Los Angeles against the Browns, then the next week the Red Sox would, and so on. But after what occurred on December 7, Barnes took the issue off the table and subsequently sold the team. The new owner, Dick Muckermann, wanted to make a go of it in St. Louis. So that was actually the first venture of a Major League Baseball club moving to the West Coast."

The trickle-down effects of such a move by the St. Louis Browns are interesting to consider. That meeting on December 8, 1941, could have seen the St. Louis move to Los Angeles approved and the start of discussions with other troubled franchises such as the Boston Braves and the Philadelphia Athletics to move to San Francisco. Had that happened, Los Angeles and San Francisco would have already had big league teams when Walter O'Malley started to look for options on the West Coast. And Horace Stoneham was already planning to move the Giants to Minneapolis before being approached by O'Malley to join him on the West Coast.

However that was not to be. The explosive and shocking entrance of the United States into World War II kept Los Angeles and San Francisco available to the Dodgers and Giants. As the postwar era continued to the mid-1950s, O'Malley was growing increasingly impatient with Brooklyn municipal officials. The lure of greener pastures in Los Angeles made it seem more and more like a real change in venue was possible. And the added interest from Horace Stoneham and the Giants was the final nail in the coffins of two proud New York franchises. "People have moved out of our city," Stoneham said. "You used to be able, at least over in Brooklyn, they could go out and get a crowd from within walking distance of the park and fill the stands. You can't do that anymore." All of the social factors and the changes happening in America's Game had combined and made this move possible.

"In '57 when they left, it was part of a troubled time in baseball history," said John P. Rossi, professor emeritus at La Salle University and author of *The National Game: Baseball and American Culture* and *A Whole New Game: Off the Field Changes in Baseball, 1946–1960*.

What generated the move as well as expansion in general were the problems that the game was experiencing. The A's had a horrible time of it and could not get the Philadelphia fans back. The same was true with the Browns.

O'Malley was in a situation where his attendance had gone from

1.8 million to 1 million in ten years. He had lost 800,000 fans and had no idea if he could build it up again in a 32,000-seat ballpark. Then a city comes along that would do anything to get baseball. He did what any businessman would have done.

What had been a very parochial country where people grew up and lived in the same neighborhood had turned into a much more mobile society with people willing to travel and explore new places.

"In the surge of prosperity after the war, people began to think about going somewhere," wrote George Vescey in *Baseball: A History of America's Favorite Game.*

People came back from their first vacation to Florida or California, raving about the weather, the new houses, the beaches, the date-nut shakes. In the frozen Midwest, people woke up on New Year's Day and turned on their brand-new television set to the Rose Bowl parade and football game from Pasadena, California, and pretty soon a family down the block packed up and moved out west. . . .

The Dodgers led the league in attendance five times after the war and were solvent mainly because O'Malley had been quick to negotiate income from television rights, but he could see himself making considerably more money somewhere else.

O'Malley soon pulled off one of the great real estate deals in the history of American sports. Insisting he wanted to replace dumpy but vibrant Ebbets Field with a new stadium in downtown Brooklyn or in Queens, O'Malley really had his eye on Los Angeles. First, he talked the Wrigley family, which owned the Cubs, into trading its minor league Los Angeles franchise to him. Then O'Malley charmed the mayor of Los Angeles into deeding him a ravine on the northern edge of downtown. Wild and crazy spendthrift that he was, O'Malley even promised to build a ballpark with his own money. He knew building a ballpark was a mere operating expense. Land was the main thing.

Land in California, where flocks of people relocated. The area had already supported Minor League Baseball for decades. It was only a matter of time until the Major Leagues spread their wings to the area.

But little did anyone know just how many dominos would fall as a result.

1 | Go West Young Men

In the 1950s there were no player agents, ballplayers didn't make the gargantuan bucks that even the most pedestrian players earn today, and they were very much part of the community. In that era, baseball players often lived in the same neighborhoods that their fans did and were active and well-known members of the community. Very few areas exemplified this as much as the borough of Brooklyn.

The players embraced Brooklyn and Brooklyn embraced the players.

"Free agency hadn't happened, and we were all on one-year contracts in those days," said former Dodger pitcher Carl Erskine. "You stayed on your team for at least a decade then. We lived in the same neighborhood as the fans. Our kids grew up together, we knew the barber, the guy in the deli, the baby sitters. We just blended in with the population. I lived in Bay Ridge. Pee Wee [Reese] lived close, as did Duke [Snider] and Preacher [Row]. I'd pitch a good game, and by the time I got home they'd have a street party for me. It was like a second home town."

That old home feeling explains part of the love affair that Brooklyn fans had for their Bums. The Dodgers were a good team that regularly reached the World Series. Successful decades that the Brooklyn players and fans enjoyed are rare in today's game.

"The Dodgers had one of its best stretches when I played there," said Erskine. "I was there for twelve seasons and I was in the World Series six times. That accounts for how we integrated so easily into the neighborhoods. But the bonding occurred because we were there for the community. We had some degree of celebrity being Dodger players, but the team was respectable and we were winning. We were there a long time and we won, but maybe we didn't win enough in the World Series."

The Dodgers were a strange combination of a successful team that was also the perennial bridesmaid. They were usually good, but with one glorious exception in 1955, not good enough to reach baseball heaven by beating the notorious crosstown rivals, the New York Yankees, in the World Series.

While the Bums were en route to their world title, Walter O'Malley fired the first of many shots across the bow of Brooklyn. On August 16 of that year, he announced that the Dodgers would play one exhibition game and seven regular season home games at Roosevelt Field in Jersey City in 1956 and seven more regular season games in 1957.

Robert Moses had shot down O'Malley's idea for a domed stadium, feeling that open space in Flushing Meadows, Queens, would be the best site for a new stadium for the Dodgers. Sound familiar? That turned out to be the future site of Shea Stadium and later, Citi Field.

"I grew up in Brooklyn," said Stan Hochman, a columnist and beat writer for the *Philadelphia Daily News* since 1959. "I know that there was a lot of politics involved in the building of a new stadium for the Dodgers. Robert Moses was very influential and wanted them in Flushing. O'Malley wanted to pick the place, and he got such a good deal from Los Angeles. It was just unbelievable that New York would only have one club, the Yankees. I was shocked that they were abandoning New York, but once I heard the details of the deal I was not surprised. That left a vacuum in New York."

There was outrage and concern over the thought of the Dodgers playing home game anywhere other than in Brooklyn. But while Roosevelt Stadium was far from a perfect venue, it offered ten thousand parking spaces. In 1956 Brooklyn went 6-1 in Jersey City, but more importantly enjoyed a 40 percent increase in attendance, averaging 21,196 fans at those games, as opposed to the 15,217 average at Ebbets Field.

After announcing the game in Jersey City, O'Malley assured his fans that almost all Dodger home games would be played at Ebbets Field. But he reiterated that his Dodgers would need a new stadium sooner rather than later.

As the defending world champions in 1956, a lot more than winning baseball games and the defense of that title was on the mind of Walter O'Malley and his fans. With the complete lack of any kind of plan for a new stadium on the horizon, rumors began to swirl. Would the Dodgers move to New Jersey? Would they relocate to another existing big league city? Or would they move somewhere else?

"We were young guys in our early to mid twenties," said Carl Erskine.

We could[n't] care less what was happening outside. We were trying to keep our jobs and stay on the team. You'd have a good year and go in to see Mr. [Branch] Rickey. You had a raise in mind but he'd just let you come back without a raise.

The players didn't have a clue what was happening. That wasn't shared with us. But we were just worried about winning the next game. I was player rep for eight years during that time period. Seldom would any owner ever call a player rep to talk about anything. We read the paper and knew what everyone else knew. The rumors would fly, but I don't think we expected to have all the information. We eventually believed that we'd be moving because it became evident that Mr. O'Malley wanted to get a new ballpark built. Then we played those games in Jersey City at Roosevelt Stadium. O'Malley said if he had to move thirty miles out of Brooklyn, he might as well move thirty thousand. I don't think that the players concerned themselves with it a whole lot. I knew we were going to do something. But we were employees who were not privy to front office information or discussions.

While maintaining a public façade that no decision had been made and that the Dodgers were still negotiating to keep the team in Brooklyn, the facts seem to indicate that Walter O'Malley was not being completely truthful.

"He said one thing, but his actions seemed like he didn't believe what he was saying," said Bob McGee, author of the book *The Greatest Ballpark Ever: Ebbets Field and the Story of the Brooklyn Dodgers.*

Before spring training in 1956, when he and Phil Wrigley exchanged notes agreeing to swap the Los Angeles and Dallas–Ft. Worth Minor League franchises, the writing was on the wall. Wrigley had a home on Catalina Island in LA and he was interested in seeing baseball in Los Angeles. He was not about to move the Cubs out of Chicago.

For all of O'Malley's talk, the Dodgers were the most profitable team in baseball by virtue of advertising and TV revenues. After the 1956 World Series, while en route to an exhibition tour in Japan, O'Malley met with Kenneth Hahn [Los Angeles County supervisor] at the Hilton Hotel in Los Angeles. O'Malley said something to the effect of although he would deny it to the press, he would move the team to LA if he got the deal he wanted.

So it is clear that Walter O'Malley was more than willing to entertain the possibility of moving the Dodgers to the West Coast fairly early in the process.

It is said that both good and bad things happen in sets of three. Following the 1956 baseball season, on Halloween, the last trolley cars in Brooklyn were retired. Then, on December 13, the great Jackie Robinson was traded to the Giants in exchange for left-handed pitcher Dick Littlefield and thirty thousand dollars. Was there any doubt that the Dodgers leaving Brooklyn would soon follow?

The draw of the West Coast was just too much to ignore. The Los Angeles and San Francisco areas had all their ducks in a row, able to make it next to impossible not to move out of New York.

"The population just boomed out here [in California] after the war," said Dick Beverage.

People settled here in droves. Citizens were clamoring for Major League Baseball, and the owners saw California as a fertile market that was untapped. If a team or teams were going to move, this was the logical place to do so.

I was living in New York at the time and didn't like it myself because I didn't want to see the Dodgers and Giants move out here. I still thought that the Pacific Coast League should be a third Major League. But when the news broke that the teams were moving there was a lot of excitement. Both teams drew well from the get go. It was tough to get a ticket in San Francisco. O'Malley just felt that he could not play in Ebbets Field any longer.

But Boston was able to salvage Fenway Park, so why couldn't they salvage Ebbets Field? Everyone thought it would be straightened out. I had a friend who would stand by the subway and hand out flyers to try to keep the Dodgers in Brooklyn. He'd do that every single day during the summer.

But despite such love and loyalty, which had been evident from their fans for decades, finally, on May 28, 1957, the National League approved the move of the Brooklyn Dodgers to Los Angeles and New York Giants to San Francisco, unanimous support by the other National League clubs. While two groups of fans were in shock and mourning, two other groups of fans were ecstatic.

"We didn't care about Brooklyn fans," said Larry Colton.

We got ours, too bad for you. It was you that let them go. They played the first couple of years in the Coliseum, which had over a hundred thousand seats. I'd go to a lot of games. It was great. Wally Moon and

Sandy Koufax were just starting to hit strides. When the Dodgers came to town everybody listened to Vin Scully on their transistor radios. You read every possible thing you could read about the team. Don Drysdale was a hometown guy. In fact, when he pitched in high school, Robert Redford was the second baseman on Drysdale's team. It was a really exciting time.

Across the country in the borough of Brooklyn, there was no such happiness or excitement. It was as if there had been a death in the family. For many, the disappointment and hurt remain even today.

"You had a sense of how the borough was never the same after they left," said Bob McGee.

Something was lost that really was essential to people's identity as far as their identification with Brooklyn was concerned. Branch Rickey once said that a baseball team is a quasi-public institution. Take away the quasi.

People identified very closely with the Dodgers because they had been playing baseball in Brooklyn for well over a hundred years. In 1858 there were fifty amateur teams in Brooklyn. In a sense baseball in Brooklyn was bread in the bone. Brooklyn without the Dodgers was unthinkable.

Say what you want about O'Malley and his choices. The one thing he wouldn't do was offer the team for sale. I think the reason he elected to move that team was that he saw an opportunity to be given all this real estate and make all this money. The lack of leadership in baseball was such that instead of expanding systematically, owners would just move franchises. That lack of leadership at the top of the game is still something that exists today. The game is brought kicking and screaming into a new era as a result of its mistakes.

While Brooklyn fans reeled over the loss of the Dodgers, the players had to finish out the season. They certainly had no say in the move of the team, and finishing out that season in Ebbets Field must have been akin to playing baseball at a wake. The borough was in shock, hurt and angry.

"In '57 it was announced that we were going to move," said Carl Erskine. "The fans were disappointed and hurt. We had lousy crowds and we didn't play all that well. The Brooklyn fans were beautiful people but they didn't mind telling you if you played bad. They were very intense about their team. A lot of people point out attendance. If you could draw a million people in those days it was a real benchmark. We did that regularly but after the move was announced it dropped off pretty big."

While all of the evidence pointed to a Dodger and Giant move to the West Coast following the 1957 season, hope always springs eternal, and you can get them next year. But would that be even a long shot in Brooklyn?

Even though the move to California was approved in May, the dog days of August brought with them a pennant race. On August 5 the Dodgers were in third place, only three games behind the first-place St. Louis Cardinals. To make matters even more interesting, they were scheduled to play seven games against the Giants over the following ten days.

Asked writer Henry D. Fetter, "Would even the most mercenary, avaricious, and unsentimental owner really pull a team out of its long-time home if they had just won the National League pennant—and, who knows, the World Series as well?"

There is little doubt that the move of both of New York's National League teams was a done deal by August 5, 1957. But against all odds, Brooklyn fans still hoped against hope. Perhaps the crucial next couple of weeks could save their beloved Bums after all.

But their hope was short lived as the Dodgers lost three of four home games to the Giants, split a four-game set in Pittsburgh against the Pirates and then lost two of three to their crosstown rivals at the Polo Grounds. By August 15, Brooklyn was eight and a half games behind the suddenly red-hot Milwaukee Braves. They finished the season eleven games off the pace, in front of paltry crowds who realized that it was finally over.

At the same time the Dodgers began losing crucial contests that ended their pennant hopes, Horace Stoneham announced that his Giants were moving to San Francisco. There was no chance they'd be moving out west alone. On October 8, 1957, the Dodgers officially announced that they were moving to Los Angeles.

The cold, harsh reality was a smack in the face to Brooklyn fans. But it was also a difficult adjustment for the players, even for a native Californian like the late Don Drysdale. In his book *Once a Bum, Always a Dodger*, Drysdale wrote of his mixed feelings upon learning that the Dodgers were moving to Los Angeles.

"Well, I was speechless," he wrote.

I used to read the papers pretty regularly and I remembered some stories about the problems Walter O'Malley was having in getting a new stadium built for the Dodgers in Brooklyn. He wanted a ballpark downtown, but the borough officials said he couldn't have it there because it was right in the middle of everything. Right in the produce center and by the railroad station. So, there were some troubles between the management of the ballclub and Brooklyn's civic leaders. But if there was ever a real threat that the Dodgers were actually contemplating a move to Los Angeles, I had missed it. At the time I heard it, I thought to myself that this had to be the best-kept secret since Pearl Harbor.

My first consideration was that I was going to my first home, California. But beyond that, I thought about Brooklyn. What about all those people who lived and died with the Dodgers? How were they going to feel about this? And all those friends I'd made in Brooklyn. I might never see them again. It was a very emotional time for me. It was an emotional time for all of us. But I don't think is really sunk in until the next year when we didn't go back to Brooklyn. Maybe I didn't want it to sink in. Maybe that's what it was.

Not only was the move of the Dodgers a move from Brooklyn to Los Angeles, but in many ways the move also ushered in a changing of the guard. The veteran players who had played so well for so long at Ebbets Field were getting older. Walter O'Malley would wait no longer to build his stadium in Brooklyn. At the same time, Father Time began to have his way with the Brooklyn players.

But even though the players had strong feelings for Brooklyn, the star-studded Los Angeles area was an exciting new place in which to play. Say good-bye to the neighborhoods of the borough and say hello to Hollywood.

"I was always pleased to have been a transition player who played in both Brooklyn and Los Angeles," said Carl Erskine.

If you asked Don Newcombe or any player who was in the group of The Boys of Summer, we had all pretty much passed our peak. But if you ask young Don Drysdale, who was going back home to California, or Sandy Koufax or Johnny Podres, those guys looked at it differently than we did. We felt, the older guys, that we had to go out there and prove ourselves and show these people all the things they had been reading about us.

All the preseason banquets that led up to Opening Day were really enthusiastic. It was Hollywood. And at the same time there were people protesting O'Malley being sold the land. People were picketing and everything. There was a welcoming at City Hall and they had to haul the protestors away. But the fans were happy they had a team. On Opening Day we had around eighty thousand fans in the Coliseum, but the crowd couldn't make as much noise as Ebbets Field with ten thousand fans. It was funny: half of my teammates would be looking behind the field into the stands to see what movie stars were there instead of watching the game. Vin Scully's broadcasting really sold the Dodgers to Southern California. He made people want to see the Dodgers.

I got to pitch the first game and beat the Giants in LA. We had eighty thousand fans come into the ballpark that day. I pitched eight innings and got the win. Clem Labine came in and got the save.

While 1958 was not a successful season on the playing field for the Dodgers, they took off midway through the 1959 season when young players such as Roger Craig, Larry Sherry, Norm Sherry, and Frank Howard began to become prime-time players. Their World Series victory in the team's second season in Los Angeles was a final slap in the face to Brooklyn fans who saw but one title in all those years.

"I think that for Brooklyn Dodger fans, the notion of the Los Angeles Dodgers is kind of akin to the two Chinas situation," said Bob McGee. "It's as if the Dodgers never existed after they left Brooklyn. The LA Dodgers have never been officially recognized as such."

The Dodgers moved to the Coliseum while Dodger Stadium was being built; similarly, the Giants played at Seals Stadium until Candlestick Park was completed for the 1960 season.

Fans in California had two Major League teams, and the future was bright. But in New York, two sets of fans left behind like a loving wife for a younger, prettier temptress wanted and needed big league baseball.

"I didn't really give a shit where the Dodgers went because I was a Yankee fan," said author Peter Golenbock.

But the people I knew, especially Brooklyn Dodger fans, were part of a community that tied everyone together. It was a conclave of neighborhoods of blacks, Italians, Greeks, and Jews. For the most part, if a fellow from one group traveled to another area, he could get beat up. But the Brooklyn Dodgers was something that everyone agreed on. They tied the whole borough together.

The Brooklyn Dodgers, the Eagle, and the Navy Yard were three important institutions in Brooklyn. But by 1957 all three were gone. Losing them, but especially losing the Dodgers, caused Brooklyn to lose a lot of its cachet. It was also a period when after the war a lot of people were making good money and decided to get out of the city and move to other areas of New York, Connecticut, and Long Island. There was a huge white, Jewish, Italian, and Irish exodus out. At the same time there was an influx of blacks and Puerto Ricans. That was a large part of the reason O'Malley moved out of Brooklyn.

On the other side of the country, New York had lost two of its three Major League teams. The powerful Yankees remained, but old feelings die hard. The powerful Yankees of the Junior Circuit had broken National League hearts for decades. How could self-respecting Dodger or Giants fans possibly switch their allegiance to the hated Yankees? C'mon!

Television enabled fans to see the Los Angeles Dodgers and the San Francisco Giants from time to time. But fans were conflicted. Writer Pete Hamill wrote in a column that the three most hated people in the history of the universe were Adolph Hitler, Genghis Khan, and Walter O'Malley. The latter's old drinking pal, Horace Stoneham, was not far removed from that list.

"Horace Stoneham was heavily influenced by Walter O'Malley," said Bob McGee.

Horace was probably someone, because of his proclivity to drink, could be spoken to after a few cocktails. Had the Giants been left to the New York market all to themselves the Stonehams might still own the Giants.

I guess when you look at things in retrospect there was more of a case for the Giants to be moving, because their attendance had fallen substantially and the team was not performing well. But that happens over a period of time for every franchise. You rebuild and become competitive again. For twenty years, George Steinbrenner maligned the location he had in the Bronx, but when the team became resurgent in the mid-1990s, you had three or four million fans going to the same location that George did not think was good enough for his franchise.

But fans still loved the players they had followed for years. After all, it wasn't Carl Erskine, Duke Snider, Pee Wee Reese, Willie Mays, or Monte Irvin who were behind the move of the two franchises. So while hatred grew toward the two owners, oddly, many fans still supported the uprooted players they had followed and cheered for throughout the years.

Following the desertion of the Dodgers and Giants to the West Coast for the 1958 season, New York mayor Robert Wagner decided to do something. A powerful politico who also enjoyed sports, the mayor decided to do something to heal his broken city. In October of 1958 he started a group called the Mayor's Baseball Committee, with William Shea, to investigate the possibility of approaching other existing franchises to encourage them to move to New York.

They were in the right church, but the wrong pew. While the group stumbled in their attempts to lure a team to New York, a group of visionaries came up with the concept of a new Major League, the Continental League. Unlike past attempts at adding a new league, this league had serious money behind it as well as a man who may have been baseball's most legendary visionary over his long life.

While he had already drastically changed the game and the business of America's Pastime, Branch Rickey had one more game-altering trick up his sleeve.

Plans were unveiled for the Continental League, which would have a team in New York. Other leagues had tried to join the Major Leagues, including the Federal League and the Pacific Coast League. Then there was a competitive push from the Mexican League. But this new upstart Continental League had serious financial backing and the credibility brought to it by Branch Rickey, named league president.

After years of sitting reactively on the sidelines, Major League Baseball was about to respond in what may have been its most decisive decision since Judge Kennesaw Mountain Landis banned seven Black Sox players for life. And the lightning rod behind the decision was a baseball lifer named Branch Rickey and a mover and shaker in the political arena named William Shea.

2 | The Continental League

Love them or hate them, no one could ever doubt the resiliency of New Yorkers. Never was that more true surrounding the tragic events of September 11, 2001, when the Big Apple was attacked with no warning and for no reason. But New Yorkers were what we've come to expect of them long before that tragic and shattering fall day. They are front-runners and the comeback kids both at the same time. Love them or hate them, if nothing else, respect them.

New Yorkers can be in your face, but will also have your back no matter what. Much is made of the experience of driving in New York, but those who drive there are usually working and just trying to get somewhere on time. Their sports teams often reflect the attitude of their fans, which can easily agitate those from other cities. But while the fans and teams can also be in your face, there is little or no acceptance in New York for anything that is second best. New Yorkers feel that they deserve the best. And to their credit, they support that belief by walking the walk and talking the talk, be it in the area of sports or anything else.

So it's easy to imagine the disappointment, heartache, and anger felt in New York when the Dodgers and Giants picked up and moved to California. Those two teams basically thumbed their noses to New York. Not surprisingly, those in "The City" were not willing to sit back and wallow in their own pity. New York took action.

From the do unto others as others have done to you department, New York mayor Robert Wagner took the defections very personally and formed a group known as the Mayor's Baseball Committee. As noted, the group was formed to find an existing big league franchise to abandon its fans and move to New York. This knee-jerk reaction is completely understandable considering the fact that New York had lost two of its three big league teams, and now as a result, did not have any representation in baseball's National League.

At the head of this committee was a politically connected attorney named William Shea. Bill Shea had raised impressive sums of money for Mayor Wagner's political campaigns. He could rub elbows with the likes of Nelson Rockefeller, Senator Prescott Bush of Connecticut, and Texas senator Lyndon Johnson. He was clearly a mover and a shaker who was as well connected as it was possible to be. Other committee members included the likes of Barnard Gimble, of department store fame; Jim Farley, the former postmaster of the United States; and Clint Blume, a real estate developer. All were well known and powerful in their own way, and all were working toward ensuring that New York had a baseball team in the National League.

Determination and connections notwithstanding, the group had little chance to convince an existing franchise to move to New York. The Dodgers and Giants were out of the mix, having just moved to the West Coast, basically telling New York to kiss their collective asses. The Philadelphia Phillies were approached and refused. The St. Louis Cardinals and Chicago Cubs were incredibly stable franchises that were not about to move anywhere. The Milwaukee Braves were also doing well. And after some discussions that never got very far, the Cincinnati Reds and Pittsburgh Pirates were going to stay put.

Branch Rickey, who had been president and general manager of the Pirates, was enlisted to approach that team's owner, John Galbreath, about the possibility of a move. Rickey later reported that he was told that money could not buy a franchise.

A lesser man might have folded, admitted defeat and called it a day. But Bill Shea was not a lesser man. He approached the venerable Branch Rickey, who was now involved in the process. Rickey had penned a magazine article suggesting that the best interests of baseball would be served if the game expanded across the country. Perhaps Rickey had an idea worth pursuing. After all, if the group could not find a team to move to New York, perhaps a new team was the answer, or perhaps a new group of teams.

"Shea's scheme involved attempting the impossible—he intended to construct a whole new baseball league from scratch, enrolling franchises in large cities that didn't have a major league presence," Peter Golenbock wrote in *Amazin'*. "He was counting on his new league putting the baseball owners in an untenable position: if organized baseball tried to crush the upstart league, Congress might lose its temper and take away baseball's sacred anti-trust exemption. But, if it chose to tread lightly, then the new league might succeed, and its impact on baseball's profits would be considerable. If a baseball executive had the Midas touch, it was the cigar-smoking, bible-quoting Mr. Rickey. With Rickey behind him, Shea's credibility was quickly established."

Good ideas and different approaches were nothing new to Branch Rickey. While he is certainly best known for breaking the color line in baseball by bringing Jackie Robinson to the Major Leagues in 1947 with the Brooklyn Dodgers and for later signing the great Roberto Clemente to the Pittsburgh Pirates, Rickey's impact on the game went much farther and deeper than just that.

"Rickey did a lot including the idea of the farm system," said Stan Hochman.

It was his idea to control as many Minor Leaguers as he could. That was how you could replenish the big league roster. He just believed in scouting at the most primitive level. The kid with promise that nobody else found could be signed and put in the farm system. He deserves a lot of credit for that. People are aware of his being behind integration in baseball and how he went about it and kept it quiet.

He and O'Malley didn't get along, so that ended his stay with the Dodgers. When the Continental League came around, he had such great knowledge of players that they could steal to make the new league viable.

Born in 1881, Rickey was a catcher at Ohio Wesleyan University and played parts of four seasons in the Major Leagues with the St. Louis Browns and the New York Highlanders. In 1906 with St. Louis, Rickey hit .284 in 65 games with 3 home runs and 24 RBIs. But the following season with the Highlanders he slipped to .182 in 52 games. For his career, he hit a meager .239 in 120 big league games. But his playing career was the least important aspect of Branch Rickey's involvement with the game of baseball.

He returned to the Browns, where he managed for three years before moving to the crosstown Cardinals in 1919. He was the skipper of that team for seven years, three of which were winning seasons. But he began investing in Minor League clubs, which were used to bring young players to St. Louis. Purchasing players had become less than economical. Rickey developed a farm system with Minor League teams purchased by the big league organization, forming a chain of teams. They were stocked by players from all over the country and would be paid seventy-five to ninety dollars a month. That was okay money is those days that afforded players the chance to eventually play in the Major Leagues.

As Cardinals general manager, it was Rickey's plan to sign numerous players to stock these Minor League teams, hoping that a handful would eventually make it to the Majors. He would then sell off players he felt were lacking to other teams. Not only did these Minor League teams feed the Cardinals with top young talent, but he made thousands and thousands of dollars selling players to other organizations.

Over time, the "Gashouse Gang," as the Cardinals were known, had become a powerful National League team. They saw Pepper Martin lead St. Louis to a World Series championship in 1931. The rookie was a player who had come through Rickey's Minor League system. He was soon joined by other future stars who had come through the organization including Dizzy Dean, his brother Paul "Daffy" Dean, and Joe Medwick. Other players to come up through the Cardinals' farm system included Enos Slaughter, Stan Musial, Marty Marion, and Billy Southworth.

But a major bump in the road continually interfered with Rickey's Minor League plans. Baseball commissioner Kenesaw Mountain Landis did not support that idea of a Minor League system being put into place by Major League clubs because he felt it would destroy most Minor League teams. His feeling was that because the parent Major League club could unilaterally call up players from Minor League teams that could be involved in pennant races, the organization was unfairly interfering with Minor League competition. He argued that the championship of each Minor League was of no less importance than the championship of the Major Leagues and that Minor League fans had the right to see their teams compete at the highest level possible.

By the end of the 1930s, he had freed from Minor League teams nearly two hundred players, including Pete Reiser and Skeeter Webb. But despite the commissioner's efforts to stymie Minor League systems, they continued to succeed and were eventually adopted by all Major League organizations. At the end, it was Rickey's groundbreaking utilization of Minor League teams as part of a farm system that has resulted in the continued health of Minor League Baseball since the advent of television.

Rickey was not done yet. With the Dodgers he began the first full-time spring training facility in Vero Beach, Florida, and also led the pack in the use of things like batting helmets, batting cages, and pitching machines.

Rickey oozed credibility for his accomplishments and for his moral fiber. His involvement with Bill Shea and the Continental League gave immediate credence and credibility to any undertaking they started. On November 12, 1958, Shea held a news conference and admitted that his efforts to induce a team to move to New York had been fruitless. But his committee favored starting a third Major League that could be in operation by 1960 or 1961. And it would include a franchise in New York.

"For years there were just sixteen Major League teams, eight and eight," said Peter Golenbock. "As the country grew, there were far more cities perfectly capable of having a Major League Baseball team. The guy who made expansion possible was Branch Rickey, by working with William Shea on the Continental League. The idea was that they were going to have eight franchises in cities that were not Major League cities such as Houston, Minnesota, and Dallas, plus New York. Rickey was a fairly old guy at the time. He had left the Pirates. He was one of the geniuses of baseball. A lot of teams all came out of that Continental League."

In addition, franchises would also be awarded to Houston, Dallas, Denver, Toronto, Miami, and Minneapolis–St. Paul. Three additional franchises were awarded to Atlanta, Buffalo, and Dallas–Ft. Worth.

"The Continental League had been talked about in different ways, and it looked like after the Dodgers and Giants moved that there was enough money around and enough target cities to have a third Major League," said John Rossi. "Initially, the people behind it had not been great businessmen, but then Shea got Branch Rickey involved, which threw a scare into Major League Baseball."

There was serious money behind the Continental League, as it would be known, as well as some good baseball personnel. Present at the press conference were Bob Howsam (Denver), Craig Cullinan Jr. (Houston), Wheelock Whitney Jr. (Minneapolis–St. Paul), Dwight David Jr. (New York), and Jack Kent Cooke (Toronto). To join the dance, $50,000 was to be paid to the league by each of the owners, in addition to a commitment of $2.5 million. Stadium costs would be extra, and any stadium would have to fit 35,000 fans.

The league was formerly announced in July of 1959, and in February 1960, it was announced that Opening Day of the inaugural season of the Continental League would be April 18, 1961. On that day, Denver, Dallas–Ft. Worth, Houston, and Atlanta would play host to Minneapolis–St. Paul, New York, Toronto, and Buffalo.

The announcement and plans for the new league were met with skepticism at best by the old boys' network. Commissioner Ford Frick said that baseball would not be sledge-hammered into putting a team in New York because of the threat of a third Major League. But the involvement of Branch Rickey clearly took the new league from a long-range fantasy league to a real entity that was going to happen.

"The thing that really got expansion going was the threat of the Continental League," said Bill Giles, chairman of the Philadelphia Phillies. "There was a lot of fear about a third league forming. The move of the Dodgers and the Giants to the West Coast left New York City without a National League team, which put a little pressure on. Branch Rickey was the president of that league, and they had a number of cities involved, with New York being the leader. So that really got the ball rolling."

After being let go by the Pirates after the 1955 season, Rickey was out of baseball, which is something akin to a fish being out of water. He served on the board of the Pacific Coast League and maintained his fervent love of the game. Although in failing health, he was ready for a new challenge. And talk of a third Major League represented just that.

Rickey joined forces with Shea and began to organize his thoughts for the prospective upstart league. He admitted up front that the league would have weaker players than the National and American Leagues. But it was also true that parity would exist in the new league, and competition would be fierce. An important factor in the success of the venture would be the willingness and ability of the league's back-ers to financially support the league long enough for it to gain momentum and a fan base.

The acquisition of players would also be difficult. Rickey felt that the combination of a draft, free agent signings, and the purchasing of players would be the most successful path to follow. While there were more than enough baseball players to supply the league with players, pretty much all of them belonged to someone else. Players were bound to the team that originally signed them due to baseball's reserve clause, which held that a player's contract was automatically renewed every year into perpetuity, or until the parent team released him.

In March of 1960, baseball blocked a proposed working agreement between Rickey and the Western Carolina League. There was also legislation in Congress that would limit the number of players a team could control to eighty, a drastic reduction in number. But the proposed bill got bogged down in the political system and died in committee.

American and National League owners realized that this upstart league might actually happen, and unlike such leagues that had mounted challenges against the baseball establishment in the past, this one seemed to be gaining momentum and credibility with Branch Rickey leading the charge. And one of the people Rickey most admired in baseball was Ban Johnson, who had started the American League.

"It may seem illogical that you can't get manpower for four extra clubs, but you can with eight," Rickey said in a magazine article. "But eight teams can compete equally while recognized as a third major league. Our new league would not pretend to be major the first year. But by the end of the third year, that would not be unthinkable."

One of the key elements in the success of the league was the concept of pay television. In 1957 *Television Age* published a report stating that 40 percent of New York families who watched television would be willing to pay to watch Major League Baseball on TV. A team in New York could conceivably make more than $8 million for a schedule of seventy-seven home games.

In the summer of that same year, the New York Giants had reached agreement with Skiatron, a pay television network, to carry their home games exclusively for paying customers.

While the chatter about this new league was increasing, the existing leagues still held most of the cards. The summer of 1960 was not one that was kind to Branch Rickey, who desperately wanted the Continental League to become a reality. In July of that year, the National League owners met to discuss expansion. On July 18 Rickey received a telegram informing him that the Senior Circuit had voted unanimously to implement expansion via the Continental League, or increased membership. He was invited to a meeting in Chicago on August 2.

Minneapolis–St. Paul had dropped out of the league on July 20, believing that Major League expansion was imminent. At the August 2 meeting, Walter O'Malley suggested a compromise that had been floated as a trial balloon earlier—Major League Baseball would take four Continental League cities in an expansion and add the others later. While the locations were not announced at this meeting, it was obvious that a National League franchise in New York would be part of the solution.

"The major league owners were unsure whether Shea and Rickey would be able to get their new league off the ground, but at the same time they were concerned that if they succeeded, the competition from the new league would cost them dearly in both players and large sums of money," wrote Peter Golenbock in *Amazin'*.

Equally important, they feared the loss of baseball's anti-trust exemption. With Lyndon Johnson, Sam Rayburn, and other powerful congressman lined up against them, and standing aside Shea and Rickey, baseball's moguls decided that the least painful and expensive tactic would be to give in to Shea's demands.

On August 17, 1960, four years after Mayor Wagner appointed Bill Shea to head his committee, the baseball owners met with Branch

Rickey at the Conrad Hilton Hotel in Chicago and agreed to add Denver and Minneapolis Continental League clubs to the American League in 1961 and the New York and Houston Continental League clubs to the National League in 1962.

There would also be a priority given to cities that did not already have Major League Baseball. The National League would expand to New York and Houston. The American League transferred the Senators to Minnesota and would add teams in Washington and Los Angeles.

When it became obvious to the owners of the proposed team in the Continental League that the National League would add a team in New York, these owners immediately accepted, basically taking away any reason for the new Continental League's being.

Bill Shea had accomplished his mission, to bring a second Major League franchise to New York. As a result, on August 2, 1960, the upstart league disbanded. While Shea was ecstatic, Rickey was anything but, as he saw his dream of a third Major League slip through his fingers.

Jimmy Cannon summed up in his column the importance of Branch Rickey to the process that made Major League Baseball take out the upstart Continentals: "The baseball people ridiculed Shea, but they were shaken when he hired Branch Rickey. They know all about Rickey and they hold no affection for him. He was too smart for them. They told themselves he was too old to put together eight 25-man squads on a field. But they never really believed what they said, because this is a guy you can never ignore."

It is impossible to underestimate the importance of the prospect of the Continental League in Major League Baseball's decision to expand. The biggest credibility factor in the upstart league was unquestionably Branch Rickey. He was all in for the project. But was the league taken as seriously by others involved, or was it simply a ploy on their part to gain leverage with Major League Baseball in their quest for expansion? And could it be that Rickey was used as a lure to make expansion happen, with the prospective owners never really serious about the new league?

"Some of the men who had joined with Branch Rickey and Bill Shea stayed on in baseball, and when they spoke of their rebellion it was with a wink and a nod, as if to dampen any illusions that they had ever been serious about striking out on their own," wrote Michael Shapiro in *Bottom of the Ninth: Branch Rickey, Casey Stengel, and the Daring Scheme to Save Baseball from Itself*. "'It was ridiculed as a sham,' Craig Cullinan once said, 'but on the contrary it was an enormous success because it ran what became the biggest bluff in the history of professional sports.'" Added Shapiro,

> The others did not disagree, and so in the years to come the league would be remembered as little more than a spectacular ruse, a con. Cullinan may have wished to be regarded as one of "Mr. Rickey's boys," and may have been sincere in the confessional letter he sent on the eve of the 1960 World Series, expressing his sorrow and his regret for the league's failure to remain united behind Rickey that August in Chicago. But as Rickey had come to suspect, the men who had enlisted in his crusade did not share his vision for the league and for the game. Rather, they were the spiritual heirs of Charlie Weeghman, who had thrown in with the Federal League so that he might win a place in the majors.

The prospective owners needed Rickey to give their upstart league immediate credibility, and despite his age and failing health, Rickey needed them as well. For Branch Rickey life without baseball was no life at all.

"Everybody was using everybody," said Branch Rickey III. "Those were the kinds of situations my grandfather most enjoyed. He didn't mind being used at all. But he wanted the ability to manage the situation. He did not want to be confined."

Throughout his lifetime, baseball unwittingly needed Branch Rickey. And his all-encompassing love of the game made him a force to be reckoned with on any level he was involved with in the game.

"Love of the game is not a phrase I would use," said Branch Rickey III.

It so filled his life. He so treasured every single facet of the game and there was nothing too small that didn't rivet him. I don't warm to the expression of loving the game, because my association with love and marriage is that you can have a broken love affair, a divorce. I would be inclined to use the word passion. It was a never-ending feeling. From the first minute he would awaken until he went to bed, every single day he could spend every single minute with a multitude of different elements of the game, or just one particular thing. He pursued it relentlessly, and he could do it on all levels. He did it for the zeal of it, the intellectuality of it, or the religion of it.

Branch Rickey got what he wanted in that he was once again involved in the game he had such passion for. And the prospective Continental League owners got what they wanted. The initial reports indicated that four Continental League cities would get big league teams. Two would be added to the American League, and New York and one other to the National League. However, only three of the cities got in immediately, New York, Houston, and Minneapolis. Four other areas eventually gained entrance to Major League Baseball through either expansion or relocation. They were Atlanta, the Dallas–Ft. Worth area, Toronto, and Denver. Only Buffalo remains from the Continental League without a big league franchise.

Even though the Dodgers and Giants has abandoned New York, the threat of the Continental League forced Major League Baseball to finally change, open its exclusive doors, and expand America's Pastime to new areas as well as return to one of its most consistent cities—New York. There would once again be a big league team in the National League—the New York Mets.

Bill Shea got the ball rolling at the behest of Mayor Robert Wagner of New York, and Branch Rickey was the fulcrum that had made it happen.

The efforts of both men have been rewarded. Rickey is immortalized in Baseball's Hall of Fame in Cooperstown New York. Bill Shea had a stadium named after him, Shea Stadium, the home of the New York Mets from 1964 to 2008.

And millions of baseball fans can thank both men for their hometown teams.

3

The First Expansion —1961

The Los Angeles Angels and the Washington Senators

Baseball expansion—a new frontier? Well, not always. While millions of baseball fans can thank the aforementioned Bill Shea and Branch Rickey for their hometown teams, not all of the added teams represented never-before-charted big-league geography. An expansion team is supposed to be a sparkling new team in a particular league going into a new area. And certainly, beginning in 1961 there were many examples of baseball expanding into new areas with new teams. But then again, that process was certainly not as pure as the driven snow. Take the case of the "expansion" Washington Senators who "entered" the American League in 1961.

A long-time AL franchise, the Senators were established by the first league president, Ban Johnson, in 1901. While they had a number of successful seasons along the way, including a World Series championship in 1924, the franchise had clearly fallen on hard times in the mid-1900s. In their last twenty-four years playing in the nation's capital, the Senators finished higher than fourth just twice, in 1943 and 1945. Calvin Griffith, the owner of the team, said that DC was not a place where he could run a successful franchise. He was hoping to move his struggling team to Minneapolis, the city that previously had lost the New York Giants when the team opted to join Walter O'Malley as his co-conspirator and major rival in San Francisco rather than the Twin Cities.

A curious solution was reached in October of 1960. Griffith was rewarded for his years of keeping his floundering team alive in Washington by being allowed by the American League to move his club to Minnesota for the 1961 season. And Washington DC, the area that did not seem to be an area capable of supporting a baseball team, was awarded with a new expansion club. The very next year! So after failing to support the likes of future Hall of Fame performer Harmon Killebrew as well as such All-Stars as slugging Bob Allison and curve-balling specialist Camilo Pascual, now the area would be asked to support a new team comprising castoffs from other organizations. So a bad team that was not supported was being replaced by a worse team.

So the old Senators moved to the Twin Cities of Minneapolis–St. Paul and became the Minnesota Twins. They were not an expansion team, but rather a relocated team getting a fresh start in a baseball-hungry area. Over the ensuing years, the Minnesota Twins have been a good team that has enjoyed the kind of fan support that they never had in Washington.

In the history of any sports franchise, there are streaks of success and streaks of failure. It is a very cyclical situation. After a team suffers through a down time, there is often talk of going through a rebuilding stage. It is during these times that things often go from bad to worse, as an organization commits itself to building toward the future. Rebuilding is not a fresh start: it is a continuation of a process. The only true fresh start, or new beginning, is an expansion franchise. Ironically, an existing team that needs to rebuild will do so with the knowledge that there will be lean times on the way toward success. And with an expansion team, it is also understood that at least for a few years, there will be some lean times.

When an expansion team begins play, it is stocked with players deemed expendable by the clubs who will make them available during a draft in which new teams choose players not protected by their current clubs. They could be proud veterans who have lost the proverbial few steps, or young players with potential who may not be ready for prime time. There are also prospects available who have become suspect. And then there are the marginal players who simply fill roles on a decent club and may be expected to take on an expanded role and become everyday players in a new city. Couple that with some financial constraints that could handcuff owners who have coughed up league fees as well as stadium costs and the hiring of front-office personnel and field coaches and managers, all of whom could be considered to be in a similar talent pool as the players they acquire.

But it's certainly not all doom and gloom. As many a true fan who lives the game of baseball will acknowledge, even bad baseball is better than no baseball at all. The nation's capital had its share of bad baseball, but it was getting a fresh start with a new ownership group. And California was getting its third big-league team in the Angels.

Los Angeles Angels

The singing cowboy Gene Autry was rich and famous thanks to his movies and records, and he had also gotten involved in the broadcasting business. After attending the 1960 winter baseball meetings to work on getting a broadcasting contract for one of his radio affiliates, he wound up being the owner of the truly new American League franchise, the Los Angeles Angels. But because of the deal that allowed the Senators to move to Minnesota, the original scheduled start of the Angels moved up a year from 1962 to 1961. When things start moving, they move quickly. The franchise was awarded to Autry on December 6, 1960. He hired a general manager in Fred Haney, who in turn hired Bill Rigney as the manager of the team. In the nation's capital, the Senators' first owner was a U.S. Air Force general, Elwood Richard Quesada, who owned the team until 1963. He hired Ed Doherty as general manager and Mickey Vernon as manager.

The first expansion draft was delayed twice, but finally happened on December 14, 1960, at the American League offices on the sixth floor of the IBM Building at 520 Boylston Street in Boston. The two new franchises had eight days to prepare for the player draft. In order to stock the expansion teams with players, each American League club had to make seven players available for the draft from its roster as of August 31, 1960, as well as eight other players from their forty-man roster. Each of the existing clubs could lose a maximum of seven players from their Major League roster.

"The thing about expansion is the protected list," said Pat Gillick. "It's too deep. To give the new teams a chance to be competitive, the existing teams should only be able to protect ten players, with the rest being available. Every time you take a player, a team can pull back three. So you'd get the sixteenth player, then the twentieth guy. I always kind of thought it might be more fair. But the ownership are so anxious to get in that they agree to the terms of the league, which can be ridiculous."

The expansion clubs would pay seventy-five thousand dollars for each of the twenty-eight players they would choose. The rules were that each team must first take ten pitchers from the list of available pitchers, followed by two catchers, six infielders, four outfielders, and then six additional players remaining available on the list. The first choice in each category would be determined by a coin toss. The table below shows the results of the first baseball expansion draft.

Los Angeles	Washington
Pitchers	

Los Angeles	Washington
1 – Eli Grba – New York	2 – Bobby Shantz – New York
3 – Duke Maas – New York	4 – Dave Sisler – Detroit
5 – Jerry Casale – Boston	6 – Johnny Klippstein – Cleveland
7 – Tex Clevenger – Minnesota	8 – Pete Burnside – Detroit
9 – Bob Sprout – Detroit	10 – Carl Mathias – Cleveland
11 – Aubrey Gatewood – Detroit	12 – Ed Hobaugh – Chicago
13 – Ken McBride – Chicago	14 – Hal Woodeshick – Minnesota
15 – Ned Garver – Kansas City	16 – Tom Sturdivant – Boston
17 – Ted Bowsfield – Cleveland	18 – Bob Davis – Kansas City
19 – Ron Moeller – Baltimore	20 – Hector Maestri - Minnesota

Catchers

21 – Ed Sadowski – Boston
23 – Bob Rodgers – Detroit

22 – Dutch Dotterer – Kansas City
24 – Red Wilson – Cleveland

Infielders

25 – Eddie Yost – Detroit
27 – Coot Veal – Detroit
29 – Bob Zipfel – New York
31 – Jim Mahoney – Boston
33 – Gene Leek – Cleveland
35 – Jim Fregosi – Boston

26 – Ken Aspromonte – Cleveland
28 – Dale Long – New York
30 – Ken Hamlin – Kansas City
32 – Bob Johnson – Kansas City
34 – Billy Klaus – Boston
36 – John Schaive – Minnesota

Outfielders

38 – Bob Cerv – New York
40 – Ken Hunt – New York
42 – Joe Hicks – Chicago
44 – Neil Chrisley – Detroit

37 – Willie Tasby – Boston
39 – Gene Woodling – Baltimore
41 – Marty Keough – Cleveland
43 – Jim King – Cleveland

Unrestricted Selections

45 – Earl Averill (c) Chicago
47 – Fred Newman (p) Boston
49 – Jim McAnany (of) Chicago
51 – Ted Kluszewski (1b) Chicago
53 – Don Ross (3b) Baltimore
55 – Julio Becquer (1b) Minnesota

46 – Chuck Hinton (of) Baltimore
48 – Dean Chance (p) Baltimore
50 – Chet Boak (2b) Kansas City
52 – Gene Green (c) Baltimore
54 – Dick Donovan (p) Chicago
56 – Rudy Hernandez (p) Minnesota

Following the draft, a number of trades were made. Even though the teams had just chosen their new players, GMs could not resist the urge to tamper with the team from the first day. Some of the trades were nondescript, and a couple of other deals proved famous from one perspective and infamous from another. But that's what trades are all about:

Washington traded Bob Davis (p) to Los Angeles for Jim Mahoney (IF).

Washington traded Ken Aspromonte (IF) to Los Angeles for Coot Veal (IF).

Washington traded Ken Hamlin (IF) to Los Angeles for Bud Zipfel (IF).

Washington traded Dean Chance (p) to Los Angeles for Joe Hicks (OF).

And following draft day . . .

Washington traded Bobby Shantz (P) to Pittsburgh for Bennie Daniels (P), Harry Bright (OF), and R. C. Stevens.

The trade of Dean Chance to the Angels was a particularly bad one for Washington. While Chance became one of the best pitchers in the game in the mid-1960s, Joe Hicks played just two seasons with the Senators, the best of which was 1962 when he hit .224 in 102 games. Chance was twice a twenty-game winner. But before expansion he was a pitching prospect in the Orioles' chain with a 22-12 Minor League record after two seasons. Roster spots were very competitive, and teams had to make tough decisions, so Chance went from Baltimore to Washington to Los Angeles in the same day. It was the best move the young Angels franchise could have made.

"I had no idea of expansion until the end of 1960," Chance said.

The Orioles said they wanted to keep me, but it came down to me and another pitcher who they just wanted more. I was happy. You want to go where somebody wants you.

We started out and had spring training in Palm Springs. Little Albie Pierson was on that team. I knew him from the Orioles organization in 1960. When I got to the Angels, our manager, Bill Rigney, said that with a name like mine I couldn't lose, because of a couple of old time players, Dizzy Dean and Frank Chance. Jimmy Fregosi came out of the Red Sox organization and was a shortstop, and Bob Rodgers came from Detroit and was our catcher. Bob Sprout came from the Tigers too.

Like many of the young prospects, Chance started the 1961 season with their Triple-A affiliate in Dallas–Ft. Worth. While he finished with a 9-12 record and a 3.66 ERA in 63 games, that Minor League campaign was a tale of two seasons for Dean Chance.

"We had an old catcher named Walker Cooper who was our manager," Chance said. "Even though I had 9 wins and 12 losses, I started out 1-8. At that rate I would have lost 32 games. But I really learned to pitch there. I had some 20 saves and got called up with Rogers, Fregosi, Sprout, and center fielder Chuck Tanner to the Angels. We played in old Wrigley Field in LA."

The decision to have the Halos play at Wrigley Field West was brought about by the move of the old Senators to Minnesota. That forced the American League to move up plans for the new team in Los Angeles by a year so that the Senators would not be the only new team, even though the Angels would not have a home stadium. So as a makeshift solution, they played their inaugural season in a park called Wrigley Field. It was not the Wrigley Field in Chicago; it was the Minor League park in Los Angeles. Cubs owner William Wrigley Jr. had purchased the Los Angeles Angels of the Pacific Coast League in 1921 and moved into the new ballpark in 1925. While the California Minor League stadium bore his name, the stadium in Chicago was at that time still called Cubs Park.

In its lone Major League season, Wrigley Field in Los Angeles saw 248 home runs sail over its fences, a record that lasted for thirty-five years. While the distances from home plate down the lines (340 feet in left field, 338 feet to right field) and center field (412 feet) were comparable to other big league parks, the alleys in left-center and right-center fields were just 345 feet. Suffice to say that it was a launching pad.

Following their inaugural season, the Angels moved across town and shared Dodger Stadium with their National League counterparts while Anaheim Stadium was being built. Because of some smart drafting, shrewd trading, and a draft system that allowed expansion teams to have access to promising young players, the Angels were an exciting and successful team. Guys like Chance, Fregosi, and Bo Belinsky got plenty of attention, but the name of Eli Grba will forever go down in the annals of the history of America's Game for being the first player ever chosen in an expansion draft.

In two seasons with the New York Yankees, Grba was 8-9 as a spot starter and reliever including a 6-4 mark in 1960. He was left unprotected by the Yankees and taken by the Angels as their first pick in the draft. Like many of the other players of his era, Grba paid little attention to the Continental League and some of the changes that were on the doorstep of Major League Baseball.

"I'm a trivia question and will go to my grave as a trivia question," said the good-natured Grba.

> All I remember was the hullaballoo about the Dodgers moving to Los Angeles. As far as the draft was concerned we found out that each team had to put fifteen players on a list who were expendable. I found out that I was on that list and could be going to Los Angeles or Washington. I had been to California, and it was really nice. I had an uncle who lived in Washington [state], so I guess that I felt like the West Coast was a better place to go.
>
> We were told to sit by our phone on draft day, and we'd find out where we were going to go. I was at my grandfather's house, and Fred Haney called me and said that the Angels selected me first. Then Mr. Autry got on the phone with me. Here was the guy I used to watch all the time at the movie shows, and now he's on the phone with me.
>
> I was glad to be a Yankee, and a real father figure to me, Ralph Houk, was going to be their next manager. So I was kind of disappointed and pissed. But then you get calls from writers and congratulations from people. I guess I had mixed emotions. It wasn't so much the attention you got, but you felt that you were really wanted. With the Yankees they all were stars and established players. And then when I got to LA, I became part of the establishment as one of the guys who had been in the league a few years.

Grba responded to his first real shot at a regular turn in a big league rotation by going 11-13 with a 4.25 ERA in 1961. The team finished in eighth place with a 70-91 record, thirty-eight and a half games behind the American League champion Yankees. But they won nine more games than their expansion partners, the Washington Senators, who finished in a last-place tie with the Kansas City Athletics.

The Halos' inaugural season got off to a great start with slugger Ted Kluszewski slugging the first of two home runs in the first inning of their first game, which saw the Angels beat Baltimore, 7–2. The opportunity to play at Wrigley Field helped the Los Angeles offense put up some gaudy stats as five players hit at least twenty home runs. Leon Wagner led the pack with twenty-eight, followed by Ken Hunt with twenty-five, Lee Thomas with twenty-four, Earl Averill Jr. who had a career year and belted twenty-one bombs, followed by Steve Bilko with twenty. Little Albie Pearson, as he was known, led the team in stolen bases, runs, walks, and on-base percentage.

Right-hander Ken McBride anchored the pitching staff with a 12-15 record. Grba was 11-13 and Ted Bowsfield went 11-8. Art Fowler was 5-8 out of the bullpen with 11 saves, and Tom Morgan went 8-2 with 10 saves. The inaugural season was quite a success.

In their second year, 1962, the Angels only got better, flirting with pennant contention for most of the season before finishing in third place with an 86-76 record. It was also the first season of Bo and Dean, Belinsky and Chance, that is. Southpaw Bo had by far his best season and went 10-11 with a 3.56 ERA, including a no-hitter against Baltimore on May 5. Dean had the first of a number of big seasons, going 14-10 with a 2.96 ERA. But their contributions on the field sometimes paled in comparison to their presence off the field.

"Dean Chance and Bo Belinsky got along like two peas in a pod," said Grba.

Bo was just Bo, a kid from New Jersey and Dean was from Wooster, Ohio. They didn't bother anybody. People thought they didn't care because of the nightlife and all that, but the two of them competed as well as anyone else. Belinsky had a good year for us in LA. And Dean Chance was the best right-handed pitcher in baseball that nobody knew about. He used to stick it to the Yankees. Mickey Mantle said he was one of the toughest right-handers he ever saw in his life. He's done wonders with his life, becoming a fight promoter and a great businessman. Belinsky was a handsome Polish-Jewish kid who used that to the max. He was street smart and really used all the publicity. They were both fun guys and good competitors.

Belinsky turned out to be a fading star, but what a star he was. A handsome, garrulous southpaw, he began that 1962 campaign 5-0, including the no-hitter. He was also the Angels' connection with Hollywood, dating the likes of Mamie van Duren, Tina Louise, and Ann Margaret. Fernandomania of a future generation had nothing on Bo Belinsky.

"Bo wound up with 10 wins and I was fourth in the league in ERA with 2.96, 14 wins, and 10 or 11 saves," said Chance.

Anybody who played on that team would say that it was the most fun year of their life. At the All-Star break we were in first place. In LA, they treated us great. We were in the Major Leagues making seven thousand dollars a year. The Yankees would come in and we'd have fifty thousand fans there supporting us.

Our manager, Bill Rigney, said he wanted everybody on that team to do just one little thing. The charisma on that team was great. We had guys like Bobby Knoop, Buck Rodgers, Leon Wagner, and Jim Fregosi. They all had great years. I led the team with fourteen wins. Eli Grba and everybody else did their jobs. That 1962 team was such a collection of great guys who played so well. Like I said, everybody on that team will tell you that it was the most fun that they've ever had.

In addition to Chance and Belinsky, Ken McBride contributed an 11-5 record and Ted Bowsfield was 9-8. Morgan and Fowler combined for a 9-5 record with 14 saves out of the bullpen, and hard-throwing Ryne Duren went 2-9 with 8 saves.

While the team's power outage was less in 1962, in no small measure because of the move from tiny Wrigley Field to the more expansive Dodger Stadium, they were still a force to be reckoned with offensively. First baseman Lee Thomas hit .290 with 26 home runs and 104 RBIs. Leon Wagner continued to be a weapon in left field, hitting .268 with 37 homers and 107 RBIs. Second baseman Billy Moran had a fine year, hitting .282 with 17 home runs and 74 RBIs, and once again Albie Pearson played well, setting the table with his .261 average.

After an outstanding first season in Los Angeles, Eli Grba began to struggle on and off the field. He was 8-9 in 1962 with an ERA of 4.54. But his problems with Rigney and a drinking problem began to take its toll.

"I got the ball a lot, but Mr. Rigney and I didn't get along," he admitted.

I was headstrong and made some comments that he didn't like. I wanted to win and was a real red ass. While I got a chance to pitch more in LA, I'm the one who screwed it up because of the drinking. As long as you do it, the nightlife and all, and still succeed, nobody says a word to you. If you drink too much and win, that's okay. I never knew I had a problem until about six months before I went to the detox place. Each year I went down further and further. It started in the army. All you did was drink.

The Angels franchise was one of the earliest success stories of any expansion team, competing for the pennant in just their second season. The team has seen its name change from the Los Angeles Angels, to the California Angels, to the Anaheim Angels, and now to the Los Angeles Angels of Anaheim.

Some great players have donned the Angels Halo, including Hall of Famers Rod Carew, Nolan Ryan, Bert Blyleven, Rickey Henderson, Eddie Murray, Frank Robinson, Don Sutton, Hoyt Wilhelm, Dave Winfield, and manager Dick Williams.

The Angels defeated the San Francisco Giants in seven games to capture the 2002 World Series championship, after reaching the American League playoffs as a wild card team. They also won the Western Division title in 2009, 2008, 2007, 2005, 2004, 1986, 1982, and 1979.

Washington Senators

What do the Minnesota Twins and the Texas Rangers have in common? Well, they both achieved a great deal of success as Major League franchises after leaving Washington DC. Season after season of losing records, with nearly a hundred losses on numerous occasions, made the Sens perennial cellar-dwellers. The well-known phrase "First in peace, first in war, and last in the American League" pretty much summed up what that woeful team was all about for decades, with very few exceptions.

Long-time owner Clark Griffith passed away in 1955 at the age of eighty-five, which saw his son Calvin take charge of the franchise. The younger Griffith had long felt that it would behoove the franchise to relocate in Minnesota, citing an aging stadium and small crowds as contributing factors for their poor play. While he convinced his fellow owners to allow the move, Major League Baseball was concerned that Congress, whose members would often take in games at old Griffith Stadium, might consider threatening baseball's antitrust exemption. So to keep its agreement with the upstart owners of the Continental League, Minnesota got a team, but not an expansion team. They welcomed in the old Senators, who would become the Twins. And oddly, along with the new Los Angeles Angels, a new and less-than-improved Washington Senators were born.

While the Angels got some young and exciting players in the expansion draft, the new Senators were not as fortunate. Because of Griffith's desire to move the existing Senators to Minnesota, the league expanded a year earlier than originally planned and had a true expansion team in Washington. They literally had a week and a day to prepare for the expansion draft.

The 1961 season saw the team finish in a last-place tie with the Kansas City Athletics with a 61-100 record. The old Senators (now the Minnesota Twins) finished in a tie for seventh place with the Angels with a 70-91 record. Whether discussing the original Senators team that had just moved or the new expansion team, Roger Kahn's words still rung true: "For the Washington Senators, the worst time of year is the baseball season."

The expansion team drew only 597,287 fans in 1961, adding even more credence to the questions about why a new team was brought into DC to replace a team that fans failed to support previously. Despite frustration on the field and disappointment at the turnstiles, there were some excellent examples of good play between the white lines. Veteran Gene Woodling led the team with a .313 batting average, and catcher Gene Green had a team-high 18 home runs, followed by first baseman Dale Long and outfielder Willie Tasby, who each added 17. And young outfielder Chuck Hinton had a fine rookie season, hitting .260 with 22 stolen bases, which was a prelude to a number of productive big league years.

Out on the mound, transplanted Pittsburgh Pirate right-hander Bernie Daniels led the team with his career high 12 wins along with 11 losses and a respectable 3.44 ERA. Another veteran, Dick Donovan went 10-10 in his only season with Washington, but tough luck Joe McClain compiled an 8-18 mark with a 3.86 ERA. Out of the bullpen, Dave Sisler went 2-8 but led the team with 11 saves in 45 appearances. Marty Kutyna led the relief staff with 50 games and a 6-8 record.

Transplanted Senators now playing in Minnesota, including Harmon Killebrew (46 home runs, 122 RBIs, and a .288 batting average), Bob Allison (29 home runs, 105 RBIs, and a .245 batting average) and young catcher Earl Battey (a team-high .302 batting average with 17 home runs and 55 RBIs) continued to become stars in the American League. Young Zoilo Versalles added a fine season as well, hitting .280.

Pitcher Camilo Pascual led the Twins with 15 wins, and southpaw Jack Kralick added 13 victories; reliever Ray Moore went 4-4 with 14 saves. The tale of two cities continued over the next few years, as the new Senators foundered with losing season after losing season while the old Senators, now the Twins, improved every year.

As an example of the exasperation that was no doubt felt in Washington, Dick Donovan, who had pitched so well for the team in 1961, was sent packing to Cleveland after the season along with catcher Green and infielder Jim Mahoney in exchange for outfielder Jimmy Piersall. Naturally, Donovan responded with his career best 20-10 record with the Indians, and Green was a solid back-up backstop. Piersall came to Washington as his career was clearly on the downside, as he hit what was up to that point a career low .244. Midway through the following season he was dispatched to the New York Mets for Gil Hodges.

The Senators' sense of futility that had been so evident prior to the expansion team continued after 1961, as the team averaged around ninety losses per season. Adding to the problems was that ownership was less than stable; Elwood Quesada was only involved for a short time, and was succeeded by Washington stockbrokers James Johnson and James Lemon. Then trucking executive Bob Short purchased the team when he outbid a group headed by comedian Bob Hope. Short became the team's general manager, and he hired the great Ted Williams as manager despite the fact that the Splendid Splinter had never managed or coached before. But the team did respond with its first winning season, with an 86-76 record in 1969.

But that lack of success on the field and in the stands once again saw ownership shift the franchise, which became the Texas Rangers for the 1972 season.

"High ticket prices to see a mediocre team and an unsafe neighborhood kept fans away to augment the losses on [owner Robert] Short's financial statements," wrote Maxwell Kates in "A Brief History of the Washington Stars." "The result—a September [1971] announcement that Short was moving the Senators to Dallas–Fort Worth Metroplex. Washington fans saved their worst for September 30, the final American League game played in Washington, when unruly behavior caused umpire James Honochick to forfeit a 7–5 lead to the visiting New York Yankees."

Heaven forbid that Major League Baseball does not have a team in the nation's capital for fans not to support. First, there was talk of the Cleveland Indians picking up and relocating there. And just two years after the Senators became the Rangers and moved to Texas, there was a serious interest in having a struggling San Diego Padres franchise move east. Padres fans at the time showed little support for their fledgling franchise, with as few as 1,413 fans showing up for a game. With new ownership in place, General Manager Peter Bavasi announced that the Padres would play their home games in Washington in 1974.

Uniforms were designed with a sky-blue road uniform with "Washington" across the chest in red block letters. The team was to be known as the Washington Stars and featured a cap with a red *W* that had a golden star on a white peak, on a blue background. Topps, the baseball card company, even printed cards in its 1974 set identifying a number of Padres as playing for the Washington National League club.

An $84 million lawsuit was filed by the city of San Diego against the Padres for breaking its lease on San Diego Stadium, which forced the team to find an ownership group that would keep the team in San Diego. One group that included Marjorie Everett, a principal stockholder in a racetrack, and songwriter Burt Bacharach, was nixed by the league.

Finally, in January of 1974 the Padres were sold to McDonald's owner Ray Kroc for $12.5 million, who kept the team in San Diego.

While the Senators franchise endured countless losing seasons, they did win the World Series in 1924 over the New York Giants, and returned nine years later only to lose to the Giants. In addition to skipper Ted Williams, numerous noteworthy players have played for the Senators, including Walter Johnson, Frank Howard, Claude Osteen, Camilo Pascual, Harmon Killebrew, Pete Richert, Moose Skowron, and Don Zimmer.

The First Expansion Part Deux—1962

The Houston Colt .45s and the New York Mets

The second phase of Major League Baseball's first expansion occurred a year after the first, in 1962. Unlike the American League, which saw owners capitulate to Calvin Griffith and allow his team to move out of Washington to Minnesota and threw yet another team into the nation's capital, the Senior Circuit followed more closely the original road map that had been drawn up after the agreement that forestalled the Continental League. As originally planned, the National League would have a new team in Houston and would once again have a team playing in New York.

On October 10, 1961, the National League expansion draft was held to stock the rosters of the Houston Colt .45s and the New York Mets. While the rules were similar to the American League expansion draft of 1960, there were some differences. Fifteen players were made available from each of the existing clubs, including seven from the twenty-five-man roster as of August 31, 1961. Both teams were required to pick two players from each roster for $75,000 each and allowed to pick a third player for $50,000. After these three rounds of picks, each existing club posted two more players from the twenty-five-man roster for a premium draft, with Houston and New York each selecting four players at a cost of $125,000 each. The table below provides the results of the National League expansion draft.

Regular Phase - $75,000 per player

Houston Colt .45s	New York Mets
1 – Eddie Bressoud (IF) San Francisco	2 – Hobie Landrith (C) San Francisco
3 – Bob Aspromonte (IF) Los Angeles	4 – Elio Chacon (IF) Cincinnati
5 – Bob Lillis (IF) St. Louis	6 – Roger Craig (P) Los Angeles
7 – Dick Drott (P) Chicago	8 – Gus Bell (OF) Cincinnati
9 – Al Heist (OF) Chicago	10 – Joe Christopher (OF) Pittsburgh
11 – Roman Mejias (OF) Pittsburgh	12 – Felix Mantilla (IF) Milwaukee
13 – George Williams (IF) Philadelphia	14 – Gil Hodges (1B) Los Angeles
15 – Jesse Hickman (P) Philadelphia	16 – Craig Anderson (P) St. Louis
17 – Merritt Ranew (C) Milwaukee	18 – Ray Daviault (P) San Francisco
19 – Don Taussig (OF) St. Louis	20 – John DeMerit (OF) Milwaukee
21 – Bobby Shantz (P) Pittsburgh	22 – Al Jackson (P) Pittsburgh
23 – Norm Larker (1B) Los Angeles	24 – Sammy Drake (IF) Chicago
25 – Sam Jones (P) San Francisco	26 – Chris Cannizzaro (C) St. Louis
27 – Paul Roof (P) Milwaukee	28 – Choo Choo Coleman (C) Philadelphia
29 – Ken Johnson (P) Cincinnati	30 – Ed Bouchee (1B) Chicago
31 – Dick Gernert (1B) Cincinnati	32 – Bobby Gene Smith (OF) Philadelphia

Regular Phase - $50,000 per player

33 – Ed Olivares (IF) St. Louis	34 – Sherman Jones (P) Cincinnati
35 – Jim Umbricht (P) Pittsburgh	36 – Jim Hickman (OF) St. Louis
37 – Jim Golden (P) Los Angeles	

Premium Phase - $125,000 per player

38 – Joe Amalfitano (IF) San Francisco	39 – Jay Hook (P) Cincinnati
40 – Turk Farrell (P) Los Angeles	41 – Bob Miller (P) St. Louis
42 – Hal Smith (C) Pittsburgh	43 – Don Zimmer (IF) Chicago
44 – Al Spangler (OF) Milwaukee	45 – Lee Walls (OF) Philadelphia

Houston Colt .45s

So much of baseball expansion has its roots in the formation of the Continental League, and that was certainly true of the new Houston franchise. Foiled in their previous attempts to secure a Major League franchise, Craig Cullinan joined forces with three other Houston power brokers, George Kirksey, Bob Smith, and Judge Roy Hofheinz. Their efforts led to Houston securing one of the original National League teams along with the New York Mets. Not all of the other cities involved in the Continental League were fortunate enough to get a Major League team, but Houston was ready to go.

Later-day Astros fans may not realize that the original name for the team, picked by fans in a name-the-team contest, was the Colt .45s, chosen for the gun that won the West. And while the most famous ballpark in Houston is certainly the Astrodome, the "Eighth Wonder of the World," the Colt .45s played their first three seasons in a venue known as Colt Stadium, which held thirty-three thousand fans and millions of mosquitos. In fact, the park was known as "Mosquito Heaven." Hall of Fame outfielder and announcer Richie Ashburn once said, "Houston is the only town where women wear insect repellent instead of perfume" (see my *Richie Ashburn Remembered*).

Colt Stadium had big outfield dimensions, as the 360-foot distance down the left- and right-field lines, as well as the 427-foot distance to center field would indicate. The stadium was also the site of the first Sunday night big league game in history in 1963. As the Astrodome was completed for the 1965 season, Colt Stadium was taken apart and shipped to Mexico, where it was reassembled and used by a team in the Mexican League in the 1970s.

As the team sweltered at Colt Stadium, Judge Hofheinz convinced his fellow National League owners of the importance of a new indoor facility, and they agreed. The oppressive summer weather conditions in Houston dictated that an indoor facility needed to be built. But while these plans and construction were underway, the team played in the largely unfriendly confines of Colt Stadium.

The inaugural season in Houston was not bad. The 1962 team under manager Harry Craft played much like their American League counterpart team of 1961, the Los Angeles Angels. The Colt .45s finished in eighth place with a 64-96 record, ahead of both the Chicago Cubs with a 59-103 mark and their fellow National League expansion team, the New York Mets, who set the standard for poor play with a disastrous 40-120 log.

One of the most popular players on the team was right fielder Roman Mejias, who hit .286 while slugging 24 home runs and 76 RBIs with 12 stolen bases. In center field, Carl Warwick had a solid season hitting .260 with 16 homers and 60 RBIs. Catcher Hal Smith hit .235 with 12 round-trippers and 35 RBIs while young third baseman Bob Aspromonte hit a solid .266 with 11 homers and 59 RBIs.

There were also some fine performances on the mound, regardless of won/lost records. Hard-throwing right-hander Turk Farrell went 10-20 but had a more-than-respectable ERA of 3.02, fanning 203 batters in 241.2 innings pitched. Bob Bruce, acquired from the Detroit Tigers, went 10-9 with a 4.06 ERA, while Ken Johnson went 7-16 with a 3.03 ERA, and Jim Golden had a 7-11 mark with a 4.07 ERA. Lefty Hal Woodeshick went 5-15 with a 4.39 ERA.

In the bullpen, Don McMahon led the team with 51 appearances, going 5-5 with 8 saves and a miniscule 1.53 ERA. Bobby Tiefenaur got into 43 games and went 2-4 with 1 save and a 4.34 ERA.

"We beat the Mets and the Cubs too," said Tal Smith, a veteran of more than fifty years in professional baseball who most recently was president of baseball operations for the Houston Astros (1994–2011). "It was not great but better than it could have been."

Being traded to an expansion team from a contending team is not what most ballplayers would hope for. But that is exactly what happened to Bob Bruce. After spending parts of three seasons trying to crack a regular spot on the Tigers' pitching staff, the Detroit native was dealt by his hometown team to Houston with pitcher Manuel Montejo in exchange for pitcher Sam Jones on December 5, 1961.

"I was really disappointed," Bruce said of the trade.

I was playing Winter Ball in Puerto Rico to rehab my arm and get in the heat and pitch. We were on a bus ride to a game and one of the guys was listening to the radio and told me I had just been traded. Oh my God, I wanted so much to do well in Detroit, which was my hometown. I was really devastated. But it turned out to be the best thing that ever happened to me. I wouldn't trade being on the first Colt .45s team and going through the experiences there in Houston. Houston was a great city. I just loved every minute of it. I had a lot of real good experiences there. Plus we learned how to fend off the mosquitoes and stuff like that.

I had a couple of winning years out of the first three of the Colt .45s, which was pretty good. I went 10-9 the first year and then 15-9 in '64. For an expansion team, that was pretty good. That first year we beat out the Mets and the Cubs. They thing about an expansion team, and this carried us for quite a few years, was that we had a pretty good nucleus of fifteen or sixteen guys who could stay competitive. After that it was a revolving door. We would get into a late-inning game and we'd be a little short. We lost a lot of one-run games with the reserves in late innings.

They have expanded again and again. I just think it gave a lot of good ball players an opportunity to play and compete. It gave guys that were outfielders behind people like Willie Mays and Will McCovey a chance to play. A real good friend of mine, Mel Corbo, was with the Dodgers organization. He got stuck behind the first baseman and had to play in Double-A and Triple-A. He could have played in the Major Leagues. He hit nothing but line drives. A guy like Norm Larker got a chance to play every day. Before expansion, if you got stuck behind a guy like Harvey Kuenn, you'd never get a chance to play.

As is the case with many regions of the country, a new baseball team also meant new experiences for the players as well as the fans. As a Detroit native, Bob Bruce had no idea what was in store for him in Houston. But before the team got to its new regular season home, they experienced Cactus League baseball in spring training in Arizona. While the Los Angeles Angels opted for Palm Springs as their preseason home a year before, Houston spent two years in Apache Junction, an experience that general manager Speck Richardson said offered "the bare minimum—and a lot of rattlesnakes."

"It was a junction in the road," Bruce said. "They had the motel we stayed at, which was very nice. There was one bar [The Red Garter] and our ballpark. We stayed out of a lot of trouble. The bar had an old miner who came there every day on a donkey and played the banjo. That was the entertainment. It was really something."

Bruce's late teammate, Turk Farrell, remembered there being two bars in the area. "There were only two bars in town," he said. "One is so bad that even I won't go there, and the other is full of coaches."

Colt .45s lore also includes stories of Farrell taking a short cut to the ballpark through the desert and shooting snakes and beer cans with a .22 caliber pistol. After two springs in Apache Junction, the team set up a new spring training home in Cocoa, Florida.

Their first experience in Houston was quite different as well. The Colt .45s not only had uniforms that they wore on the field, but the players were required to wear cowboy uniforms when they traveled. Every day was like Halloween for the players.

"The first year there we all had to wear cowboy uniforms," Bruce recalled. "The boots they put on us were about ten inches long and were horrible. We were made to wear these outfits on the road when we traveled. We had these big ten-gallon hats, and being a Yankee, I didn't even know how to wear the hat. I think my uniform is in the museum in Houston. We didn't enjoy wearing them."

While they didn't realize it at the time, the outfits and uniforms were all part of a larger plan to gain acceptance for the brand. Of course, that distinction was lost on the players, who felt that they were dressed to knock on doors and say, "Trick or treat!"

"Judge Hofheinz made them wear that," said Tal Smith. "He was a master promoter and gave everything a theatrical flair. He was a great showman. He wanted everyone to recognize the players as Colt .45s for marketing the team. He'd do anything he could to create better ad revenue and radio revenue. He paid a lot of attention to those things. We all had distinct apparel on and off the field. The players tired of it, but we got a lot of mileage out of it."

Considering their experiences in spring training and their travel garb, the best part of the first season for the Colt .45s may have been on the field. Of course, Colt Stadium offered challenges of its own. Not even the clubhouse met anywhere near minimal Big League standards.

"The club house was an experience also," said Bruce. "It had eight-foot ceilings and was just sitting there in the sun, and in Houston, it was unbelievably hot. The air conditioning could get the clubhouse a little below 80 degrees. You'd come in after a game and just sit there and sweat for an hour. It was a very steamy, very smelly place."

Still, the team overcame the heat, mosquitoes, and country/western garb to forge a successful first season by expansion team standards. In 1963 the team treaded water with a 66-96 record and a ninth-place finish in the National. And best of all, the team finished fifteen games ahead of the Mets.

The second-year team did not have the offensive weapons that the previous team did. Home run leader Mejias was dealt to the Boston Red Sox for infielder Pete Runnels, who hit .253 in 124 games. Aspromonte slumped to .214, and Carl Warwick hit just .209. New catcher John Bateman hit .210. Some important young players had their debuts in 1963, however. While their rookie seasons were not spectacular, Rusty Staub (.224 average), Jimmy Wynn (.244 average), and future Hall of Famer Joe Morgan (.240) all got their first taste of the big leagues.

Farrell once again led the staff with a 14-13 record, followed by Johnson at 11-17, Bruce with 5-9, and newcomer Don Nottebart, who went 11-8. It was Nottebart who became the first pitcher to throw a no-hitter for a National League expansion team on May 17, when he held the Phillies hitless in a 4–1 win.

Those early years in Houston were also times of history and tragedy. The Colt .45s and later the Astros were a franchise that seemed to have a steady stream of young players coming up in their Minor League system. And on September 27, 1963, they took that bevy of young prospects and played them all in one game. On that night against the New York Mets, Houston had the first all-rookie lineup in the history of the game.

That rookie lineup comprised pitcher Jay Dahl (seventeen years old), catcher Jerry Grote (nineteen years old), first baseman Rusty Staub (nineteen years old), second baseman Joe Morgan (twenty years old), third baseman Glenn Vaughan (nineteen years old), shortstop Roland "Sonny" Jackson (nineteen years old), and outfielders Brock Davis (nineteen years old), Aaron Pointer (twenty-one years old), and Jimmy Wynn (twenty-one years old). Also during that game, two left-handed relief pitchers made their Major League debuts, Joe Hoerner and Danny Coombs.

While his big league debut was not successful, as he gave up seven runs in three innings en route to his first and last big league loss (Mets 10, Colt .45s 3), less than two years later, Jay Dahl became the youngest former Major League player to die. While pitching for Salisbury of the Western Carolina League, with a 5-0 record, Dahl had pitched his team into first place by beating Gastonia, 7–3, on June 19, 1965. Later that evening, the Salisbury Astros' players were the guests at a dinner at the home of G. M. Hamilton, the Salisbury club president. Dahl and Gary Marshall, a nineteen-year-old pitcher also on the team, left to attend a movie with Patricia Ann Troutman, a twenty-year-old secretary.

As the ballplayers were returning Troutman to her home, the auto, which is believed to have been driven by Marshall, was traveling at high speed when it hit a patch of sand on a Salisbury street and went out of control, hitting a tree. Troutman was killed instantly.

Jay Dahl died of internal injuries hours after the accident at Rowan Memorial Hospital. Marshall, a native of Hutchinson, Kansas, was taken to a hospital in Winston-Salem. He was suffering from a broken right arm and a broken right leg. His injuries also forced the removal of his left eye, and the vision in his right eye was lost as it was damaged beyond repair.

Interestingly, a North Carolina prisoner offered one of his eyes in a transplant to Marshall in the hope he would be able to see again. But doctors felt that the transplant would not result in Marshall regaining his vision.

Jay Dahl was not the only Houston player to die young. Fourteen months before his untimely death, the Colt .45s suffered the loss of one of their best relief pitchers, Jim Umbricht. The big right-hander had been up and down between the Pittsburgh Pirates and their Minor League affiliates for three years and had found a home with Houston. He got the call to the Colt .45s in July of 1962 and went 4-0 with a miserly 2.01 ERA in 34 appearances.

He was at the height of his career, pitching well for the expansion Houston team. It was in spring training of 1963, during one of the team's golf outings, that Umbricht confided to general manager Paul Richards that a small lump had appeared on his leg. Richards sent the pitcher back to Houston's M. D. Anderson Cancer Clinic, where he learned that he had lymphoma, which had spread to his leg, thigh, and groin. On March 8 he underwent more than six hours of surgery at Methodist Hospital in Houston to remove the cancerous tumors.

Two months later, he was back on the mound pitching for the Houston Colt .45s with more than a hundred stitches in his leg.

"After he had the surgery, we all thought he was going to be all right," said his teammate, pitcher Ken Johnson. "He thought so too. He was such a competitor. During games when he was pitching, blood would start to come through his uniform, from where he had the surgery and the stitches were. He'd have to go into the clubhouse and put on a new bandage to keep the blood from showing through his uniform. He would just never quit."

While the initial prognosis after surgery was encouraging, Umbricht soon learned that he was dying. Despite the bleak outlook, he continued to pitch and pitch well, with a 4-3 record in 35 games with a 2.61 ERA. In fact, he yielded just fifty-two hits in seventy-two innings. But that November, he was back in the hospital and learned that the rapidly spreading cancer was incurable.

Although he had a burning desire to live until the Opening Day of the 1964 baseball season, Jim Umbricht passed away at the age of thirty-three on April 8, just five days before the Colts' opening game against the Cincinnati Reds. In the years since then, pitcher Don Wilson, former Colt .45s slugger Walt Bond, and former Astros pitcher Darryl Kile all passed away at tragically young ages.

The Houston franchise was renamed the Astros in 1965 and moved into the Eighth Wonder of the World, the Astrodome. Baseball's first enclosed stadium was a wonder, but not without its issues. Because of the ceiling, which comprised skylight panels to help fielders see the baseball once it was hit in the air, the grass died. This led to yet another new innovation to the sports world—AstroTurf.

While the Houston franchise had the typical growing pains of an expansion team, the player selections of general manager Paul Richards helped the club finish ahead of the New York Mets in six of seven years. While the Astros have never won a World Series, they did play in the Fall Classic in 2005, only to be swept by the Chicago White Sox. The Astros won the National League pennant that year as a wild card team, which they had also done in 2004. In addition, Houston won the Central Division title in 2001, 1999, 1998, and 1997 and were Western Division title winners in 1986 and 1980. Those two years saw them lose heartbreaking series first to the Phillies and then to the Mets, barely missing chances to advance to the World Series.

The Houston franchise has had a collection of fantastic players, including Hall of Famers Nolan Ryan, Nellie Fox, Eddie Matthews, Joe Morgan, Don Sutton, and Robin Roberts. Other notable players include Mike Scott, Don Wilson, Larry Dierker, Jimmy Wynn, Crag Biggio, Jeff Bagwell, Jose Cruz, Roy Oswalt, Lance Berkman, Roger Clemens, and Andy Pettitte.

"It's been exciting throughout," said Tal Smith.

I was young and early in my career when we went to Houston. I remember driving through Houston when I was going to spring training, working with the Reds. Two and a half years later I was living there permanently. It was so different from the standpoint of culture, with a real southwestern flavor of oil and cattle. Today Houston is quite metropolitan. Major League Baseball was new to everyone. It was exciting to see the reaction of the people. Then we had the first year in the Astrodome, which I was so proud of because I was a project manager of that since its inception. It was like a big theater. People were coming to the game all dressed up and would sit there politely like they were waiting for intermission before they applauded.

The franchise has had a lot of great moments, and we struggled too. We've finished sixty-four games out of first place and then turned it around. I still maintain that there is such a thin line between winning and losing. Games are often decided by a single run, and you can turn a loss into a win very easily. You can rebuild without having a huge payroll. Just an addition here and there can make a big difference. A lot of fine players have come through here such as Bagwell, Biggio, Ryan, Pettitte, Cedeno, Cruz, and others.

New York Mets

Of the four expansion teams that entered the Major Leagues in 1961 and 1962, no other franchise experienced more frustration on the playing field than the New York Mets. And ironically, the Mets were the first of the teams to win a world championship just seven years later.

The Mets might never have even become a reality had the proposed move of the St. Louis Browns come to fruition at the Major League owners meeting scheduled for December 8, 1941, but the attack on Pearl Harbor began a long process that saw New York lose both its National League teams in 1957 and get a new franchise for the 1962 season. Make no mistake: the first New York Mets team was bad. But they were just good enough to keep you interested. While they were absolutely blown out of some games early, more often than not they stayed in games long enough to be competitive. Their fans were interested and grateful to have their new team, no matter how bad it might have been. But this team was new and fun. They just had trouble winning.

The first game in the history of the New York Mets, scheduled for April 10, 1962, in St. Louis, was rained out. One could say that this was a harbinger of things to come. They played their first of two seasons at the home of the old New York Giants, the Polo Grounds, before moving into the new Shea Stadium in 1964. The team drew 922,530 fans in its inaugural season and more than a million in 1963. Not bad for a team with a 40-120 record that finished sixty and a half games behind the National League pennant winner, ironically, the aforementioned Giants. Their 120 losses was the most since the Cleveland Spiders actually went 20-134 in 1899. Yes, 20-134! Following that season, the team folded. No one can accuse the New York Mets of being quitters.

While the futility of the team is well documented, they still had some pretty good players. Left fielder Frank Thomas had hit twenty or more home runs eight times in his nine previous big league seasons with the Pirates, Cubs, and Milwaukee Braves. The big slugger stepped right in and led the Mets with 34 round trippers, 94 RBIs, and hit .266. Veteran Richie Ashburn, the former Phillie and Cub, led the team with a .306 average, along with a career high 7 home runs and 28 RBIs. Marv Throneberry hit .244 at first base with 16 homers and 49 RBIs. And third baseman Felix Mantilla hit a more-than-respectable .275 with 11 homers and 59 RBIs.

But despite some respectable offensive performances, the team had the lowest batting average in the National League at .240. Only the Houston Colt .45s scored fewer runs, and only the Chicago Cubs struck out more. The Mets also finished last in the league in hits and doubles.

While the team had trouble scoring runs, they certainly had no problem giving them up, as the Mets staff led the Majors, allowing 948 runs to score against them. Roger Craig led the team with 10 wins, but also led the league in losses with 24 while posting a 4.51 ERA. It was the most losses a pitcher endured in a single season since Ben Cantwell, of the Boston Braves, dropped 25 decisions in 1935. Joining Craig in the starting rotation were Bob Miller, who went 1-12, Al Jackson with an 8-20 record, and Jay Hook, who finished at 8-19.

Craig Anderson appeared in 50 games, mostly out of the bullpen, sporting a 3-17 mark with a 5.35 ERA and 4 saves. Southpaw Ken MacKenzie had the only winning record on the staff with a 5-4 record in 42 relief appearances. When he was traded to St. Louis late in the 1963 season, MacKenzie had an 8-5 Mets career record in 76 games. And they traded him!

Not only did the team have trouble hitting and pitching, but their fielding was abysmal. With the initials of his name, there was no way that former Yankee Marvin Eugene Throneberry would not be a Met. Nicknamed "Marvelous Marv" by teammate Richie Ashburn, Throneberry could hit. But he also committed 17 errors in 116 games at first base. Second base wasn't any better, as Charlie Neal and "Hot Rod" Kanehl had a combined 35 miscues. Shortstop Elio Chacon committed 22 errors. The Mets' infield totaled 144 errors.

This collection of players may have suffered through the worst baseball season in decades, but one man made the losing a little less cumbersome, the Mets' first manager, former Yankee skipper Casey Stengel. The man who guided the crosstown Yanks to seven World Series championships and ten American League pennants during a twelve-year stretch had been basically forced out of his job after the Yankees were upset in the 1960 World Series by the Pittsburgh Pirates, when Bill Mazeroski homered off of Ralph Terry. The tactical moves, such as platooning and pinch hitting early in games that Stengel made so often during his tenure had not been as successful and at the age of seventy, he was forced out of the Yankees picture. Never mind that fourteen other teams would have cherished the opportunity to lose Game Seven of the World Series to the Pirates.

While he was certainly looked at as a genius by many baseball people, dubbed "The Old Professor," there were those who considered Stengel's moves less than stellar.

"I was in shock over the '60 Series," said pitcher Eli Grba, who compiled a 6-4 record with the Yankees during the regular season, appearing in 24 games.

I was also kind of peeved because I didn't get a chance to pitch in it. Stengel screwed up the World Series. You have Whitey Ford as your ace. You are supposed to have your best pitcher go in the first game of the Series because then he could pitch three times in a seven-game Series. But he had Art Ditmar pitch the first game and we lost.

In Game Seven, he had Terry warm up three or four different times during the game and never went in. Now, here he is in the ninth inning and has nothing. Ryne Duren was sitting there and could have given us a couple of innings.

Criticisms such as Grba's were not isolated. In fairness to Stengel, his style of managing had led to an incredible string of successful seasons for the Yankees. And even his decision to start Ditmar over Ford could be explained, since it could be argued that Ditmar was the ace of the '60 squad with his 15-9 record, rather than Ford, who went 12-9.

So after a year out of the game following being replaced at the helm of the Yankees by Ralph Houk, Stengel was named the first manager of the New York Mets. While it was obvious that the team had little chance of winning, just how much they would lose was quite a surprise.

"I actually thought we were going to have a better team than we ended up having," said pitcher Jay Hook.

We had a lot of name guys like Ashburn and Hodges who had been around. I thought this could be a really good team. It turned out we weren't. I don't think we ever assumed we were as bad as we were. One of the great things about baseball is that it's a new game every day. We may have lost a lot of games, but I never thought we didn't have a chance to win tomorrow and I know a lot of the guys thought that too.

We had won the pennant with Cincinnati the year before, in '61, but I didn't get a chance to pitch in the Series. I came up with a really bad case of the mumps during the season, which really wiped me out for most of the year. All the guys were upset, because they had to get shots. The Reds put me up on the expansion list as a premium draft choice, which meant the new clubs had to pay $125,000 as opposed to $75,000. The Reds' strategy was that since Hook didn't pitch much, he might not get picked up. But the Mets took me, and I was disappointed to leave the Reds. But on the other side of the coin, look at the New York market. So I went there with mixed feelings.

The losses at the Polo Grounds mounted, but the Mets were a phenomenon, and the leader of the pack was Stengel. His malaprops and odd statements that left people shaking their heads were a language of their own, known as Stengelese. While managing the Yankees, he once said, "If we're going to win the pennant, we've got to start thinking we're not as smart as we think we are."

Upon being fired by the Yankees basically for being seventy, he quipped, "I'll never make that mistake again."

But once he arrived on the scene with the Mets, Casey took Stengelese to new levels, often entertaining the beat writers in the clubhouse and at hotel bars on the road late into the evening. One of his gems was, "I've been in this game a hundred years, but I see new ways to lose I never knew existed before."

When describing his three catchers with the Mets, he said, "I got one that can throw but can't catch, one that can catch but can't throw, and one who can hit but can't do either."

Reading about Stengel gives one level of enjoyment, but playing for him took it to a new level. And for all of the funny things he would say, it was part of his master plan to get some of the pressure off of his players. He may very well have been "The Old Professor."

"He was one of the quickest-witted people I've ever known," said Jay Hook. "He had his sayings and Stengelese. Casey was seventy at the time. He would be talking on a subject and then was thinking about what he would say next and would jump to that topic and then go back to the previous subjects. He had several topics in a conversation that paralleled each other."

Hook won eleven games for the Reds in 1960 and went 8-19 for the expansion Mets. He was one of the brightest people in the game, having earned a master's degree in thermodynamics at Northwestern. While playing for the Mets, he participated in an article about what makes a baseball curve.

"It was the time of Sputnik, which was a spheroid, just like a baseball," Hook said.

We worked up the physical dynamics of making a ball curve. It's the same law that makes a wing lift an airplane. One of the young writers from the *New York Times* needed me to explain why a baseball curves. So I drew up a schematic for him and discussed the pressure gradients and linear velocity, and I wrote up the law for him. He won fifty bucks for [that] article in the *Times*. So then I get knocked out of a ballgame, and Casey says, "You know, if Hook could only do what he knows." I'm seventy-four now, and that expression I've used I don't know how many times. Its application is universal.

In fairness to Hook, he was also pretty good at what he knew. On April 23, 1962, after the Mets lost the first nine games of the season, Hook threw a five-hit 9–1 victory over the Pittsburgh Pirates, earning the first win in the history of the New York Mets franchise. He also led the team that season with thirty-four starts and thirteen complete games.

"Winning that first game means more now than it did then," he said. "I wasn't looking at it as anything other than, 'We won a game.'

But since then it certainly achieved higher recognition than back then. I never thought it would be a defining moment in my life. But the recognition of me and my career is much more because of that game. That's what people remember about my career."

While being part of the losing-ist team in modern history may have been challenging at the time, it is a badge of honor for the players who gave it their best shot and continued to show up every day in the hope that this was the tomorrow that would be a better day.

"The Mets organization must have given my name to publications a few years ago when the Detroit Tigers were on the cusp of losing more than 120 games," said Hook.

The *Los Angeles Times* asked me to write an op-ed piece for them. One of the things I focused on was that baseball wasn't the end of the world and used examples of what some of the guys who had been in baseball had done with their lives. Look at how Roger Craig has done as a manager, pitching coach, and with the split-finger fastball. Richie Ashburn had a second career announcing and writing. Hobie Landrith became a vice president with Volkswagen. Just because that team lost 120 games didn't mean that the people on the team necessarily felt like losers. They went on and had successful lives in other avenues.

Alan Trammell was the manager of the Tigers that year, and people compared him to Casey. People asked me if I wanted them to lose more than us. I really hoped that they wouldn't, because even though we lost all those games, it wasn't going to change Casey's reputation as a good manager. If a first-time manager like Trammell beat that record, the stigma would be with him his whole life. For us, losing 120 games was not the end of the world.

Although they were not the least bit successful on the playing field, the team won over the fans of New York. National League fans in the Big Apple had been without a team for five years, and they were happy to embrace the Mets. Winning was expected for the Yankees, across the river. It was kind of a bonus for the expansion New York Mets.

In his book *Once More around the Park: A Baseball Reader*, author Roger Angell recounted attending a Mets game against the Los Angeles Dodgers at the Polo Grounds in 1962. The Mets got creamed, but Angell realized the difference between a Mets fan and a Yankees fan. He was able to discern what made the Mets lovable. Turns out, it is something in each of us:

"These [Yankees] fans expect no less than perfection. They coolly accept the late-inning rally, the winning homer, as only their due. They are apt to take defeat with ill grace, and they treat their stars as though they were executives hired to protect their interests. During a slump or a losing streak, these capitalists are quick and shrill with their complaints: 'They ought to damn well do better than this, considering what they're being paid.'

"Suddenly the Mets fans made sense to me," he wrote.

What we were witnessing was precisely the opposite of the kind of rooting that goes on across the river. This was the losing cheer, the gallant yell for a good try—antimatter to the sounds of Yankee Stadium. This was a new recognition that perfection is admirable but a trifle inhuman, and that a stumbling kind of semi-success can be much more warming. Most of all, perhaps, these exultant yells for the Mets were also yells for ourselves, and came from a wry, half-understood recognition that there is more Met than Yankee in every one of us. I know for whom that foghorn blew; it blew for me.

The following season, 1963, saw the Mets improve to a 51-111 mark in their final season at the Polo Grounds, which played host to 1,080,108 fans, fourth best in the National League. While the Mets still finished in last place, forty-eight games behind the eventual World Series champion Los Angeles Dodgers, a changing of the guard had begun. Second baseman Ron Hunt led the team with a .272 average, adding 10 home runs and 42 RBIs in his rookie season. He also was hit by pitches 13 times, something that would happen to him 243 times during his twelve-year big league career. In fact, Hunt led the league in being hit by pitches for seven consecutive seasons, from 1968 to 1974, including an astounding 50 times in 1971. No doubt, Ron Hunt was a player who would take one for the club.

Jim Hickman hit .229 but added 17 homers and 51 RBIs, and Frank Thomas hit .260 with 14 dingers and 60 RBIs. Veteran Duke Snider added 14 round trippers along with 45 RBIs and a .243 average. But he made history on June 14, 1963, when he hit his 400th career home run against the Cincinnati Reds, off pitcher Bob Purkey.

The Mets' pitching staff evolved in 1963. Holdover Al Jackson led the staff with a 13-17 record and a 3.96 ERA. Luckless Roger Craig was again a twenty-game loser with a 5-22 mark. Carlton Willey went 9-14, and Tracy Stallard went 6-17. Galen Cisco was 7-15 in 51 games, and Hook went 4-14 in 41 games. The top man out of the bullpen was Larry Bearnarth, who was 3-8 with 4 saves, appearing in a team-high 58 games for the Mets.

After two seasons at the Polo Grounds, in 1964 the Mets moved into a sparkling new stadium in Flushing, New York, named for the man responsible for bringing National League baseball back to the city that never sleeps, Bill Shea. Ironically, the park was built in the area that Robert Moses had suggested that Walter O'Malley house the Brooklyn Dodgers.

The early ineptitude of the Mets was exemplified in the 1966 amateur draft, when the club passed over outfielder Reggie Jackson to select catcher Steve Chilcott, who would never play in the Major Leagues. But certainly every franchise has numerous examples of such unfortunate moves. The Mets have actually become one of the most successful expansion franchises, winning the World Series in 1969 and 1986. They, the Toronto Blue Jays, and the Florida Marlins are the only expansion teams to win two championships.

An oddity concerning the Mets is that none of their pitchers had ever thrown a no-hitter until June 1, 2012, when Johan Santana hurled a gem.

They won National League pennants in 1969, 1973, 1986, and 2000.

The Mets were East Division champs in 1969, 1973, 1986, 1988, and 2006, and wild card teams in 1999 and 2000.

Numerous Hall of Famers have played with the team, including Roberto Alomar, Richie Ashburn, Yogi Berra, Gary Carter, Rickey Henderson, Willie Mays, Eddie Murray, Nolan Ryan, Tom Seaver, Duke Snider, Warren Spahn, and, of course, "The Old Professor," manager Casey Stengel. But the history of the franchise is replete with many other notable players, including Gil Hodges, Jerry Koosman, Tom Glavine, Keith Hernandez, Ron Darling, Ed Kranepool, Dwight Goodin, Darryl Strawberry, Jon Matlack, Cleon Jones, Tommy Agee, and Ron Swoboda.

The Second Wave
—1969

The Kansas City Royals, Seattle Pilots,
San Diego Padres, and Montreal Expos

The expansions of 1961 and 1962 had solved some of baseball's problems. Once again, America's Game had a National League club in New York and a new club in California. And for some reason, there was still a team in the nation's capital. But there were still issues troubling the game.

There was not the widespread interest in the game that had been hoped for by the previous expansion. Eight years into the 1960s, baseball attendance had exceeded that of 1960 by just three million. At the same time, a trend toward dual-earner families, in which both the man and women worked, resulted in additional family income and increased recreational spending. Watching televised sports was certainly one of the most popular recreational activities in the country, and this also led to increased attendance at games. As a result, more bodies went through the turnstiles and more profits came from television and radio revenue, so times were good for club owners. But they could be better.

Owners agreed on the subject of expansion, but once again, in what would be a recurring theme, baseball would be held hostage by legislators threatening to challenge the game's antitrust exemption. You can always count on a politician to be at the forefront of any such battle.

When Calvin Griffith moved the Senators to Minnesota, that failing franchise was replaced by an expansion franchise destined to fail. The Milwaukee Braves moved to Atlanta in 1966, causing unhappiness in Wisconsin, and then the Kansas City Athletics moved to Oakland after the 1967 season. Major League Baseball owners agreed to a four-team expansion at their winter meeting of 1967 but once again found their hands tied, to a degree.

U.S. senator Stuart Symington of Missouri was so angered by the departure of Charles O. Finley's Athletics of to Oakland that he drew up legislation to remove baseball's antitrust exemption if Kansas City did not get a team to replace the A's.

Baseball's antitrust exemption is one of those gray areas that everyone recognizes but few understand. It seems like every time a particular legislature becomes angry or upset with Major League Baseball, this trump card is used.

Peter Bendix wrote an illuminating explanation of antitrust exemption on Beyondtheboxscore.com, saying:

> The United States currently has antitrust laws in order to prevent businesses from monopolizing a given market. However, throughout its history, major league baseball has monopolized the baseball market, preventing upstart competitors from ever really getting off the ground. And the Supreme Court has upheld MLB's right to their monopoly several times. In many ways, major league baseball is the only true monopoly in the United States, and has been since its inception. . . .
>
> When the National League joined forces with the American League in 1903, the partnership proved to be fruitful immediately. And one of the main rules of business is: success breeds imitation.
>
> Thus, it should be no surprise that another baseball league soon had intentions of challenging the AL/NL monopoly. The Federal League started out as a minor league, but it had major intentions. In 1914, in

fact, many people considered the Federal League to be a Major League. And the Federal League wanted to make it official.

An antitrust lawsuit against MLB was filed by the prospective Federal League owners, who claimed there was a conspiracy to destroy the upstart league. A court agreed with the plaintiffs in April of 1919 and awarded $240,000 in damages. Two years later an appellate court overturned the lower court's decision. They stated that baseball was not the type of commerce that federal law was intended to regulate. The Supreme Court then upheld this decision, allowing baseball's antitrust exemption to continue.

This ruling held in place until former St. Louis Cardinals outfielder Curt Flood sued baseball in 1972 and saw his case heard by the United States Supreme Court. Flood was an outstanding player who refused to report to the Philadelphia Phillies after being traded there by St. Louis and was attempting to have baseball's Reserve Clause overturned. The Reserve Clause bound a player to the organization that originally signed him in perpetuity, unless he was released or traded.

While Flood lost his case in the high court, the process resulted in baseball players getting arbitration, which not only drastically increased player salaries but eventually led to the players getting free agency, when an arbitrator ruled against baseball and in favor of pitchers Andy Messersmith and Dave McNally, who were both ruled free agents. This opened up the floodgates, which allowed players a system of free agency that has resulted in the enormous salaries that players earn today, as well as the continual movement of players from one team to another.

It was in this contentious era that threats over baseball antitrust legislation continued and Major League Baseball continually chose to give in to the special interests of those who threatened their antitrust exemption. When a city was abandoned, protests by fans and litigation influenced which franchises were awarded and where they were awarded. The original concept of mirroring the teams envisioned in the Continental League became less a reality.

It was also at this time of heightened social awareness that baseball began to reflect the charged atmosphere in the country demanding civil rights and more personal freedom, which will be treated in the next chapter. Suffice it to say that society and baseball were changing. Looking back, it's possible to look at baseball players today, as well as society today, and reference the cigarette commercial of the day that attracted women with the tagline, "You've come a long way, baby!"

Many changes would be seen in baseball in 1969. The size of the strike zone was lessened and the pitching mound was lowered in response to the "Year of the Pitcher," 1968, which had brought a cycle of overpowering pitching to its zenith. There would also be a totally different look to the game based on both the American and National Leagues splitting into two six-team divisions. The original plan had scheduled this expansion for 1971, but the Symington antitrust threat caused MLB to move that up to 1969, similar to what happened in 1961 when the Angels and Senators started a year earlier than the original planned.

The first-place finishers from each six-team division would play a best-of-five league championship series with the two winners facing off in the World Series. While many baseball purists thought this plan nothing short of sacrilege, the visionaries had this one right. America's Game was losing fans because two ten-team divisions often saw no real pennant race down the stretch of the season. Two six-team divisions in each league doubled the number of teams reaching the postseason, and the addition of the league championship series opened up whole new avenues as far as rivalries are concerned.

The American League divisions were basically geographic, while in the National League, parity between the two divisions was a consideration, as there was the fear that one division would be much stronger than the other. So the Atlanta Braves and the Cincinnati Reds were both placed in the West Division, while the St. Louis Cardinals and Chicago Cubs were in the East. Such a geographic snafu was not without precedent in sports. The Atlanta franchise of the National Football League, the Falcons, were also in the West Division, while the Cincinnati Bengals were in the AFL Central Division. Conversely, the St. Louis Cardinals football team was part of the NFL East.

Once again, with the antitrust gun held to its head, Major League Baseball embarked on its second expansion in 1969. The Kansas City Royals and Seattle Pilots would join the American League, while the Montreal Expos and San Diego Padres would be their National League counterparts.

In Kansas City, owner Ewing Kauffman named his team the Royals, after the American Royal livestock show held in that city since 1899. The Seattle Pilots were named for the harbor pilots of the maritime industry in Puget Sound. An ownership group headed by Dewey Soriano and William Daley were in for rough waters.

In the National League, the owner of Seagram, Charles Bronfman, was the owner of the new Montreal Expos, the first Major League Baseball franchise outside the United States. The team was named the Expos for the World's Fair that Montreal hosted that year. The owner of the Pacific Coast League San Diego Padres team, C. Amholdt Smith, won the bidding for the new NL San Diego team and kept that name.

So the revamped baseball divisions were as follows:

American League East: Baltimore Orioles, Boston Red Sox, Cleveland Indians, Detroit Tigers, New York Yankees, and Washington Senators.

American League West: California Angels, Chicago White Sox, Kansas City Royals, Minnesota Twins, Oakland A's, and Seattle Pilots.

National League East: Chicago Cubs, Montreal Expos, New York Mets, Philadelphia Phillies, Pittsburgh Pirates, and St. Louis Cardinals.

National League West: Atlanta Braves, Cincinnati Reds, Houston Astros, Los Angeles Dodgers, San Diego Padres, and San Francisco Giants.

The rules for the draft were different for each league. In the American League, Kansas City and Seattle each paid a $100,000 franchise fee to join the Junior Circuit. Each team picked thirty players, three from each team, in the expansion draft for $175,000 each. The established teams could protect fifteen players, plus three more after each round. And the new teams agreed not to share in the national television revenue from 1969 to 1971, which cost them $2,062,500.

In the National League, Montreal and San Diego paid a $4 million franchise fee to join the league and had to prove that they had an additional $2.5 million in working capital. They also picked thirty players in the draft, three from each team, for $200,000 each. The established teams could also protect three additional players after each round. But unlike their American League counterparts, the Expos and Padres were allowed to share in national television revenue immediately.

On October 15, 1968, the American League held its expansion draft, the day after the National League had filled its two new teams. The results appear in the tables below.

Kansas City Royals

1 – Roger Nelson (P) Baltimore
4 – Joe Foy (IF) Boston
6 – Jim Rooker (P) New York
8 – Joe Keough (OF) Oakland
10 – Steve Jones (P) Washington
12 – Jon Warden (P) Detroit
13 – Ellie Rodriguez (C) New York
15 – Dave Morehead (P) Boston
17 – Mike Fiore (OF) Baltimore
19 – Bob Oliver (OF) Minnesota
22 – Bill Butler (P) Detroit
23 – Steve Whitaker (OF) New York
25 – Wally Bunker (P) Baltimore
27 – Paul Schaal (IF) California
29 – Don Haynes (IF) Chicago
31 – Dick Drago (P) Detroit
34 – Pat Kelly (OF) Minnesota
36 – Billy Harris (IF) Cleveland
38 – Don O'Riley (P) Oakland
40 – Al Fitzmorris (P) Chicago
42 – Moe Drabowsky (P) Baltimore
43 – Jackie Hernandez (IF) Minnesota
45 – Mike Hedlund (P) Cleveland
47 – Tom Burgmeier (P) California
49 – Hoyt Wilhelm (P) Chicago
51 – Jerry Adair (IF) Boston

Seattle Pilots

2 – Don Mincher (IF) California
3 – Tommy Harper (OF) Cleveland
5 – Ray Oyler (IF) Detroit
7 – Jerry McNertney (C) Chicago
9 – Buzz Stephen (P) Minnesota
11 – Chico Salmon (IF) Cleveland
14 – Diego Segui (P) Oakland
16 – Tommy Davis (OF) Chicago
18 – Marty Pattin (P) California
20 – Gerry Schoen (P) Washington
21 – Gary Bell (P) Boston
24 – Jack Aker (P) Oakland
26 – Rich Rollins (IF) Minnesota
28 – Lou Piniella (OF) Cleveland
30 – Dick Bates (P) Washington
32 – Larry Haney (C) Baltimore
33 – Dick Baney (P) Boston
35 – Steve Hovley (OF) California
37 – Steve Barber (P) New York
39 – John Miklos (P) Washington
41 – Wayne Comer (IF) Detroit
44 – Darrell Brandon (P) Boston
46 – Skip Lockwood (P) Oakland
48 – Gary Timberlake (P) New York
50 – Bob Richmond (P) Washington
52 – John Morris (P) Baltimore

54 – Jerry Cram (P) Minnesota
56 – Fran Healy (C) Cleveland
58 – Scott Northey (OF) Chicago
60 – Ike Brookens (P) Washington

San Diego Padres

1 – Ollie Brown (OF) San Francisco
3 – Dave Giusti (P) St. Louis
5 – Dick Selma (P) New York
7 – Al Santorini (P) Atlanta
9 – Jose Arcia (IF) Chicago
12 – Clay Kirby (P) St. Louis
14 – Fred Kendall (C) Cincinnati
16 – Jerry Morales (OF) New York
18 – Nate Colbert (IF) Houston
20 – Zolio Versalles (IF) Los Angeles
22 – Frank Reberger (P) Chicago
24 – Jerry Davanon (IF) St. Louis

26 – Larry Stahl (OF) New York
28 – Dick Kelley (P) Atlanta
30 – Al Ferrara (OF) Los Angeles
31 – Mike Corkins (P) San Francisco
33 – Tom Dukes (P) Houston
35 – Rick James (P) Chicago
37 – Tony Gonzalez (OF) Philadelphia
39 – Dave Roberts (P) Pittsburgh
42 – Ivan Murrell (OF) Houston
44 – Jim Williams (OF) Los Angeles
46 – Billy McCool (P) Cincinnati
48 – Roberto Pena (IF) Philadelphia
50 – Al McBean (P) Pittsburgh
51 – Rafael Robles (IF) San Francisco
53 – Fred Katawczik (P) Cincinnati
55 – Ron Slocum (IF) Pittsburgh
57 – Steve Arlin (P) Philadelphia
59 – Cito Gaston (OF) Atlanta

53 – Mike Marshall (P) Detroit
55 – Jim Gosger (OF) Oakland
57 – Mike Ferraro (OF) New York
59 – Paul Click (P) California

Montreal Expos

2 – Manny Mota (OF) Pittsburgh
4 – Mack Jones (OF) Cincinnati
6 – John Bateman (C) Houston
8 – Gary Sutherland (IF) Philadelphia
10 – Jack Billingham (P) Los Angeles
11 – Donn Clendenon (IF) Pittsburgh
13 – Jesus Alou (OF) San Francisco
15 – Mike Wegener (P) Philadelphia
17 – Skip Guinn (P) Atlanta
19 – Bill Stoneman (P) Chicago
21 – Maury Wills (IF) Pittsburgh
23 – Larry Jackson (P) Philadelphia
   (retired) Bobby Wine (IF)
25 – Bob Reynolds (P) San Francisco
27 – Dan McGinn (P) Cincinnati
29 – Jose Herrera (IF) Houston
32 – Jimy Williams (IF) Cincinnati
34 – Remy Hermoso (IF) Atlanta
36 – Jim Mudcat Grant (P) Los Angeles
38 – Jerry Robertson (P) St. Louis
40 – Don Shaw (P) New York
41 – Ty Cline (OF) San Francisco
43 – Garry Jestadt (IF) Chicago
45 – Carl Morton (P) Atlanta
47 – Larry Jaster (P) St. Louis
49 – Ernie McAnally (P) New York
52 – Jim Fairey (OF) Los Angeles
54 – Coco Laboy (IF) St. Louis
56 – John Boccabella (IF) Chicago
58 – Ron Brand (C) Houston
60 – John Glass (P) New York

Following the draft, both teams selected other notable players in various ways. San Diego purchased catcher Freddie Velazquez from Oakland and signed pitchers Johnny Podres and Jack Baldschun as free agents. Infielder Bobby Klaus was a Rule 5 draftee from Philadelphia. The Expos purchased outfielder Don Bosch from the Mets and infielder Bob Bailey from the Dodgers. They also selected outfielder Don Hahn (San Francisco), infielder Juan Rios (New York), and pitchers Carroll Sembera (Houston) and Floyd Wicker (St. Louis) in the Rule 5 draft.

So perhaps it was a signal for the new teams that fortunes could quickly turn around.

Kansas City Royals

Based on the quality of the players chosen, the odds were very much against the new Kansas City Royals becoming a laughing stock, and the new team certainly got off on the right foot. Their inaugural 1969 season saw them finish in fourth place in the American League West Division, with five more wins than their expansion brethren, the Seattle Pilots, and one win more than the Chicago White Sox.

Not only did the team fare well in the draft, but they made some key player moves that proved to be fruitful. On April 1 outfielder Lou Piniella was acquired from Seattle in exchange for outfielder Steve Whitaker and pitcher John Gelnar. All Piniella did was win the Rookie of the Year Award, hitting .282 with 11 home runs and 68 RBIs. The team then sent veteran reliever Hoyt Wilhelm to the California Angels in exchange for Ed Kirkpatrick and Dennis Paepke. Kirkpatrick hit .257 with 14 homers and 49 RBIs.

First baseman Mike Fiore hit a solid .274 with 12 dingers, Bob Oliver hit 13 homers with a .254 batting average, and third baseman Joe Foy had a solid season, hitting .262 with 11 home runs and 71 RBIs.

The pitching staff also did its part, with none of its top five starters having an ERA over 3.90. Former Oriole Wally Bunker led the staff with a 12-11 record and a 3.23 ERA. Dick Drago went 11-13 with a 3.77 mark. Bill Butler was 9-10 with a 3.90 ERA, while Roger Nelson went 7-13 with an ERA of 3.31. And hard-luck lefty Jim Rooker went 4-14 with a more-than-respectable 3.75 ERA.

Out of the bullpen, Moe Drabowsky led the team with 52 appearances with an 11-9 record and 11 saves along with a 2.94 ERA. Southpaw reliever Tom Burgmeier got into 31 games and finished up with a 3-1 mark and a 4.17 ERA.

Although the 1970 version of the Royals lost four more games than the previous season, sporting a 65-97 record, they were on their way to being a much better team. Tied for fourth place with the Milwaukee Brewers, the former Seattle Pilots, the Royals once again finished ahead of the hapless Chicago White Sox, winning nine more games than that struggling team.

During the off-season, Kansas City made one of the best trades in franchise history, sending third baseman Joe Foy to the New York Mets in exchange for outfielder Amos Otis and pitcher Bob Johnson. Otis responded with a solid season, hitting .284 with 11 home runs and 58 RBIS and was one of the best players in the history of the franchise.

There was no sophomore slump for Lou Piniella, who led the team with a .301 average along with 11 round-trippers and 88 RBIs. First baseman Bob Oliver had another big year, hitting .260 while leading the team in home runs with 27 and RBIs with 99. And a pair of infielders, Cookie Rojas (.260) at second base and Paul Schaal (.268) at third base, were solid.

Lefty Jim Rooker bounced back with a 10-15 season and a 3.54 ERA, and Dick Drago went 9-15 with a 3.75 ERA. Newly acquired Bob Johnson went 8-13 with a 3.07 ERA, while Bill Butler (4-12) and Wally Bunker (2-11) struggled. Ted Abernathy went 9-3 out of the bullpen, with a team-high 12 saves and a 2.59 ERA, while young Al Fitzmorris led the staff with 43 appearances and went 8-5 with a 4.44 ERA.

Kansas City had its first winning season the following year with a second-place finish. The continued success of the team was guaranteed by a strong farm system that sent such outstanding players to the parent club as pitchers Paul Splittorff and Steve Busby, as well as second baseman Frank White, outfielder Al Cowens, and of course, Hall of Fame third baseman George Brett.

The franchise has been very successful over the years, despite the fact that it is not what is commonly referred to as a big market team.

The Royals won West Division titles in 1985, 1984, 1980, 1978, 1977, and 1976. They won the American League pennant in 1985 and 1980, and won the World Series title in 1985.

Hall of Famers to don the Royals blue include Brett, Orlando Cepeda, Harmon Killebrew, Gaylord Perry, and managers Whitey Herzog, Bob Lemon, and Joe Gordon.

Other key players in the history of the Kansas City team include Otis and Piniella, Fred Patek, Willie Wilson, Hal McRae, and two-sport star Bo Jackson; pitchers Dennis Leonard, Bret Saberhagen, Mark Gubicza, and Dan Quisenberry; and manager Dick Howser.

One of the most entertaining moments in team history occurred on July 24, 1983, when the Royals were playing the Yankees in New York in what has become known as "The Pine Tar Incident." Brett hit a home run off Goose Gossage to give the Royals a 5–4 lead in the top of the ninth inning. But Yankees Manager Billy Martin pointed out to home plate umpire Tim McClelland that Brett had used a bat with illegal placement of pine tar (more than eighteen inches up the handle) to hit the home run.

After conferring with his fellow umpires, McClelland pointed to Brett in the Kansas City dugout and gave the out sign. An irate Brett stormed onto the field and had to be restrained. He was ejected from the game.

The home run was later reinstated by American League President Lee MacPhail, and the Royals went on to win the game when it was completed weeks later. Brett often jokes that he'd much rather be known for the Pine Tar Incident than the hemorrhoid pain that caused him to leave Game Two of the 1980 World Series against Philadelphia.

Seattle Pilots

While hemorrhoids were not necessarily a problem with the Seattle Pilots, that team's one-year existence was very much a pain for all involved. The team seemed hexed from day one. Quite frankly, that was a surprise because Seattle had long supported its Pacific Coast

League team, the Rainiers. But Minor League success does not necessarily transfer to the Major Leagues.

Seattle was actually perceived as a desirable location for a baseball franchise. The Cleveland Indians flirted with a move to Seattle in 1965, as had the Kansas City Athletics in 1967. But both times it was the condition of the Rainiers' ballpark, Sicks Stadium, that foiled any such flirtation. In fact, after deciding against moving to Seattle, A's owner Charles O. Finley made the comment that Sicks Stadium was aptly named.

The park, which first opened in 1938, had a seating capacity of just 11,000. But Seattle had agreed to expand that capacity to 30,000 in 1969 as part of the deal to bring the Pilots to town. But bad weather and other problems delayed the completion of the project so that on Opening Day of the season, only 18,000 seats were almost ready. Almost ready? That's because some of the 17,150 fans who showed up for Opening Day had to wait until the third inning to sit down because their seats were not assembled yet.

Water pressure was so weak at the stadium that players often showered in their hotel rooms following games. The clubhouses were pathetic, and announcers had only a partial view of the field, needing to install mirrors to see the third base line and left field.

In fairness, a big factor in some of the issues in Seattle were a direct result of the Symington factor, named for Senator Symington, who insisted that baseball expand in 1969 in Kansas City rather than wait until 1971, which had been the original plan. The trickle-down effect of that capitulation was that Seattle would have to be admitted two years earlier than planned because the American League would not agree to having one team enter the league since that would result in an unbalanced schedule.

A former pitcher for the Rainiers, Dewey Soriano, who had been president of the Pacific Coast League, became the Pilots' chairman of the board. But he was in need of investors and reached out to William R. Daley, who had been involved with the Indians when that organization considered a move to Seattle. He bought 47 percent of the team.

Marvin Milkes, the team's general manager, hired St. Louis Cardinals coach Joe Schultz as the Pilots' first skipper. The organization had high hopes for the first team they were to put on the field. And they stayed in the mix, flirting with a .500 record for most of the first half of the season. At the end of June, the Pilots were in third place in the West Division, just six games out of first place. But a cruel month of July saw them win just nine games while losing twenty. They finished the season in last place, with a 64-98 record, thirty-three games out of first.

Of the regular players, former Dodger Tommy Davis played left field and led the team with a .271 average, adding 6 home runs and 80 RBIs. Powerful left-handed hitting Don Mincher led the team with 25 home runs, adding 78 RBIs with his .246 average. In center field, Wayne Comer had a productive year, hitting .245 with 15 home runs and 54 RBIs. And while the speedy veteran Tommy Harper hit just .235, he made the most of every hit, leading the team with 73 stolen bases. And young outfielder Steve Hovley provided a spark off the bench with a .277 average in 91 games.

Out on the pitching mound, big right-hander Gene Brabender led the staff with a 13-14 record and a 4.36 ERA. Marty Pattin went 7-12 with a 5.62 ERA, and Fred Talbot was 5-8 with a 4.16 ERA. Veteran southpaw Steve Barber was 4-7 with a 4.80 ERA.

If the Pilots' pitching staff had a real strength, it was the bullpen. Diego Segui put up impressive numbers in 66 games with a 12-6 record, a team-high 12 saves, and an ERA of 3.35. Bob Locker went 3-3 in 51 games with a 2.18 ERA and 6 saves. And lefty John O'Donoghue had a 2-2 mark in 55 games with a 2.96 ERA and 6 saves.

Despite these impressive numbers, it was another relief pitcher with the team who got much more attention over the years and has almost become a cult figure. Former Yankee star Jim Bouton was holding on by the time 1969 rolled around and had become a knuckle-ball pitcher. A former flame-thrower, nicknamed "Bulldog," Bouton was purchased by Seattle from New York in October of 1968. He was effective, sporting a 2-1 record and 1 save, with a 3.91 ERA in 57 games. But he also compiled a daily diary of the season, which became the best-selling book *Ball Four*.

Cincinnati Reds pitcher Jim Brosnan had previously written two books that chronicled baseball seasons: *The Long Season*, about the 1959 season, and *Pennant Races*, about the happenings of 1961. But these books were interesting, harmless, uncontroversial recounts of baseball seasons.

Ball Four offered an insider's view of what really went on behind the scenes on a baseball team, as well as what happened on the field. It was from a player's perspective, full of sarcasm and a player's view of the whole picture, offering criticisms while painting an honest picture. Bouton wrote not just of home runs and baseball strategy, but also of pre-steroid drug and alcohol use and abuse, womanizing, dirty jokes and tricks, and how teammates really interact during the long 162-game season.

Phrases such as "Pound that Budweiser" and "Shitfuck," used often by the team's manager and players, became a part of the baseball culture. While the book was incredibly interesting and humorous for true fans, the baseball establishment was not thrilled with the work.

Baseball commissioner Bowie Kuhn said that the book was a detriment to baseball and asked that Bouton say that the happenings in the book were fictional. But Bouton refused, insisting that the stories were all true. Following publication of the book, he was shunned by many of his former teammates and baseball people, who considered him a traitor who betrayed a baseball axiom that states, "What you see here, what you say here, what you do here, let it stay here."

While it made for fun reading, the lone season of the Seattle Pilots was a long process that saw all of the hope and optimism that a new team experiences nearly gone by the end of the season. The attendance was much less than expected, and the team was nearly out of money by the end of the season. A potential cash cow, a new stadium was scheduled to be built, but a petition by opponents of the project delayed it.

The team was in deep financial trouble and needed a bridge of new ownership for it to survive long enough to play in the new stadium.

Ever since Milwaukee had lost the Braves to Atlanta for the 1965 season, car dealer Bud Selig had been at the forefront of the efforts to bring big league baseball back to Milwaukee. He offered to buy the Pilots for between $10 and $13 million and move the struggling team to Milwaukee. But the deal was turned down because of, once again, politicians. Washington state's U.S. senators, Warren Magnuson and Henry Jackson, both tried to stand in the way of the sale. State Attorney General Slade Gorton was part of the Washington state contingent that wanted Soriano to find a local buyer for the team and keep it in Seattle.

Numerous efforts were made to find a local person or group. Theater chain owner Fred Danz was interested but lacked the necessary financing. Westin Hotels owner Eddie Carlson was also in the mix, but no agreement could be reached.

Schultz was replaced as manager of the club by Dave Bristol, and the team arrived at spring training having no idea where they would play in the regular season. The pending sale of the team to Selig in Milwaukee was held up by an injunction that the state of Washington got to put a halt to the deal. At that point, Soriano filed for bankruptcy, which would protect him from any legal action following the sale of the team.

In a bizarre bankruptcy hearing, general manager Milkes reported that there was not enough money available to pay the players, coaches, or office staff. If the players were paid ten days late, they would have all become free agents, leaving Seattle with no money and no players. Federal bankruptcy referee Sidney Volinn ruled on April 1 that the Pilots were bankrupt and cleared the move of the team to Milwaukee just six days before the first game of the season.

The team's equipment was actually on trucks in Utah, as the drivers waited for instructions about where to go with their loads. The word came very late in the day. So late, in fact, that the new Brewers had to wear the old Pilots uniforms for a short time.

When the team moved to Milwaukee, the first improvement was attendance, which took a jump of nearly 40 percent in 1970. Tommy Harper rebounded from a disappointing 1969 by putting up a solid .296 average with a team-leading 31 home runs and 82 RBIs with 38 stolen bases. Left fielder Danny Walton hit .257 with 17 homers and 66 RBIs, and Ted Savage hit at a .279 clip with 12 home runs and 50 RBIs.

Marty Pattin led the pitching staff with a 14-12 record and a 3.39 ERA. He was joined by Lew Krausse, who went 13-18 with a 4.75 ERA. But Skip Lockwood (5-12), Bobby Bolin (5-11), Gene Brabender (6-15), and Al Downing (2-10) did not fare as well.

Ken Sanders was solid out of the bullpen, with a team-high 13 saves and a 5-2 record in 50 games with a 1.75 ERA. John Gelnar went 4-3 in 53 games with 4 saves and a 4.13 ERA. And Bob Humphreys went 2-4 with 3 saves in 23 games with a 3.15 ERA.

The Brewers continued to struggle in the standings and did not have a winning season until 1978. But they won the AL East crown in 1982 and the American League pennant that same year. More recently, the team earned a wild card berth in 2008, and in 2011 they finished first in the NL Central and their NL division series, though they lost the league champion series to the Cardinals.

Hall of Fame players who spent time with the Brewers include Hank Aaron, Rollie Fingers, Paul Molitor, Don Sutton, and Robin Yount. The radio voice of the team is former big league catcher Bob Uecker, a winner of the Ford C. Frick Award from the Baseball Hall of Fame. Uecker has been with the team since it moved to Milwaukee in 1970.

Other outstanding Brewers include Mike Caldwell, Francisco Cordero, Ben Sheets, Cecil Cooper, Geoff Jenkins, Ben Oglivie, Gorman Thomas, Don Money, and Jim Gantner.

San Diego Padres

The San Diego Padres had been in existence since 1936 in the Pacific Coast League. The following season, an eighteen-year-old Ted Williams helped guide them to the PCL title. So there was a long tradition of professional baseball in San Diego prior to the Padres joining the Major Leagues. Whereas the Padres did better than the hapless Seattle Pilots, they endured six consecutive last-place finishes, losing a hundred or more games four times.

The Padres got off to a great start, winning their first game, 2–1, over the Houston Astros behind right-hander Dick Selma, who threw a complete game five-hitter with twelve strikeouts. But Selma was dispatched to the Chicago Cubs three weeks later in exchange for Joe Niekro, Frankie Libran, and Gary Ross. The team had a difficult 52-110 record in 1969, forty-one games behind the NL West champion Atlanta Braves. But to put the season in perspective, the Padres not only finished in sixth and last place in the division, but they trailed the fifth-place Houston Astros by thirty-nine games.

Some of the Padres put up some decent numbers, but the team was often overmatched. Downtown Ollie Brown led the regulars with a .264 average, with 20 home runs and 61 RBIs. Big first baseman Nate Colbert slugged 24 round trippers, with 66 RBIs and a .255 average. Left fielder Al Ferrara hit a respectable .260, adding 14 homers and 56 RBIs. And future World Series winning manager Cito Gaston hit .230 for the first-year Padres, with 2 home runs and 28 RBIs.

Clay Kirby was the ace of the staff and went 7-20 with a 3.80 ERA. After being acquired from the Cubs, Niekro went 8-17 with a 3.70 ERA, and Al Santorini had an 8-14 mark with a 3.95 ERA.

The bullpen was anchored by Billy McCool, who led the staff with 7 saves in 54 games, with a 3-5 record and a 4.30 ERA. Frank Reberger was a workhorse, appearing in 67 games and achieving 6 saves and a 1-2 record with a 3.59 ERA. And veteran screwball specialist Jack Baldschun appeared in 61 games, sporting a 7-2 record with 1 save and a 4.79 ERA.

The early seasons in San Diego were as frustrating as the first. In 1970 Pittsburgh Pirates pitcher Dock Ellis threw a no-hitter against the Padres and admitted to being under the influence of LSD during the game.

Young right-hander Steve Arlin had a no-hitter going on July 18, 1972, against the Philadelphia Phillies with two outs in the ninth inning, but then Denny Doyle singled to break up the gem. Arlin had a 34-67 career record in the Major Leagues, and a lifetime ERA of 4.33. He won 32 games with San Diego, 11 of which were shutouts. After having two brief cups of coffee with the Padres in 1969 and 1970, with a 1-1 record in 6 games, Arlin made it to the Show full time in 1971, going 9-19 with a fine 3.48 ERA but leading the league in losses. He was the prototypical pitcher who constantly kept his team in the game. In this case, a bad team.

"It was a struggle," said Arlin.

We had Buzzie Bavasi running the show. The owner, C. Amholt Smith, gave Buzzie 10 percent of the club. So he became a cheapskate who wouldn't spend any money and would not get new players. It was a struggle and a half. You had guys who did not belong in the Major Leagues. For a pitcher it was a nightmare. You were getting no run support and then they couldn't field behind you.

They brought in Roger Craig to be the pitching coach. His job was to keep our heads on straight. He was there to tell us that we were going to lose games, but just keep our heads on straight and develop. That's what happens with expansion teams. I lost ten games in a row at one point and didn't give up more than three runs in any of those games. It was rough.

The same thing happens over and over, and then you start to try to strike people out all the time. Our staff had a great ERA. We had Clay Kirby and Dave Roberts, who fought Tom Seaver for the ERA lead. The toughest part about that was after pitching as well as I had pitched, I was included in a magazine article about the worst pitchers in baseball.

It was rough, and Arlin continued to take the ball and make quality starts. In 1972 his reputation as a top-notch pitcher continued, but once again he led the league in losses, with a 10-21 mark. And once again he pitched in bad luck, as his 3.60 ERA indicates. It wasn't perfect, but it was still a dream come true.

"Hey, it was the Major Leagues," Arlin said.

I felt privileged to be there. The first year I'd been to spring training and here I'm meeting guys I have baseball cards of. Those were big things. I had no problem going out there and pitching. I had gone to dental school and could have quit the game and been a doctor sooner than I did. But that thought never entered my mind until my last year when I hurt my shoulder.

It was so cool standing behind the batting cage and talking to guys like Willie Mays and Hank Aaron. I was getting a chance to pitch to them and have them make an out. I faced Mays fourteen times and struck him out eleven times. It was the seven- and eight-hole hitters that got me. I'd throw them a fastball down the middle.

I had a battle with Willie Stargell of the Pirates one time. I had him full count and he fouled off ten straight fast balls. I ended up walking him. Roberto Clemente comes up as a pinch hitter, and I struck him out on three pitches. Pat Corrales, my catcher, knew how to pitch to Clemente. He said that he couldn't hit the inside pitch. He said to throw a fast ball down and in and he can't see it. I had his number. But Stargell was a different story. I threw him a curve ball that would have bounced, a waste pitch. He flipped his wrists at the ball and hit it into the second deck.

Arlin went 11-14 in 1973 but injured his pitching shoulder. He struggled in 1974, going 1-7 with San Diego before being traded to the Cleveland Indians, where he went 2-5. He retired after that season to become a dentist, but he still has nothing but fond memories of his big league career.

The team continued to founder, and while attendance was not a flop, topping more than five hundred thousand the first year and rising over the ensuing seasons, club owner C. Amholt Smith was not pleased with the fan support he was receiving, and he began to investigate unloading his underperforming team. In 1974 he had agreed to sell the team to Joseph Danzansky, who planned to move the team to Washington DC. But at the eleventh hour, when new uniforms had been manufactured and Washington baseball cards had been printed, Ray Kroc, the founder of McDonald's, came to the rescue and made a last ditch offer to buy the Padres and keep them in San Diego, which Smith accepted.

During that 1974 season, Kroc once was so frustrated with what he saw on the playing field that he grabbed the public address announcer's microphone and apologized to the fans for the team's inept play. It was no coincidence that in Kroc's second year at the helm of the franchise that the team escaped the cellar in the National League West for the first time.

Helping the Padres turn the corner were young stars such as Dave Winfield, Ozzie Smith, Tony Gwynn, Kevin McReynolds, and Randy Jones, who took the team to levels of success it had never enjoyed previously. The acquisition of established players such as Rollie Fingers, Gaylord Perry, Steve Garvey, Graig Nettles, and Goose Gossage also made the team a contender.

The team won the West Division title in 2006, 2005, 1998, 1996, and 1984, advancing to the World Series by winning the National League pennant in 1998 (where they lost to the New York Yankees) and 1984 (where they lost to the Detroit Tigers).

For all the time it took the Padres franchise to gain momentum and produce winning seasons, they have always have had notable talent on the field. Hall of Famers who have played for San Diego include Roberto Alomar, Rollie Fingers, Goose Gossage, Tony Gwynn, Rickey Henderson, Willie McCovey, Gaylord Perry, Ozzie Smith, Dave Winfield, and former skipper Dick Williams. Former Yankee infielder Jerry Coleman, who managed the Padres for one season, has been the team's long-time broadcaster and is a winner of the Baseball Hall of Fame Ford C. Frick award.

Other fine players who have spent time with San Diego include Steve Garvey, Randy Jones, Rick Wise, Mickey Lolich, Nate Colbert, Benito Santiago, Eric Show, Ed Whitson, Kevin Brown, Fred McGriff Garry Templeton, career saves leader Trevor Hoffman, and the popular (though unofficial) mascot of the team, The Famous Chicken, aka the San Diego Chicken. And the Padres are currently the only team without a no-hitter.

Montreal Expos

The beautiful city of Montreal, Quebec, was a good place to be in the 1960s. As the decade unwound, a string of good things were happening there. Expo 67, the World's Fair that was hosted April–October 1967, was a stunning success. The sparkling new subway system, the Montreal Metro, opened. The city was about to be named to host the 1976 Summer Olympics when in December of 1967 Montreal was awarded one of the four new expansion franchises.

This was a significant moment in baseball history, as the Montreal Expos, named for the World's Fair, became the first franchise awarded to a Canadian city. Seagram owner Charles Bronfman had made it happen, and the face of baseball changed.

"Montreal is such a great city to visit," said Bill Stoneman, now a consultant for the Los Angeles Angels of Anaheim, and who was then a pitcher and an original Montreal Expo. "When they formed the club, Montreal was the most influential city in all of Canada. A lot of the big banks were there, Sun Life insurance was there. Going to Montreal was like going to Europe. We made our living playing baseball, but it's like we were being treated to a European vacation at the same time. It was such a cosmopolitan city. A fun place."

There had been a long tradition of baseball in Montreal, which was the home of the Dodgers' Triple-A affiliate, the Royals, from 1939 to 1960. But the parent club decided to leave Montreal after the 1960 season to move its top farm club closer to the West Coast. The victory of the Expos franchise capped a seven-year effort by Montreal City Council member Gerry Snyder. He had previously been instrumental in bringing the Olympics and Formula One Racing north of the border.

Snyder appeared at the Major League Baseball owners' meeting in December of 1967 in Mexico City to promote Montreal as the best place for a new expansion team. It seems reasonable to assume the Dodgers' president Walter O'Malley may have rewarded Montreal for its years as the Dodgers' top farm club by helping the city win a franchise. And it was O'Malley who on May 27, 1968, announced that San Diego and Montreal would be joining the National League in 1969.

Gerry Snyder's work was still not done, as he reached out to Bronfman to help fund the project. Other investors and directors included Lorne Webster, Paul Beaudry, his brother Charlemagne Beaudry, and team president and executive director, John McHale.

Since the Kansas City franchise had already adopted the name of the Royals, that historic moniker was not available to the new Montreal franchise. But "Expos" proved to be a popular choice, which fortuitously was the same in both English and French, the two languages of the city.

The new team had a working agreement with the Atlanta Braves, who shared their spring training facility in Palm Beach, Florida. That site is filled with memories for Bill Stoneman: "The Braves had built a stadium in Palm Beach in the 1960s, and John McHale and Jim Fanning came to our organization from the Braves," he said. "Atlanta gave the Expos a couple of back fields. We stayed at a little Ramada Inn that was a three-minute walk to the park, right across the street from a mall. It worked for us, and we loved to play baseball."

Stoneman continued,

The clubs had the option of giving us meal money or feeding us. The Expos made a deal with the Ramada Inn where the team had its own dining room, and they paid for our breakfast and dinners. So that was good, but we didn't get any meal money. And the food was pretty good. We'd go in there and there would be a mimeographed sheet of paper with a choice of three entrees. But the desserts never changed. It was always jello or ice cream. Our traveling secretary was Gene Kirby, and if you had a problem or a complaint about hotels and travel you went to him. After being in camp about three weeks, one day I asked him if he could do something about the dessert menu. This Ramada Inn was famous for its cheesecake and it looked really good. Kirbs was funny and he jumped all over me about it.

We started the season and went into Philadelphia, where I threw a no-hitter against the Phillies. My next start was in St. Louis, and after getting my first win against the Phillies, then I shut the Cardinals out. After doing some radio interviews I came back to my locker and there was a huge box on my chair. It was the biggest cheesecake I ever saw in my life. It was from the Chase Park Plaza Hotel, and Kirby was in the corner laughing. He was so funny.

While the Expos prepared for the regular season in Palm Beach, the finishing touches were being made on their new home in Montreal. But it was a lot more involved than most people realized.

The former home of the Montreal Royals, Delorimier Stadium, was deemed too small to host Major League Baseball even temporarily. After investigating other alternatives, executives finally settled on a 3,000-seat community ballpark, Jarry Park. In order to make it work, the venue's seating capacity was increased to 28,500 prior to the start of the 1969 season.

"Jarry Park was a really different place to play," said former San Diego pitcher Steve Arlin. "It was a really loud place to play and it was always a little colder up there. But it didn't stop those amazing Montreal fans. They were so loud, cheering with their Canadian accents. What a different place to play."

Montreal put of fun and likable team on the field that first year, which only equaled the success of San Diego, with a 52-110 record.

But the Expos more than doubled the Padres' attendance figures, with more than 1.2 million fans jamming Jarry Park. Players such as Maury Wills, Bob "Beatles" Bailey, Mack Jones, Rusty "Le Grand Orange" Staub, Coco Laboy, Jim "Mudcat" Grant, and Bill Stoneman became fan favorites.

Even though the team finished forty-eight games behind the NL East champion New York Mets, they were a hit in Montreal. In just the team's ninth game, right-hander Stoneman pitched his no-hitter against the Philadelphia Phillies on April 17. He won the game 7–0, striking out eight Phillies. Rusty Staub was the offensive hero of the game, smashing a home run and three doubles. Stoneman led the team in wins with an 11-19 record and an ERA of 4.39.

Steve Renko went 6-7 with a 4.01 ERA, Jerry Robertson was 5-16 with a 3.96 ERA, and young Mike Wegener rounded out the rotation going 5-14 with a 4.40 ERA.

Lefty Dan McGinn led the team with 74 appearances and went 7-10 with a team-high 6 saves and a 3.94 ERA. Howie Reed went 6-7 with a 4.84 ERA, and Elroy Face went 4-2 with 5 saves. But the team began what was to be a long and harmonious relationship when they acquired pitcher Claude Raymond from the Atlanta Braves on August 19. A native of St. Jean Quebec, the bilingual reliever pitched out of the Montreal bullpen for three years. After his playing career ended, Raymond became the Expos' French-language broadcaster and served in that function from 1972 to 2001, and then he was the club's English-language broadcaster in 2004, their last season in Montreal.

The Expos' first manager was Gene Mauch, known as "The Little General." It was quite ironic that Mauch would be the first manager of an expansion club. When he managed the Phillies in the early 1960s, he made it a point to beat up on the expansion Mets and Colt .45s, often changing his pitching rotation to ensure that his ace hurlers, Jim Bunning and Chris Short, would start against the new teams. Make no mistake, Mauch was old school.

"I broke into the Major Leagues in Chicago under Leo Durocher," said Bill Stoneman. "If you want to look at hard-nosed managers, it was Leo and Gene. For me, I got along really well with Gene. I was used to the kind of manager he was. If you made a mistake, you heard about it—especially mental mistakes. He might even embarrass you. But he always talked to you and he expected a lot out of his players. Again, I never had a problem with that, because he just wanted the game played the right way."

The Expos finished in last place again in 1970, but their record improved to 73-89 under Mauch. An influx of young talent brought the team to new levels. By the end of the decade they were an exciting team led by the likes of Gary Carter, Ken Singleton, Tim Raines, Andre Dawson, Larry Parrish, Tim Wallach, Bill Gullickson, and Steve Rogers. In fact by 1979, Manager Dick Williams had Montreal contending for the division title all season long, eventually finishing second to Pittsburgh.

In 1980 Montreal was barely defeated by Philadelphia, who won the final series of the season. In 1981 Montreal made its only postseason appearance by defeating the Phillies in a special playoff format invented to sort out confusion over a work stoppage during the season. But they lost to Los Angeles in the league championship series.

Over the next decade the Expos were good, but never quite good enough. After a particularly heartbreaking fourth-place finish in 1989, a year in which Montreal led the NL East from June until August, owner Charles Bronfman said he was burnt out and announced his intention to sell the team, which he did to a consortium of fourteen owners on June 14, 1991, who were represented by managing partner Claude Brochu. Adding to his frustration over the '89 collapse was losing star players Mark Langston, Hubie Brooks, Pasqual Perez, and Bryn Smith to free agency following the season.

The team continued to struggle through the 1990s, unable to afford to keep young stars that had been brought up through the Montreal Minor League system, such as John Wetteland, Ken Hill, Larry Walker, and Marquis Grissom.

In December of 1999, Jeffrey Loria became managing general partner and CEO of the team when he bought out Brochu. His plans to build a new stadium in downtown Montreal were foiled when he was unable to get government funding for the project. When the proposed new stadium failed, the Montreal Expos were doomed and on life support.

Two years later a deal was orchestrated that would strip the franchise of any chance to succeed. A group headed by John Henry, owner of the Florida Marlins, agreed to buy the Boston Red Sox in December 2001. Henry would then sell the Marlins to Loria, who had Major League Baseball buy the Expos from him. After the deal was consummated, Loria took the Expos' front office personnel and the on-field staff with him.

In 2003, Montreal played twenty-two of its home games in San Juan, Puerto Rico, in a move similar to when the Brooklyn Dodgers played seven home games at Roosevelt Field in Jersey City, New Jersey, in 1956 and 1957. Montreal also continued to play part of their home games in San Juan in 2004.

As that season progressed, there were numerous suitors who were involved in discussions with Major League Baseball about acquiring the Expos franchise. Cities involved in negotiations included San Juan, Monterrey (Mexico), Portland, Charlotte, Norfolk, Las Vegas, and, of course, Washington DC. It was announced on September 29, 2004, the date of the Expos' final home game, that the Expos would move to the nation's capital starting in 2005; they were later renamed the Nationals.

The Montreal Expos played the final game in franchise history on October 3, 2004, at Shea Stadium in New York, losing to the Mets, 8–1. Ironically, the once-proud franchise had come full circle. Its first game back in 1969 was also against the Mets.

6 | The Pendulum of Power Swings to the Players

The face of baseball was changing rather dramatically as expansion became a new aspect of the game. New cities were being empowered with their own teams, and baseball truly was having an impact on every area of the country. It was certainly a big change from the days just a decade before, when there were eight teams in each league.

While in those days the game was parochial, centered on a particular geographic area, expansion put a new face on America's Game. It was now a game enjoyed by the masses.

Baseball saw many changes on and off the field, just a real life changed so much for all of us at the same time. Race relations, Vietnam, gender equality, and a bevy of other social equality issues were at the forefront of society. And much like the old cigarette commercial spoke to women, the same phrase could be extended to the Grand Old Game: "You've come a long way, baby."

Absolutely nobody expected to see just how far the game was about to progress. It all started innocently enough, in the October before the start of the 1970 season when a big trade was made by two of the original clubs in the National League. But it was a trade that would change the game forever.

As four new teams assessed their rookie campaigns and prepared for their second season of Major League play, two old-time ball clubs pulled off a blockbuster of an old-fashioned trade on October 8, 1969. The Philadelphia Phillies traded slugging but troubled first baseman Richie Allen, pitcher Jerry Johnson, and infielder Cookie Rojas to the St. Louis Cardinals in exchange for catcher Tim McCarver, pitcher Joe Hoerner, and outfielders Byron Browne and Curt Flood.

It was looked at as a trade that would immediately help both clubs. Allen had reached the end of the line in Philadelphia and was the poster boy of a player who needed a change of scenery. And while McCarver, Hoerner, and Browne all made the Phillies a better team, it was smooth-fielding and clutch-hitting Curt Flood who was the key to the trade for Philadelphia. On October 8, 1969, they were already a much-improved team for the upcoming 1970 season. And the Cardinals were hoping that the family atmosphere that their franchise was known for would turn Allen into a player who finally felt appreciated and could make it easier for him to reach his enormous potential. There was only one problem. Curt Flood didn't want to leave St. Louis.

Vietnam War protesters were shouting, "Hell no, we won't go!" Flood had a similar refrain. Here was a guy who was willing to give up his annual salary of nearly a hundred thousand dollars. He met with Phillies general manager John Quinn, who felt that he had convinced the talented center fielder to give the City of Brotherly Love a try. But the head of the player's union, Marvin Miller, eventually advised Flood that the union was prepared to pay the cost of a lawsuit, should he decide to file an antitrust suit against Major League Baseball.

Two and a half months after the trade was made, Flood sent a Christmas Eve letter to Commissioner Bowie Kuhn demanding his freedom. The letter read in part:

After twelve years in the major leagues, I do not feel I am a piece of property to be bought and sold irrespective of my wishes. I believe that any system which produces that result violates my basic rights as a citizen and is inconsistent with the laws of the United States and of the several States.

It is my desire to play baseball in 1970 and I am capable of playing. I have received a contract offer from the Philadelphia club, but I believe I have the right to consider offers from other clubs before making any decision. I, therefore, request that you make known to all Major League clubs my feelings in this matter, and advise them of my availability for the 1970 season.

His request was denied because of baseball's reserve clause. The reserve clause stated that once a player signed a contract with a big league organization, that player was property of that club into perpetuity even when his contract expired. They only way to go to a different team was to be traded or released. Here is baseball's reserve clause as it originally appeared in all player contracts:

10. (a) On or before February 1st (or if a Sunday, then the next preceding business day) of the year following the last played season covered by this contract, the Club may tender to the Player a contract for the term of that year by mailing the same to the Player at his address following his signature hereto, or if none be given, then at his last address of record with the Club. If prior to the March 1 next succeeding said February 1, the Player and the Club have not agreed upon the terms of such contract, then on or before 10 days after said March 1, the Club shall have the right by written notice to the Player at the said address to renew this contract for the period of time of one year on the same terms, except that the amount payable to the player shall be such as the Club shall fix in said notice; provided, however, that said amount, if fixed by a Major League Club, shall be an amount payable at a rate not less than 75 percent of the rate stipulated for the preceding year.

(b) The Club's right to renew this contract, as provided in subparagraph (a) of this paragraph 10, and the promise of the Player not to play otherwise than with the Club have been taken into consideration in determining the amount payable under paragraph 2 hereof.

The clause came into being in 1879 and was written into the standard player's contract in 1887. Players made little money and had even less leverage when negotiating with their team. You would see a very good player hold out—not sign his contract and skip part of spring training until an agreement could be reached. But that ploy didn't always work out the way that a player hoped, because in most cases any pay raise that he was able to muscle away from the organization was given right back fines that the player owed for showing up late to the Grapefruit or Cactus League. There was no free agency, and players went where they were told to go. Or they got a real job.

"What the reserve clause brought in was that the players were now controlled," said author and baseball historian Jerrold Casway. "The collusion of the owners to protect their investment and property is how they determined the fate of a ballplayer. That only worked because of the tacit agreement amongst the owners that they would all recognize the rights and responsibility of each other and they would not violate that. The onus was not on the player."

Those two run-on paragraphs were at the core of the business of Major League Baseball for decades, and were always a source of heartache and pain for a huge majority of players. The extent to which organized baseball could control the game and its players represented a raw nerve for the players, who grew more uncomfortable with every year that passed.

Actually, a decision made in the Supreme Court in 1922 gave Major League Baseball the whole deck of cards to deal as they chose. In the case of *Federal Baseball Club of Baltimore v. National League of Professional Clubs*, Supreme Court justice Oliver Wendell Holmes created an exemption for professional baseball from the application of anti-trust laws. The Baltimore team, which was a member of the Federal League, had filed suit because that organization deemed its inability to sign players was due to antitrust violations. Any business that operates across state borders and participates in interstate commerce is subject to antitrust legislation. Any attempt to control or monopolize trade may be illegal under the Sherman and Clayton Acts.

The Holmes decision was based on the determination that baseball did not involve interstate commerce, and as a result federal courts did not have the power to regulate it.

Speaking for a unanimous court in *Federal Baseball*, Holmes concluded that baseball was a business involved in giving exhibitions, which are purely state affairs. The court also held that baseball was not commerce. While teams played in different states and equipment had to cross state lines, the exhibition was not trade or commerce in the commonly accepted use of those words. The transportation of players and equipment across state lines was deemed merely incidental to the business conducted at baseball parks.

"Well it made more sense in 1922," said author Brad Snyder in *A Well-Paid Slave: Curt Flood's Fight for Free Agency in Professional Sports*.

Holmes didn't like the Sherman Act and thought it was a foolish law. It said that Congress can only regulate things between two or more states. They cannot regulate the state of Maryland cattle farming, but they can regulate cattle farming between Maryland and New Jersey. That is the basis for the Sherman Act. Holmes didn't go out of his way to broadly interpret its statute.

He didn't know anything about baseball. He said that the baseball games were like a lecture circuit where a lawyer or lecturer traveled to distant cities as proof that travel alone did not make baseball games interstate commerce.

In Holmes' defense, there were no real radio broadcasts of games in 1922 and there was no television as the first television broadcast of a major league game was not until 1939. The farm system concept did not become popular until the 1930s.

The U.S. Constitution does allow Congress to regulate commerce among the states. Federal antitrust law applied only to acts of interstate commerce as opposed to what Holmes considered baseball to be, intrastate commerce, occurring within a single state. He said that intrastate commerce such as baseball was outside the regulation of the Sherman Act. Baseball had a legal monopoly status. The reserve clause was a huge example of restraint of trade.

"In 1922, the United States Supreme Court heard a complaint by the Baltimore team from the upstart Federal League, alleging that the major leagues illegally wielded a reserve clause on players, in restraint of free trade and in violation of the Sherman Act of 1890," wrote George Vecsey in *Baseball: A History of America's Favorite Game.*

Chief Justice Oliver Wendell Holmes delivered an opinion for the unanimous majority that baseball did not constitute interstate commerce. "The business is giving exhibitions of baseball, which are purely state affairs," wrote Justice Holmes, who added, "Owners produce baseball games as a source of profit, [they] cannot change the character of the games. They are still a sport, not trade."

That opinion would strengthen club owners for more than half a century, handing them legal control of their players, whose only options were to accept the contract offered them or not play at all. By defining baseball as a sport, the Supreme Court had essentially turned it into a national asset.

That is not to say that there were not challenges to the antitrust exemption. In 1953 the Supreme Court once again got involved in baseball's monopoly status. In *Toolson v. New York Yankees,* George Toolson, a disgruntled Minor League player for the Yankees, sued baseball and challenged the reserve clause in federal court. The plaintiffs argued that radio and television broadcasts, train and air travel, and the expansion of the Minor Leagues had made it quite clear that baseball had become a prime example of interstate commerce.

As Snyder wrote in *A Well-Paid Slave*,

> The Supreme Court, however, is extremely reluctant to reverse its own decisions. It is a principle known as stare decisis, which means let the decision stand. Supreme Court decisions, or precedents, are interpretations of American law that are relied on year after year by judges, lawyers, businessmen and scholars. This is particularly true when the Court interprets the meaning of federal legislation such as the Sherman Act. The general immutability of these decisions is based on stare decisis.

The Court's unsigned, one-paragraph opinion in *Toolson* refused to reexamine the "underlying issues" about whether Major League Baseball in 1953 had risen to the level of interstate commerce. It claimed to be a reaffirmation of Holmes' opinion. Yet, in a single paragraph, it completely changed *Federal Baseball's* meaning. The Court, in *Toolson*, offered three additional reasons for baseball's legal monopoly:

1. Congress had done nothing to correct *Federal Baseball* despite hearings in 1951 about baseball's monopoly status;
2. Baseball had developed for the last 30 years under *Federal Baseball* and had relied on the assumption that it was a legal monopoly; and
3. Any future action on baseball's antitrust exemption should be taken by Congress.

Brad Snyder relates a commentator's description of the *Toolson* decision as the first step in "the greatest bait-and-switch scheme in the history of the Supreme Court." Part of the decision alluded to the idea that Congress had no intention of including the business of baseball within the scope of antitrust laws.

"The *Toolson* suit was the next big one," Snyder said.

> Here is where the Court really screwed up. Congress had intended to exclude baseball from the Sherman Act. Holmes had said that professional professional baseball as it operated in 1922 was not interstate com-

merce. But this decision by the Court was to make it clear that Congress had the right to regulate baseball if and when it desires to do so.

Toolson also made it possible for baseball to enforce the reserve clause. Before and even after *Federal Baseball*, lower courts had been reluctant to enforce the reserve clause because the contracts were so one-sided against the players. *Toolson*, by redefining *Federal Baseball*, further insulated the reserve clause from legal challenges.

At the end of the day, respecting prior precedents is a big thing with the Supreme Court. They look after the decisions of previous courts and can probably expect the same respect years down the line when challenges are made.

So years later, trying to reverse the upholding of the reserve clause made Curt Flood's prospects rather bleak on the surface, but he was a man on a mission. On January 16, 1970, he filed a $4.1 million lawsuit against Kuhn and Major League Baseball. Not only was he willing to walk away from a six-figure contract, the legal proceeding also most assuredly meant the end of his playing career.

"All of his friends were very helpful in trying to get him to realize what he was doing," said Flood's longtime St. Louis teammate and friend, Tim McCarver. "What many of them didn't realize was that he didn't need any help. He knew what he was doing."

Flood and his attorney, Arthur Goldberg, made their case, which eventually made it to the U.S. Supreme Court. In the long history of baseball, collusion was a way of life. The argument was made that the Thirteenth Amendment to the Constitution and the Sherman Antitrust Act were violated by the reserve clause. Players, economists, and others testified in favor of Flood and his crusade. Baseball continued its tradition of stating that the reserve clause was in place for the good of the game. How could the reserve clause be in violation of the Thirteenth Amendment when the players were more than capable of finding other employment? they asked.

The owners contended that free agency would destroy the game and forever change it from the pastime that generations of fans had come to know and love. The good of the game was their mantra, and the reserve clause was clearly for the good of the game.

In August of 1970 Federal Judge Ben Cooper ruled against Flood reaffirming the reserve clause. But he noted that players and owner should negotiate the issue. The U.S. Court of Appeals rejected Flood, as did the Supreme Court, by a 5–3 decision in 1972. The courts all affirmed that the reserve clause was not a matter to be decided by a point of law, but by collective bargaining. Even though Flood lost his case and all of his appeals, it was his efforts that marked the first cracks in the armor of the owners when they agreed to negotiate the subject of the reserve clause.

When Flood refused to report to the Phillies, on April 8, 1970, the Cardinals sent first baseman/outfielder Willie Montanez to the Phillies to complete the trade. Flood sat out that entire season, but in November 1970 the Phillies traded him to the Washington Senators along with a player to be named later, pitcher Jeff Terpko, in exchange for Greg Goossen, Gene Martin, and interestingly, Jeff Terpko.

Flood agreed to the deal because he was anxious to try to resume his career and signed a $110,000 contract with Washington. But the year off had affected his skills, and he retired after playing just thirteen games and hitting .200. He passed away in 1997.

"What he did led to the changes in the reserve system," said Tal Smith, of the Houston Astros. "Historically, it is one of the most important things in the annals of the game."

The owners' decision to negotiate the reserve clause through collective bargaining was disastrous from management's point of view. This led to an agreement struck with the players in 1973 that created an arbitration system that allowed players with just two years of big league experience to have salary disputes decided by an impartial arbitrator.

Since the arbitrator had to pick either the player's salary request or the number offered by the team, this process immediately raised the money earned by players. If the teams made an offer ridiculously low, they would lose since the arbitrator could not allow the two sides to meet both ways. It was a choice of one offer or the other. So the process saw salaries hike.

Even though Flood alienated some when he referred to himself as a ninety-thousand-dollar-a-year slave, his stance is something that his fellow players lauded. The late 1960s were a time in our society where people were striving for greater individual rights. Race riots were still a regular occurrence, and opposition to the war in Vietnam had literally driven President Lyndon B. Johnson out of the White House when he decided not to run for reelection in 1968.

The complexion of baseball was rapidly changing, as by the end of the 1960s teams were increasingly having numerous black and Latin American players up and down their rosters. The civil rights movement brought huge legal changes in American society, and the players were influenced by what was going on outside of the game of baseball as well. But it was a change that was very slow in coming. In fact, not everyone felt that baseball was keeping up.

"Society was changed and I didn't think that baseball was changing with it," said pitcher/author Larry Colton.

My last few years they were constantly telling me to get my hair cut. But compared to normal society, I had short hair. I lived in Berkeley at the time, and people looked at me like I was from Lawrence Welk or something.

I still felt that baseball was important, but to be a great athlete you have to be so hundred percent dedicated. I'd go out and watch guys pitch and think that they barely graduated from high school and could barely spell "dog." Yet, they'd go out there so zoned in. I had equal physical skills but they were better because they could focus in better. Maybe I just had some sort of attention deficit disorder. I could concentrate for four straight pitches, but not the fifth.

I think that the civil rights stuff, Vietnam, and all that was going on in society affected me more than most other players. I had come from Berkeley, and my wife at the time was a real left-winger. The music and the pill and everything else had changed the playing field for me. Then Curt Flood did his thing and a little while later came Messersmith and McNally.

Those two pitchers were to take what Curt Flood started to a new level. But that is not to say that things were not getting better for the ballplayers. By 1970, the average player's salary rose to $25,000 from the $17,000 figure in 1965. More than twenty players were earning more than $100,000 a year.

Baseball attendance was flat however. While 15 million fans came through the turnstiles at National League ballparks in 1966, that figure dropped to 11.7 million in 1968. Not only did baseball have four new teams coming into the mix in 1969, but the powers-that-be realized that while good pitching stopping good hitting was an acceptable axiom of the game, the pitching in 1968 was just too good, and it seemed to be taking some fan interest away.

Cardinals flamethrower Bob Gibson was overpowering in 1968, with a 1.12 ERA. He was also dominating in the World Series, striking out thirty-five Detroit Tiger hitters in three games. And Tigers right-hander Denny McLain went 31-6 in the Motor City, the first pitcher to win thirty games since St. Louis Cardinal Dizzy Dean in 1934. And back in the National League, Don Drysdale of the Los Angeles Dodgers threw fifty-eight consecutive shutout innings. As a result of this pitching dominance, the strike zone was narrowed, and the pitching mound was lowered from fifteen inches to ten in an effort to make it a more level playing field and to take some of those pitching advantages away. At some fields such as Dodger Stadium, the pitching mound may have been as high as twenty inches, giving the hurler an even bigger advantage.

Changes such as the size of the strike zone and the lowering of the pitching mound were very subtle rules to help add offense to the game. But a dramatic change was adapted in 1973—for half of the teams at least. On January 11 of that year, Oakland's Charles O. Finley convinced his fellow American League owners to adopt the designated hitter (DH) beginning that season. The rule allows a team to have a DH in the lineup to basically pinch hit for the pitcher throughout the game, while allowing the pitcher to remain in the game. Thus, the weakest offensive link in the lineup is replaced by a much better hitter. The idea significantly changed the strategy involved in the game as well as adding more runs.

While Finley was looked at as a renaissance man in many instances, the DH idea was nothing all that new. Another A's owner, the legendary Connie Mack of the Philadelphia A's, had suggested the designated hitter as far back as 1906.

While the rule changes bandied about were all about helping the hitters add more offense to the game, the aforementioned Andy Messersmith and Dave McNally were about to give pitchers and position players alike a huge advantage by playing the 1975 season without a signed contract. Their teams, Messersmith's Dodgers and McNally's Expos, forced them to report to spring training and renewed their contracts, as the reserve clause stipulated. That they played the season without a signed contract convinced the players that they were now free agents and should be able to sign with any club they chose. Marvin Miller attempted to give the owners an opportunity to make changes to the reserve clause, but they had never lost a dispute over the subject and continued their imperial attitude.

"This was a very important happening because this was the first time the players really took on the owners," author Jerrold Casway said in Zimniuch's book *Going, Going, Gone! The Art of the Trade in Major League Baseball.* "Had the owners given the players just a little more freedom and respect, you would not have had the Flood situation, the unions and the strikes. From the 1903 merger of the two leagues up until the Curt Flood incident, the owners did exactly what they wanted to do. On each occasion, the owners put their foot in their mouth and either overreacted or underreacted."

The owners accepted arbitration, which led to drastically higher salaries, and shortly thereafter, free agency. Messersmith and McNally played without signed contracts, thus claiming the right to free agency. Naturally the owners objected. But the tide in the country and the arbitration process were about to deal them and their attitude a crushing blow.

The case went before a three-man panel of arbitrators that included Marvin Miller from the union, John Gaherin the owners' representative, and chairman Peter Seitz.

"The whole case was rather interesting," said Tal Smith. "One day, Gabe Paul called me into his office when he was on a conference call with John Gaherin, when they were discussing selecting an arbitrator. Gabe and I both urged them not to put this case in the hands of Seitz. I didn't have a lot of confidence in Seitz's understanding of baseball. Both Gabe and I argued it. I just think that Seitz was not well informed with baseball issues. He was very liberal. It was just not something I felt comfortable with."

Both pitchers submitted their grievances to arbitration, and then on December 23, 1975, Seitz declared that the Major League Baseball players' contracts bound them to a team for only one year after the prior contract expired. This decision rendered the reserve clause ineffective, ending the enormous power and control it had given the owners for decades.

"The grievances of Messersmith and McNally are sustained," Peter Seitz wrote in his decision. "There is no contractual bond between these players and the Los Angeles and Montreal clubs, respectively. Absent such a contract, their clubs had no right or power under the Basic Agreement, the uniform player contract of the Major League Rules, to reserve their services for their exclusive use for any period beyond the 'renewal year' in the contracts which these players had heretofore signed with their clubs."

That was strike 1.

Baseball appealed the ruling to the U.S. District Court for Western

Missouri, but the ruling was upheld in February 1976 by Judge John Oliver.

That was strike 2.

Then, the Eighth Circuit Court of Appeals also upheld the rulings.

That was strike 3. The owners had struck out, and the players and their union had taken control of their destiny away from the owners.

Major League Baseball and the players' association negotiated and agreed that players with six years of experience could become free agents. That agreement on the part of the union was incredibly fair and gave the teams an opportunity to reap the harvest from the players who they brought through their farm systems into the Major Leagues. Teams that lost free agents would receive amateur draft picks in exchange. While the reserve clause still exists in player contacts, it has no bearing on the comings and goings of players as it did in the past.

Two popular songs of the era were "A New World Comin'," by Mama Cass Eliot, and "People Just Gotta Be Free," by the Rascals. While baseball often lagged behind society in many instances, suddenly America's Pastime was leading the way in individual rights and worker rights.

With a bevy of free agent players looming in its future thanks to the Seitz decision, baseball planned a draft for teams to pick free agent players they'd like to negotiate with. On November 1, 1976, some of the biggest names in the game became available. They included the likes of Rollie Fingers, Willie McCovey, Wayne Garland, Bobby Grich, Reggie Jackson, Bill Campbell, Steve Stone, Doyle Alexander, Dave Cash, Richie Hebner, and Garry Matthews.

Teams were also forced to begin locking up their best players rather than risk losing them to free agency. After earning $155,000 pitching for the Dodgers in 1976, ace right-hander Don Sutton landed a $1 million four-year deal. It was happening all over the game. Owners were bidding huge sums of money to sign veteran free agents who could have an immediate impact on their team. And the gains of the players upped the ante for other players, no matter what their level of achievement.

Players were making more money, and they had achieved a level of freedom of movement that their predecessors could never have imagined. The owners continued to make money. Television revenue was staggering, and the popularity of baseball was increasing, with numerous cities attempting to get a baseball team. It seemed like a ripe time to spread the wealth and the joy of the game. As the 1970s progressed, another expansion was on the horizon.

7 North by Northwest —1977

The Toronto Blue Jays and the
Seattle Mariners

The early success of the Montreal Expos franchise and the excitement of their fan base proved to Major League Baseball that Canadian cities could support a team. And Toronto, considered the New York of the North seemed the logical place. During January of 1976, the San Francisco Giants were at it again. Owner Horace Stoneham agreed to sell the Giants to a Toronto group that included Labatt Brewery, Vulcan Assets, and Canadian Imperial Bank of Commerce for $13.25 million. The team would move to Toronto and play the 1976 season at Exhibition Stadium.

The deal never came to fruition, as San Francisco's Bob Lurie stepped up and purchased the team and kept it in the city by the bay. It should be noted that by 1992, Lurie himself had seen enough and agreed to sell the Giants to a group of investors from St. Petersburg, who planned to move the franchise to Florida. But Lurie's fellow owners blocked that sale.

"Toronto was a situation where I went over there in 1976 and our first year was 1977," said Pat Gillick, who served as general manager of the Blue Jays from 1977 to 1994.

They were almost about to get the San Francisco Giants, but the mayor stepped forward and Bob Lurie kept the Giants there. Toronto lobbied very hard to get in the National League because of a natural rivalry with the Montreal Expos. The lawsuit in Seattle over the loss of the Pilots was to be dropped if they got a team. They had nobody to pair Seattle with, so that's when Toronto came in. People in Toronto were so happy to get a Major League franchise. We had a honeymoon for four years or so. They wanted to see the Yankees or the Red Sox more than they wanted to see the Blue Jays.

The Tigers, White Sox, Red Sox, and Yankees were teams [in cities] that also had hockey teams, and that helped. Then in year five and six, the press started getting more critical, and the fans were more knowledgeable. It was the right situation, though, as the team started to improve as the criticism began. So it all came together at the same time. By 1982 we knew we were headed the right way. It all meshed.

That was also a time frame in which the American League wanted to investigate the possibility of interleague play, an idea that was dashed by the National League, which wanted to continue its current set-up of two six-team divisions. In February of 1976 the American League voted 11–1 to expand. Their hope was to convince the Senior Circuit to join them in expanding. The two new teams would be split, with Seattle joining the American League and Toronto becoming a National League team. But the NL turned the idea down, and the AL accepted both new franchises, bringing its membership to fourteen teams while the NL remained at twelve.

The addition of the Seattle Mariners in 1977 was a direct result of the loss of the Pilots franchise to Milwaukee and Bud Selig after the disastrous 1969 season. When the Pilots became the Milwaukee Brewers, the city of Seattle, King County, and the State of Washington sued the American League for breach of contract. After the lawsuit, the city was promised a franchise by Commissioner Bowie Kuhn, and the awarding of this franchise was evidence that baseball was true to its word and that politics and litigation once again held the game hostage.

While it may have seemed a risky proposition to put yet another franchise in Seattle, Major League Baseball spotted the potential. In addition to his tenure in Toronto, Pat Gillick also served as general manager of the Mariners from 2000 to 2003 and has an understanding of all the potential the area had to offer baseball.

"Seattle is really a great sports town, and the fans are very supportive," he said.

Now they lost the Supersonics because they didn't have a basketball facility to support enough revenue. Their facility, revenue wise—seating capacity and from a luxury box standpoint—just didn't work in the current National Basketball Association model. They couldn't get the city to build another arena and lost the Supersonics.

But it's a really good sports town and the Mariners are a great franchise. The closest team is about a thousand miles away and that's Oakland. They have an area that is not densely populated but can attract fans from Portland, Vancouver, and other areas. So they can include Portland and Vancouver as part of their territory.

Seattle was just a good potential drawing area. When Boeing was there, income was good too. If you put a pretty good product on the field, you will draw in Seattle. The last six or seven years they have not been as competitive. You don't have to win there. Just put a competitive team on the field, and you'll draw. It's a better market than Kansas City, Cincinnati, Milwaukee, Oakland, or San Diego. I'd put it in the middle of the pack as far as a place to own a franchise.

The city fathers were so confident that Seattle would get another baseball team that the Kingdome was built. A huge improvement over Sicks Stadium, the home of the Pilots, the Kingdome would also become the home of the NFL's Seattle Seahawks.

So despite the discord between the two leagues, on November 5,

1976, the American League held its player draft to stock its new franchises, the Toronto Blue Jays and the Seattle Mariners.

Looking at draft choices decades later can be an interesting proposition in a Monday-morning quarterbacking sense. But teams have strategies whether they are existing clubs trying to hold on to their best players, or expansion clubs trying to build a winner faster.

While an early team like the New York Mets seemed to go after more veteran players to attract fans and possibly win more quickly, the early Houston Colt .45s simply went for the best player on the board. In that case, Houston came away the winner but it isn't always as simple as a fan might think.

New organizations literally sell their souls to get a franchise, and the financial commitment necessary to land a big league team can often hinder their ability to put a winning product on the field.

Seattle Mariners	**Toronto Blue Jays**
1 – Ruppert Jones (OF) Kansas City	2 – Bob Bailor (1F) Baltimore
3 – Gary Wheelock (P) California	4 – Jerry Garvin (P) Minnesota
5 – Bill Stein (3B) Chicago	6 – Jim Clancy (P) Texas
7 – Dick Pole (P) Boston	8 – Gary Woods (OF) Oakland
9 – Dan Meyer (1B) Detroit	10 – Rico Carty (DH) Cleveland
11 – Grant Jackson (P) New York	12 – Butch Edge (P) Milwaukee
14 – Dave Collins (OF) California	13 – Al Fitzmorris (P) Kansas City
16 – Frank MacCormack (P) Detroit	15 – Al Woods (OF) Minnesota
18 – Stan Thomas (P) Cleveland	17 – Mike Darr (P) Baltimore
20 – Juan Bernhardt (OF) New York	19 – Pete Vuckovich (P) Chicago
22 – Rick Jones (P) Boston	21 – Jeff Byrd (P) Texas
24 – Glenn Abbott (P) Oakland	23 – Steve Bowling (OF) Milwaukee
25 – Bob Stinson (C) Kansas City	26 – Dennis DeBarr (P) Detroit
27 – Carlos Lopez (OF) California	28 – Bill Singer (P) Minnesota
29 – Dave Pagan (P) Baltimore	30 – Jim Mason (SS) New York
31 – Roy Thomas (P) Chicago	32 – Doug Ault (1B) Texas
33 – Tom McMillan (SS) Cleveland	34 – Ernie Whitt (C) Boston
35 – Peter Broberg (P) Milwaukee	36 – Mike Weathers (1F) Oakland
38 – Steve Braun (OF) Minnesota	37 – Steve Staggs (2B) Kansas City
40 – Leroy Stanton (OF) California	39 – Steve Hargan (P) Texas
42 – Bob Galasso (P) Baltimore	41 – Garth Iorg (3B) New York
44 – Steve Burke (P) Boston	43 – Dave Lemanczyk (P) Detroit
46 – Joe Lis (1B) Cleveland	45 – Larry Andersen (P) Milwaukee
48 – Alan Griffin (P) Oakland	47 – Jesse Jefferson (P) Chicago

50 – Bill Laxton (P) Detroit	49 – Dave McKay (IF) Minnesota
52 – Julio Cruz (2B) California	51 – Tom Bruno (P) Kansas City
54 – Steve Barr (P) Texas	53 – Otto Velez (OF) New York
56 – Puchy Delgado (OF) Boston	55 – Mike Willis (P) Baltimore
58 – Tommy Smith (OF) Cleveland	57 – Sam Ewing (OF) Chicago
60 – Greg Erardi (P) Milwaukee	59 – Leon Hooten (P) Oakland

Toronto Blue Jays

Under the leadership of manager Roy Hartsfield, the Blue Jays had a typical first year for a new expansion team. They went 54-107, good enough for seventh place in the American League East, forty-five and a half games behind the New York Yankees. They finished twelve and a half games behind sixth-place Milwaukee.

And as is also typical of expansion teams, a number of players stepped up to the plate and performed well for the Blue Jays. Veteran outfielder Ron Fairly smacked a team-high 19 homers with 44 RBIS and a solid .279 average. Right fielder Otto Velez hit .256 with 16 homers and 62 RBIS, while first sacker Doug Ault his a solid .245 with 11 home runs and 64 RBIS. Roy Howell led the regulars with a .316 average at third base, hitting 10 round trippers with 44 RBIS, and utility man Bob Bailor hit .310, with 5 homers and 32 RBIS. He also hit the first leadoff home run in Blue Jays history.

Dave Lemancyk led the pitching staff with a 13-16 record and a 4.25 ERA. Jerry Garvin went 10-18, 4.19; and Jesse Jefferson was 9-17, 4.31.

Out of the bullpen, Pete Vuckovich led the staff with 53 appearances and went 7-7, with a 3.47 ERA and 8 saves. Mike Willis (2-6, 3.94, 5 saves) and Jerry Johnson (2-4, 4.60, 5 saves) both got into 43 games.

"We knew when we had the expansion draft that there were a lot of experienced players available," said Gillick.

But they were not going to be there when you got good, as they ran out of time. So in Toronto we went for as many young people as we possibly could. We drafted Jim Clancy, who pitched on our division championship team in 1985. Brad Corbett, who owned the Texas club, had promised his catcher who had gotten hurt, John Ellis, that he'd protect him in the draft. He did, and we got Clancy. Ernie Whitt was there in '85 too. We got some young guys in the draft who at twenty-five would still be with us when we got better.

In their second season, 1978, the Blue Jays improved, but not enough to escape the cellar of the American League East Division. But they improved to 59-102, forty games behind the New York Yankees, but they closed the gap to eleven games behind sixth-place Cleveland. And as is always the case with a new team, some different players found their way to prominence on the field.

The Jays acquired John Mayberry from Kansas City, and the former Houston Astro responded to his North-of-the-Border digs by leading the team with 22 home runs and 70 RBIs, hitting a very solid .250. Rico Cary hit .284, with 20 homers and 68 RBIs before being dealt to Oakland in August. Roy Howell had another good season, with a .270 average, 8 homers, and 61 RBIs. Newcomers Rick Bosetti hit .259 with 5 round-trippers and 42 RBIs while Willie Upshaw began what was to be a fine ten-year career hitting .237 with 1 homer and 17 RBIs in 95 games.

Right-hander Jim Clancy established himself as the ace of the staff with a 10-12 record and a 4.09 ERA. Jesse Jefferson went 7-16 with a 4.38 ERA, lefty Tom Underwood was 6-14 and 4.10, Jerry Garvin had a 4-12 mark and 5.54, and Dave Lemanczyk slumped to 4-14, with an ERA of 6.26. Newcomer Bailor Moore was 6-9 and 4.93.

The bullpen became more of a strength for the 1978 Blue Jays, with the emergence of Tom Murphy and Victor Cruz. Murphy led the staff with 50 appearances and had a 6-9 record with a 3.93 ERA and 7 saves. Cruz went 7-3, with a 1.71 ERA in 32 games and a staff-high 9 saves. And holdover Mike Willis appeared in 44 games with a 7-7 mark, 4.56 ERA with 7 saves.

The team showed slow but steady improvements. Pat Gillick

replaced Peter Bavasi after the first season and built a strong team that had its first winning season in 1983, with an 89-73 mark, good enough for a fourth-place finish. They went on to win East Division titles in 1985, 1989, 1991, 1992, and 1993, as well as American League pennants and World Series titles in both 1992 and 1993.

The '93 World Series victory was especially memorable. Leading the Philadelphia Phillies 3 games to 2 in the Series, Toronto trailed 6–5 with one out in the bottom of the ninth inning when Joe Carter slugged a game-winning, World Series–winning walk-off three-run home run against Phillies closer Mitch Williams to cinch the title. It was only the second time in Major League history that a team won the World Series on a walk-off homer. The other time occurred in 1960 when Bill Mazeroski of the Pittsburgh Pirates homered off Ralph Terry of the New York Yankees to earn the upset victory for the Pirates.

Hall of Famers who spent time in the Toronto organization include Roberto Alomar, Rickey Henderson, Phil Niekro, Dave Winfield, Paul Molitor, and general manager Pat Gillick.

Some other outstanding Blue Jays players include Alfredo Griffin, Tony Fernandez, George Bell, Joe Carter, Dave Stieb, John Olerud, Carlos Delgado, Lloyd Moseby, Tom Henke, Roy Halladay, Roger Clemens, and Jimmy Key.

Seattle Mariners

One of the teams brought into being by the numerous lawsuits filed by disenfranchised cities that lost baseball teams, the Mariners became a reality eight years after the Seattle Pilots took off for Milwaukee after one season in the Pacific Northwest.

The Mariners joined the American League's West Division, and on Opening Day of April 6, 1977, some things were different as far as Seattle baseball was concerned, while other things stayed the same. The big difference was that the first game was a sell-out, as 57,762 fans jammed the Kingdome. The familiar scenario was that the Mariners were handily defeated by the Los Angeles Angels, 7–0.

All things considered, it was not a bad inaugural season for Seattle's second big-league team. The M's finished in sixth place with a 64-98 record, thirty-eight games behind the Kansas City Royals but a half game ahead of seventh-place Oakland, which had a 63-98 record.

Seattle could score some runs. Right fielder Leroy Stanton led the team with 27 home runs and 90 RBIs with a .275 average. Ruppert Jones hit .263 with 24 homers and 76 RBIs, while first baseman Dan Meyer turned into a fine everyday ballplayer, hitting .273 with 22 home runs and 90 RBIs.

Outfielder Carlos Lopez hit .283 for manager Darrell Johnson, with 8 round-trippers and 34 RBIs, and Dave Collins chipped in with a .239 average with 5 homers and 28 RBIs.

Out on the mound, Glenn Abbott led the pitching staff with a 12-13 record and a 4.45 ERA. Dick Pole went 7-12, 5.15; John Montague was 8-12, 4.29; and Gary Wheelock had a 6-9, 4.89 mark. While veteran Diego Segui was a disappointing 0-7 in 40 games with a 5.69 ERA, the Opening Day starter became the only player who was both a Seattle Pilot and a Seattle Mariner. Given the Opening Day start, he earned the nickname of "The Ancient Mariner" at the ripe old age of thirty-nine.

Out of the bullpen, Enrique Romo was the team leader in both appearances with 58 and in saves with 16; he was 8-10 with a 2.83 ERA. Lefty Bill Laxton went 3-2, with 3 saves and a 4.95 ERA in 43 games. And veteran former Yankee Mike Kekich got into 41 games, going 5-4, 5.60.

In the Mariners' second season, they took a step back with a 56-104 record, which set them firmly in the basement of the West Division, thirty-five games behind the first-place Kansas City Royals and twelve games behind the Oakland A's.

Leon Roberts led the regulars with a .301 average, 22 home runs, and 92 RBIs. Bob Stinson was solid behind the plate, hitting .258 with 11 homers and 55 RBIs. Shortstop Craig Reynolds chipped in with a .292 average, along with 5 home runs and 44 RBIs. But first baseman

Dan Meyer slipped to a .227 average, with 8 dingers and 56 RBIs. And Ruppert Jones hit .235, with 6 home runs and 46 RBIs.

But off the bench, Tom Paciorek hit .299, adding 4 home runs and 30 RBIs in 70 games, and Bob Robertson hit .230 with 8 round trippers and 28 RBIs in 64 games.

The starting pitchers were led by Paul Mitchell, who was 8-14 with a 4.18 ERA. Glenn Abbott was 7-15, 5.27; Rick Honeycutt went 5-11, 4.89; and Dick Pole was 4-11, 6.48.

Enrique Romo continued to be a force out of the bullpen with a team-high 56 appearances and 10 saves to go along with his 11-7, 3.69 record. Tom House was 5-4, 4.66; and newcomer Shane Rawley went 4-9, with a 4.12 ERA and 4 saves in 52 games.

While the Mariners have become a solid franchise, they have never achieved baseball's promised land—the Fall Classic. They won the American League wild card in 2000 and were West Division title winners in 2001, 1997, and 1995. The 2001 campaign was particularly heartbreaking for Seattle fans as the team matched the all-time win total of the 1906 Chicago Cubs when they went 116-46. But they were defeated in the American League championship series 4 games to 1 by the New York Yankees.

Hall of Fame members from the organization include Gaylord Perry, Goose Gossage, Rickey Henderson, manager Dick Williams, and general manager Pat Gillick. There seems little doubt that some other Mariners players will also be part of the Cooperstown elite, including Ichiro Suzuki, Alex Rodriguez, Ken Griffey Jr., and Edgar Martinez. And many other fine ballplayers have also been Mariners, including Jamie Moyer, Freddie Garcia, Harold Reynolds, Mark Langston, Randy Johnson, and Jay Buhner.

8 | Thin Air and Immediate Success—1993

The Colorado Rockies and the
Florida Marlins

Toward the middle of the final decade of the twentieth century, the National League finally agreed that it was time for both leagues to have the same number of teams. As would be expected, a number of seemingly deserving cities were in the hunt for the two new franchises. Cities vying for the new teams included Buffalo, Charlotte, Denver, Miami, Nashville, Orlando, Phoenix, Sacramento, Tampa Bay, and, of course, Washington DC.

After much discussion it was announced on July 5, 1991, by the baseball expansion committee led by Pirates chairman Doug Danforth that the two new National League teams would be based in Denver—the Colorado Rockies—and in South Florida, in Miami, the new home of the Florida Marlins. They would begin play in the 1993 season.

The acceptance of a franchise in Denver had its roots in the Continental League, and a new team in Florida was a grand experiment to see if the home of the Grapefruit League in spring training could actually support a club for an entire Major League season.

There had been a number of unsuccessful attempts to bring baseball to Colorado. In the late 1980s, the Pittsburgh Pirates had considered a move to the Denver area. Attendance was down, and the drug trials that included Pittsburgh players had seemingly opened up the door for a possible relocation. But the proud history of the Bucos franchise prevailed, however, and any big league club in Denver would have to be an expansion team.

In Florida, in the spring of 1990, Wayne Huizenga of Blockbuster Entertainment purchased 15 percent of the Miami Dolphins' Joe Robbie Stadium. He reportedly spent approximately $30 million on the acquisition, which he hoped would help in his plan to get an expansion team in South Florida. Baseball had an active interest in pursuing a new team in Florida, the only question was where it would be located. Miami, Orlando, and Tampa Bay were all viable choices for a new National League team. But it was Huizenga's group that won the competition.

On November 17, 1992, New York hosted the expansion draft conducted by Major League Baseball to stock the Colorado Rockies' and Florida Marlins' rosters. Colorado would join the NL's West Division, while the Marlins would be part of the National League East.

The rules for this draft were different as well. In the past, only teams from the league in which expansion teams would play were forced to participate and lose players in the draft. So when the American League expanded with two teams in 1977, only teams from the Junior Circuit lost players. But in 1992, both leagues were forced to put players in the pool to be chosen from.

This new procedure was fair to the league in question and also gave the new teams a better opportunity to be competitive sooner, as they had a larger group of players to choose from. Each team was able to protect fifteen players from its roster, and each team could lose only one player in each round. At the end of each round, the National League teams could call back and protect three additional players, while the American League teams could protect an additional four players.

Colorado Rockies

1 – David Nied (P) Atlanta
4 – Charlie Hayes (3B) New York Yankees
6 – Darren Holmes (P) Milwaukee
8 – Jerald Clark (OF) San Diego
10 – Kevin Reimer (OF) Texas
12 – Eric Young (2B) Los Angeles Dodgers
14 – Jody Reed (2B) Boston
16 – Scott Aldred (P) Detroit
18 – Alex Cole (OF) Pittsburgh
20 – Joe Girardi (C) Chicago Cubs
22 – Willie Blair (P) Houston
24 – Jay Owens (C) Minnesota
26 – Andy Ashby (P) Philadelphia
28 – Freddie Benavides (SS) Cincinnati
30 – Roberto Mejia (2B) Los Angeles Dodgers
32 – Doug Bochtler (P) Montreal
34 – Lance Painter (P) San Diego
36 – Butch Henry (P) Houston
38 – Ryan Hawblitzel (P) Chicago Cubs
40 – Vinny Castilla (SS) Atlanta
42 – Brett Merriman (P) California
44 – Jim Tatum (3B) Milwaukee
46 – Kevin Ritz (P) Detroit
48 – Eric Wedge (C/1B) Boston
50 – Keith Shepherd (P) Philadelphia
52 – Calvin Jones (P) Seattle
54 – Brad Ausmus (C) New York Yankees
56 – Marcus Moore (P) Toronto
58 – Armando Reynoso (P) Atlanta
60 – Steve Reed (P) San Francisco
62 – Mo Sanford (P) Cincinnati
64 – Pedro Castellano (3B) Chicago Cubs
66 – Curtis Leskanic (P) Minnesota
68 – Scott Fredrickson (P) San Diego
70 – Braulio Castillo (OF) Philadelphia
72 – Denis Boucher (P) Cleveland

Florida Marlins

2 – Nigel Wilson (OF) Toronto
3 – Jose Martinez (P) New York Mets
5 – Bret Barberie (SS) Montreal
7 – Trevor Hoffman (P) Cincinnati
9 – Pat Rapp (P) San Francisco
11 – Greg Hibbard (P) Chicago White Sox
13 – Chuck Carr (OF) St. Louis
15 – Darrell Whitmore (OF) Cleveland
17 – Eric Helfand (C) Oakland
19 – Bryan Harvey (P) California
21 – Jeff Conine (1B/OF) Kansas City
23 – Kip Vaughn (P) Baltimore
25 – Jesus Tavarez (OF) Seattle
27 – Carl Everett (OF) New York Yankees
29 – Dave Weathers (P) Toronto
31 – John Johnstone (P) New York Mets
33 – Ramon Martinez (SS) Pittsburgh
35 – Steve Decker (C) San Francisco
37 – Cris Carpenter (P) St Louis
39 – Jack Armstrong (P) Cleveland
41 – Scott Chiamparino (P) Texas
43 – Tom Edens (P) Minnesota
45 – Andres Berumen (P) Kansas City
47 – Robert Person (P) Chicago White Sox
49 – Jim Corsi (P) Oakland
51 – Richie Lewis (P) Baltimore
53 – Danny Jackson (P) Pittsburgh
55 – Bob Natal (C) Montreal
57 – Jamie McAndrew (P) Los Angeles Dodgers
59 – Junior Felix (OF) California
61 – Kerwin Moore (OF) Kansas City
63 – Ryan Bowen (P) Houston
65 – Scott Baker (P) St. Louis
67 – Chris Donnels (3B) New York Mets
69 – Monty Fariss (OF) Texas
71 – Jeff Tabaka (P) Milwaukee

Both new clubs made a number of player transactions following the expansion draft. Some of the major moves that affected both teams are as follows:

Florida traded Danny Jackson to Philadelphia in exchange for Joel Adamson and Matt Whisenant.

Colorado sent Jody Reed to the Los Angeles Dodgers for Rudy Seanez.

Florida traded Greg Hibbard to the Chicago Cubs for Gary Scott and Alex Arias.

Colorado sent Kevin Reimer to the Milwaukee Brewers for Dante Bichette.

Florida traded Eric Helfand and Scott Baker to the Oakland A's for Walt Weiss.

Florida traded Tom Edens to the Houston Astros for Hector Carrasco and Brian Griffiths.

Colorado Rockies

After being the bridesmaid for so many years, the city of Denver seemed to have its ducks all in a row. Banking executive Larry Varnell headed the Colorado Baseball Commission and convinced Denver voters to approve a 0.1 percent sales tax to help finance a new baseball stadium. Governor Roy Romer formed an advisory committee in 1990 to help recruit an ownership group. They selected a group led by Ohio beverage distributor John Antonucci and Phar-Mor drugstore executive Michael Monus, along with regional entities Erie Lake, Hensel Phelps Construction, KOA Radio, and the *Rocky Mountain News* to complete the group. Finally, in a process that began in 1960 with Branch Rickey and William Shea's Continental League came to fruition on July 5, 1991, when the National League approved Denver as one of the two expansion teams to begin play in 1993.

As the franchise prepared for its inaugural season, in 1992 a scandal (not related to baseball) rocked both Monus and Antonucci, who were forced to sell their shares in the team to Jerry McMorris, a trucking executive who owned the team until 2005.

Despite the ownership shuffle, the team got underway in 1993 and finished in sixth place in the National League West Division with a 67-95 record, thirty-seven games behind division champion Atlanta.

But the Rockies finished six games ahead of the lowly San Diego Padres, who were at 61-101. Like all expansion teams, Colorado had some challenging times in its first year, including a 2-17 run during the month of May. But their sixty-seven wins set a National League record for victories for a first-year expansion club. And after waiting more than thirty years to get a Major League franchise, when they finally got one, fans came out in droves to see their Rockies. The team set a Major League record for home attendance that first year, bringing in 4,483,350.

Offensively the team was led by Andres Galarraga at first base, who had a phenomenal season, leading the team by winning the batting title with a .370 average with 22 home runs and 98 RBIs. Manager and hitting guru Don Baylor convinced Galarraga to use an open batting stance in which he faced the pitcher and saw pitches much more clearly than he did with a regular stance. Third baseman Charlie Hayes hit .305 and led the team with 25 homers and 98 RBIs. Dante Bichette hit .310 with 21 round trippers and 89 RBIs, while Jerald Clark hit .282 with 13 homers and 67 RBIs. Catcher Joe Girardi hit a solid .290 with 3 homers and 31 RBIs. Daryl Boston added 14 home runs and 40 RBIs to go along with his .261 average.

The pitching staff was headed by Armando Reynoso, who went 12-11 with a 4.00 ERA. David Nied was 5-9, 5.17, Butch Henry went 2-8, 6.59, and Ken Bottenfield had a 3-5 mark with a 6.10 ERA.

In the bullpen, Darren Holmes was solid, appearing in 62 games with a 3-3 record and 4.05 ERA, leading the staff with 25 saves. Lefty Bruce Ruffin went 6-5 in 59 games with 2 saves and a 3.87 ERA. Gary Wayne led the staff with 65 appearances and a 5-3, 5.05; and Steve Reed went 9-5, 4.48 in 64 games.

Great hitting statistics and less-than-stellar pitching was the theme of the team. They truly were a team of two cities—Denver, the Mile High City, and every other National League town. While in Colorado, hitting reigned supreme and pitching was an afterthought. Hits and lots of long home runs were the order of any day in Denver.

The reason for the hitting hysteria in Denver is the high altitude of both Mile High Stadium, where the team first played, and the team's current Coors Field. There the very thin air affects the baseball's movement. A curve ball tends to flatten out, making it an invitingly hittable pitch. And in a maddening case of double jeopardy for hurlers, a batted ball travels farther. There were no years of the pitcher in Denver, to be sure.

The trend continued in 1994, with the Rockies powering their way into contention in the National League West Division. Just how close they might have come to winning the division will never be known, as a player strike cost them forty-five games during the year. But they finished with a 53-64 mark, good enough for third place, just six and a half games behind the division champion Los Angeles Dodgers and three games behind second-place San Francisco.

Andres Galarraga firmly established himself as a star performer, hitting .319 with 31 home runs and 85 RBIs. Dante Bichette slugged his way to a .304 average with 27 homers and 95 RBIs, and Charlie Hayes had another good season, hitting .288 with 10 dingers and 50 RBIs. But in its second season, the Rockies saw some newcomers begin to make a dramatic impact.

Mike Kingery played right field and hit .349 with 4 home runs and 41 RBIs. Walt Weiss played a dependable shortstop and hit .251. Ellis Burks hit .322 with 13 homers and 24 RBIs in 42 games, while Manny Castilla hit at a .331 clip with 3 homers and 18 RBIs in 52 games.

On the war zone known as the pitcher's mound, free agent signee Marvin Freeman went 10-2 with a 2.80 ERA. David Nied rebounded nicely with a 9-7, 4.80 season; and Kevin Ritz went 5-6, 5.62. Greg Harris, 3-12 with an ERA of 6.55, and lefty Lance Painter, 4-6 and 6.11, rounded out the rotation.

In the bullpen, Bruce Ruffin appeared in 56 games, with a 4-5 record with a 4.04 ERA and a team-high 16 saves. Steve Reed appeared in a team-leading 61 games, with a 3-2, 3.94 mark and 3 saves. Mike Munoz went 4-2 and 3.74 in 57 games, and Darren Holmes finished the season at 0-3 with 3 saves and a 6.35 ERA in 28 games.

The effect of the conditions in Denver had some interesting side-lights. The team changed hitting coaches five times in the first five years of the franchise. No one seemed to have the key to putting up the same kind of offensive stats on the road as they did at home. As a result, the Rockies were a team that played far worse when they were out of the friendly confines of Mile High Stadium and then Coors Field.

Only six pitchers from the Opening Day roster of the team in 1993 lasted two seasons with the Rockies. The seemingly out-of-this-world pitching conditions took their toll.

But over the years the franchise has enjoyed success. They won wild card berths in 1995, 2007, and 2009. The Rockies won the National League pennant in 2007, but in the World Series they were swept 4 games to 0 by the Boston Red Sox.

While no members of the Hall of Fame have ever played for the Rockies, numerous outstanding athletes have played in Denver. They include Andres Galarraga, Dante Bichette, Vinny Castilla, Larry Walker, Todd Helton, Matt Holliday, Garret Atkins, Troy Tulowitzki, Jason Jennings, Huston Street, and Darryl Kile.

Kile signed a big-money contract after going after going 19-7 with a 2.57 ERA with Houston. In his two seasons in Colorado, Kyle under-performed, going 13-17 with a 5.20 in 1998, and 8-13, 6.61 the follow-ing season. The pitching conditions even had a negative effect on an All-Star caliber such as Darryl Kile.

Following the 1999 season, the Rockies dealt him with Luther Hick-man and Dave Veres to the St. Louis Cardinals in exchange for Man-uel Aybar, Grent Butler, Rich Croughore, and Jose Jimenez. Kile responded with a 20-9 season in St. Louis in 2000. He went 16-11 the following season and was off to a 5-4 start with a 3.72 ERA after 14 starts in 2002.

On June 21, 2002, while the Cardinals were in Chicago for a series against the Cubs, Kile went to dinner with his brother Dan and some friends. As the team prepared to take the field the following afternoon in Wrigley Field, they began to grow concerned when Kile did not arrive at the ballpark by 11 a.m. Security was asked to make sure that he was all right. Sadly, the popular right-hander was found dead in his bed. An autopsy revealed that he had died of a massive heart attack caused by severe coronary atherosclerosis, which caused a significant blockage of the arteries that supply blood to the heart.

The Rockies have addressed the situation that caused havoc with the baseball in Denver. Coors Field, affectionately referred to as Coors Canaveral by hitters (not such a pleasant moniker by pitchers), continued to be a venue for sending baseballs into Earth orbit. In 1996 an astounding 271 round trippers were hit at Coors. That's an average of nearly three and a half homers per game.

But a study found that dry air contributed to the number of home runs hit in Denver. Baseballs stored in drier areas are harder and more elastic to the bat. So before the 2002 season, a room-sized humidor was installed in the stadium to store the baseballs. Since that installation, the number of homers at Coors Field has decreased and is more in line with other Major League parks. Since 2005 the total number of home runs hit there has dropped below two hundred.

Of course, even this adjustment is not without intrigue. It seems that some visiting clubs wondered if humidor baseballs were used when they were hitting and if the former super-baseballs were used when Colorado was hitting. As a result, Major League Baseball has intervened. The powers-that-be are protecting the integrity of the humidor-stored baseballs as if they were the presidential nuclear launch codes.

According to a tweak from the commissioner of baseball's office,

All teams have received a memo regarding the new procedures, which are as follows: An authenticator employed by MLB meets the umpire-room attendant at the humidor before the game, watching as the baseballs are removed. The authenticator follows the attendant to the umpire room, where the baseballs are rubbed down. He then accompanies the attendant as the baseballs are placed in the Rockies' dugout.

During the game, the authenticator sits in the photo well just to the right of the Rockies' dugout with the ball bag in sight. Because the authenticator cannot leave his post, an MLB-contracted security officer meets the umpire-room attendant at the humidor if more baseballs are required during the course of the game.

Hopefully, the conspiracy theorists can put this latest threat to national security to rest.

Florida Marlins

When Blockbuster CEO Wayne Huizenga purchased 15 percent of the National Football League's Miami Dolphins and 50 percent of their stadium, Joe Robbie Stadium, for approximately $30 million in March of 1990, he made it clear that a Major League Baseball franchise was his long-term goal. Even though his top competitor for a franchise, St. Petersburg–Tampa already had erected a stadium, the Florida Suncoast Dome, in 1990, MLB awarded Huizenga a franchise in Miami on June 10, 1991.

The team has been well known as the youngest franchise to win a World Series, in just its fifth season. They were also the first wild card team to win a World Series championship. And they have won the World Series the only times they made it to the postseason, in 1997 and 2003. But that 1997 championship team was then decimated by a fire sale, where Huizenga unloaded many of his high-priced players.

In their inaugural season of 1993, the Marlins finished in sixth place in the National League East Division with a 64-98 record, thirty-three games behind the division champion Philadelphia Phillies. But they did finish five games ahead of the New York Mets.

Jeff Conine had a solid season, hitting .292 with 12 home runs and 79 RBIs. After being acquired in a trade with San Diego in late June, Gary Sheffield hit .292, with 10 homers and 37 RBIs. First baseman Orested Destrade led the Marlins with 20 home runs to go along with 87 RBIs and a .255 average. Second baseman Bret Barberie hit .277, with 5 home runs and 33 RBIs; and Chuck Carr hit .267 with 4 round-trippers and 41 RBIs. Alex Arias (.269, 2 home runs, 20 RBIs) and Dave Magadan (.286, 4 home runs, 29 RBIs) were key players off the bench.

Chris Hammond led the pitching staff with an 11-12 record and a 4.66 ERA. Charlie Hough was 9-16 at 4.27, Jack Armstrong went 9-17 with 4.49, and Ryan Bowen filled out the rotation going 8-12 and 4.42.

In the bullpen, Bryan Harvey appeared in 59 games with a 1-5 record, but he had an ERA of 1.70 and led the staff with 45 saves. Joe Klink also got into 55 games, going 0-2 and 5.12. Future Hall of Famer and eventual career saves leader Trevor Hoffman was dealt to San Diego in the Gary Sheffield trade. But he went 2-2 with 2 saves in 28 games for the Fish prior to the trade.

The following season, Rene Lachemann's squad went 51-64 in a strike-shortened season, twenty-three and a half games behind the division champion Montreal Expos. Pitcher Charlie Hough became the second-oldest pitcher in the history of the game to be an Opening Day starter, at the age of forty-six. The only hurler who was older was Jack Quinn of the Brooklyn Dodgers, who pitched on Opening Day of 1931 at the age of forty-seven.

While the strike-shortened season certainly stalled the team's progress to a degree, 1994 also saw continued progress by players who were to play important roles.

Catcher Benito Santiago hit .273, with 11 home runs and 41 RBIs. At second base, Bret Barberie had another good season, hitting .301 with 5 homers and 31 RBIs. Third baseman Jerry Browne hit .295 with 3 home runs and 30 RBIs.

The Marlins' outfield was a mix of speed and power. Gary Sheffield hit .276, with a team-high 27 round-trippers and 78 RBIs. Jeff Conine led the regulars with a .319 average, adding 18 homers and 82 RBIs. Speedy Chuck Carr hit .263 and led the team with 32 stolen bases.

The aforementioned Charlie Hough went 5-9 with a 5.15 ERA. Joining him in the starting rotation were David Weathers, 8-12 with a 5.27

ERA, Pat Rapp, 7-8 and a 3.85 ERA, and Chris Hammond, 4-4 with a 3.07 ERA.

Hard-throwing right-hander Robb Nen was the closer. He appeared in 44 games, sporting a 5-5 record with a 2.95 ERA and 15 saves. Richie Lewis appeared in a team-high 45 games and went 1-4 with a 5.67 ERA. And lefty Yorkis Perez went 3-0 and 3.54 in 44 games.

The Marlins showed a steady improvement that would move them gradually but steadily toward the top of the standings. They went 67-76 in 1995, 80-82 in 1996, and 92-70 in 1997. That was their first wild card season, in which they finished nine games behind the National League East champion Atlanta Braves, who went 101-61.

Huizenga had brought in some high-priced talent to get the team to the apex of a title. Bobby Bonilla led the regulars with a .297 average with 17 home runs and 96 RBIs. Moises Alou hit .292 and led the team with 23 homers and 115 RBIs. Two steady holdovers were Gary Sheffield, who hit .250 with 21 round-trippers and 71 RBIs; and Jeff Conine, who added 17 home runs and 61 RBIs along with his .242 average.

But some experienced newcomers acquired to strengthen the team did just that. Jim Eisenreich hit .280, Craig Counsell .299, Darren Daulton .262, and Cliff Floyd .234, and all played key roles off the Florida bench.

The pitching staff consisted of Alex Fernandez, who led the team with a 17-12 record and a 3.59 ERA. Money pitcher Kevin Brown was 16-8, with a 2.69 ERA; Al Leiter went 11-9, with an ERA of 4.34; Livan Hernandez was 9-3, with a 3.18 ERA; and holdover Pat Rapp went 4-6, 4.47 ERA.

In the bullpen, Robb Nen was firmly entrenched as one of the premier closers in the game, appearing in 73 games with a 9-3 record, a 3.89 ERA, and a team-high 35 saves. Jay Powell was in a team-high 74 games sporting a 7-2, 3.28 ERA mark with 2 saves. And Dennis Cook was 1-2, with a 3.90 ERA in 34 games.

Florida defeated the San Francisco Giants, 2 games to 0, in the National League division series and then went on to trip the Atlanta

Braves in six games in the National League championship series before defeating the Cleveland Indians in an exciting seven-game World Series.

But saying that the world championship team had lost $34 million, Huizenga quickly stripped the team. Alou, Nenn, Brown, and Cook would be joined by Sheffield, Bonilla, and Eisenreich, who were all gone by May of 1998. That team went from 92-70 to 54-108.

Huizenga sold the club to John Henry, a Boca Raton commodities trader who later sold the team to Jeffrey Loria. The 2003 team rebounded nicely, and once again won the wild card and captured their second World Series title. Those two championships equal the New York Mets and the Toronto Blue Jays for the most titles for an expansion team.

Tony Perez and Andre Dawson are Hall of Fame members who have played for the Marlins franchise. Other key players in the franchise's history include Gary Sheffield, Derrek Lee, Miguel Cabrera, Luis Castillo, Jeff Conine, Kevin Brown, Josh Beckett, A. J. Burnett, Brad Penny, Mike Lowell, and Dontrelle Willis.

The team changed its name to the Miami Marlins in 2012 as they moved into a new stadium on the site of the Orange Bowl.

9 | Baseball's Final Expansion?—1998

The Arizona Diamondbacks and the
Tampa Bay Devil Rays

Thanks to the success enjoyed by both the Colorado Rockies and
the Florida Marlins (who entered the Major Leagues in 1993), the
following spring in March 1994, Major League Baseball created an
expansion committee to look into yet another expansion that would
add one team to the National League and one team to the American
League, increasing the number of teams from twenty-eight to
thirty.

While it was felt from the outset that Phoenix and St. Petersburg
were the favorites to receive big-league franchises, other cities were
encouraged to vie for the two spots. In addition to the favorites, Buffalo, Mexico City, Monterrey, Nashville, Northern Virginia, Orlando,
and Vancouver all submitted bids. Charlotte, Washington DC, and
Guadalajara were also mentioned as possible venues.

The expansion committee narrowed it down to a grouping of four
finalists, with Phoenix and St. Petersburg beating out Orlando and
Northern Virginia. On March 9, 1995, nearly a year to the day of the
formation of the committee, it was announced that Phoenix and St.

Petersburg would begin play in the 1998 season and pay a $130 million expansion fee for the honor.

Baseball has gotten expansion down to a science, and these two new teams were the beneficiaries of that knowledge. While the Los Angeles Angels had a full eight days to prepare for baseball's first expansion draft, these two new franchises had three years to prepare for their first season of play.

The expansion also forced a realignment of leagues. Without such a move, each league would have had fifteen teams, forcing interleague play every day of the season. So after the Kansas City Royals rejected such a move, the Milwaukee Brewers moved to the National League in 1998.

Before this move, Commissioner Bud Selig had proposed a radical realignment of teams based on geography, which would have had interleague play on a daily basis. Under his plan, baseball would have four divisions. Here is how Selig's baseball map would have looked:

American League East: Baltimore Orioles, Boston Red Sox, Montreal Expos, New York Mets, New York Yankees, Philadelphia Phillies, Toronto Blue Jays.

American League Midwest: Atlanta Braves, Cincinnati Reds, Cleveland Indians, Detroit Tigers, Florida Marlins, Pittsburgh Pirates, Tampa Bay Devil Rays.

National League Central: Chicago Cubs, Chicago White Sox, Houston Astros, Kansas City Royals, Milwaukee Brewers, Minnesota Twins, St. Louis Cardinals, Texas Rangers.

National League West: Anaheim Angels, Arizona Diamondbacks, Colorado Rockies, Los Angeles Dodgers, Oakland Athletics, San Diego Padres, San Francisco Giants, Seattle Mariners.

Numerous clubs objected to the plan, and as mentioned previously, the Brewers changed leagues to bring the game to its present alignment of two leagues, each with three divisions, featuring sporadic interleague play during the season. Here is the current alignment:

National League East: Atlanta Braves, Miami Marlins, New York Mets, Philadelphia Phillies, Washington Nationals.

National League Central: Chicago Cubs, Cincinnati Reds, Houston Astros, Milwaukee Brewers, Pittsburgh Pirates, St. Louis Cardinals.

National League West: Arizona Diamondbacks, Colorado Rockies, Los Angeles Dodgers, San Diego Padres, San Francisco Giants.

American League East: Baltimore Orioles, Boston Red Sox, New York Yankees, Tampa Bay Rays, Toronto Blue Jays.

American League Central: Chicago White Sox, Cleveland Indians, Detroit Tigers, Kansas City Royals, Minnesota Twins.

American League West: Los Angeles Angels of Anaheim, Oakland Athletics, Seattle Mariners, Texas Rangers.

Two new cities were to be part of baseball in 1998 as expansion franchises were awarded to Tampa Bay and Phoenix.

The draft was held on November 18, 1997. Each franchise paid a $130 million fee to baseball's central fund. In addition, both new expansion teams gave away their rights to $5 million from baseball's central fund for the first five years following the draft, 1998 to 2002. The total franchise fee for each team was $155 million, a far cry from the early days of expansion when the Los Angeles Angels and the Washington Senators had joined Major League Baseball for the 1961 season.

The draft consisted of three rounds. For the first and second rounds, each team would select fourteen players from the list of available players. In the third round they would choose seven new players, so each new team would pick thirty-five players. Existing teams could protect fifteen players from the rosters of their entire organizations. Each team could add three more players to their protected list after each round. Players chosen in the 1996 and 1997 amateur drafts were automatically exempt from the draft, as well as players who were eighteen or younger when signed in 1995. And players who were free agents at the end of the 1997 season did not have to be protected.

Tampa Bay Devil Rays

1– Tony Saunders (P) Florida
4– Quinton McCracken (OF) Colorado
6– Bobby Abreu (OF) Houston
8– Miguel Cairo (IF) Chicago
10 – Rich Butler (OF) Toronto
12 – Bobby Smith (3B) Atlanta
14 – Jason Johnson (P) Pittsburgh
16 – Dimitri Young (1B) Cincinnati
18 – Eseban Yan (P) Baltimore
20 – Mike DiFelice (C) St. Louis
22 – Bubba Trammell (OF) Detroit
24 – Andy Sheets (IF) Seattle
26 – Dennis Springer (P) Anaheim
28 – Dan Carlson (P) San Francisco
30 – Brian Boehringer (P) New York Yankees
32 – Mike Duvall (P) Florida
34 – John LeRoy (P) Atlanta
36 – Jim Mecir (P) Boston
38 – Bryan Rekar (P) Colorado
40 – Rick Gorecki (P) Los Angeles Dodgers
42 – Ramon Tatis (P) Chicago Cubs
44 – Kerry Robinson (OF) St. Louis
46 – Steve Cox (1B) Oakland
48 – Albie Lopez (P) Cleveland
50 – Jose Paniagua (P) Montreal
52 – Carlos Mendoza (OF) New York Mets
54 – Kevin Sefcik (OF) Philadelphia
56 – Santos Hernandez (P) San Francisco
58 – Randy Winn (OF) Florida
60 – Terrell Wade (P) Atlanta
62 – Aaron Ledesma (IF) Baltimore
64 – Brooks Kieschnick (OF) Chicago Cubs
66 – Luke Wilcox (OF) New York Yankees
68 – Herbert Perry (IF) Cleveland
70 – Vaughn Eshelman (P) Oakland

Arizona Diamondbacks

2 – Brian Anderson (P) Cleveland
3 – Jeff Suppan (P) Boston
5 – Gabe Alvarez (3B) San Diego
7 – Jorge Fabregas (C) Chicago White Sox
9 – Karim Garcia (OF) Los Angeles Dodgers
11 – Edwin Diaz (1B) Texas
13 – Cory Lidle (P) New York Mets
15 – Joel Adamson (P) Milwaukee
17 – Ben Ford (P) New York Yankees
19 – Yamil Benitez (OF) Kansas City
21 – Neil Weber (P) Montreal
23 – Jason Boyd (P) Philadelphia
25 – Brent Brede (OF) Minnesota
27 – Tony Batista (IF) Oakland
29 – Tom Martin (P) Houston
31 – Omar Daal (P) Toronto
33 – Scott Winchester (P) Cincinnati
35 – Clint Sodowsky (P) Pittsburgh
37 – Danny Klassen (IF) Milwaukee
39 – Matt Drews (P) Detroit
41 – Todd Erdos (P) San Diego
43 – Chris Clemons (P) Chicago White Sox
45 – David Dellucci (OF) Baltimore
47 – Damian Miller (C) Minnesota
49 – Hector Carrasco (P) Kansas City
51 – Hanley Frias (SS) Texas
53 – Bob Wolcott (P) Seattle
55 – Mike Bell (3B) Anaheim
57 – Joe Randa (3B) Pittsburgh
59 – Jesus Martinez (P) Los Angeles Dodgers
61 – Russ Springer (P) Houston
63 – Bryan Corey (P) Detroit
65 – Kelly Stinnett (C) Milwaukee
67 – Chuck McElroy (P) Chicago White Sox
69 – Marty Janzen (P) Toronto

At the conclusion of the draft, numerous trades were made. Trades by existing clubs could not be made until the conclusion of the draft, since newly acquired players would not be on their protected player list. The post-draft deals are as follows:

Tampa Bay traded Bobby Abreu to Philadelphia in exchange for Kevin Stocker.

Tampa Bay traded Andy Sheets and Brian Boehringer to San Diego in exchange for John Flaherty.

Tampa Bay traded Dmitri Young to Cincinnati in exchange for Mike Kelly.

Tampa Bay purchased Fred McGriff from Atlanta.

Arizona traded Gabe Alvarez, Joe Randa and Matt Drews to Detroit in exchange for Travis Fryman.

Arizona traded Scott Winchester to Cincinnati in exchange for Felix Rodriguez.

Arizona traded Jesus Martinez to Florida in exchange for Devon White.

Arizona traded Chuck McElroy to Colorado in exchange for Harvey Pulliam.

Arizona Diamondbacks

Cactus League baseball in Arizona had been a successful spring training alternative to Florida's Grapefruit League since 1946. There was a history between America's Game and Arizona for such a long period that any talk about an expansion team being located there had instant credibility. Phoenix had hosted the San Francisco Giants Triple-A farm team for years and had been such a draw for new residents that it had become the nation's sixth largest city by the early 1990s.

In 1993 Jerry Colangelo, owner of the Phoenix Suns National Basketball Association team, formed an ownership group known as Arizona Baseball Inc., to approach Major League Baseball for an expansion team.

The influential Colangelo got some important support in his pursuit of a Major League franchise from his friend Jerry Reinsdorf, owner of the Chicago White Sox and the Chicago Bulls NBA team, along with the then-acting commissioner of baseball, Bud Selig.

Plans were made for a new ballpark with a retractable roof, Bank One Ballpark, which was renamed Chase Field in 2005. The new park was built across the street from the Phoenix Suns' U.S. Airways Center.

Colangelo and his group confidently held a name-the-team competition before they were awarded a franchise. The contest, announced in the February 13, 1995, edition of the *Arizona Republic* newspaper, would see the first-place winner receive a pair of lifetime season tickets for the new team's home games. The winning choice was the Diamondbacks, named for the western diamondback, a rattlesnake native to the area.

On March 9, 1995, three weeks following the announcement of the name-the-team contest, Major League Baseball awarded Colangelo's group a franchise to begin play in 1998.

This new franchise operated differently from any of its predecessors. Two years before the team's first game, Colangelo hired former New York Yankees manager Buck Showalter as the Diamondbacks' skipper.

Arizona had a typical inaugural season, finishing in last place in the National League West Division with a 65-97 mark. But they acquired talented veteran players such as Matt Williams, Devon White, Jay Bell, and Travis Fryman through trades or free agency before the start of the season, which was a harbinger of things to come.

White led the regulars with a .279 batting average, with 22 home runs and 85 RBIs. First baseman Travis Lee also smashed 22 home runs, with 72 RBIs and a .269 average. Williams hit .267, with 20 homers and 71 RBIs. And shortstop Bell hit .251 with 20 dingers and 67 RBIs.

Right-hander Andy Benes led the pitching staff with a 14-13 record and a 3.97 ERA. Brian Anderson went 12-13 and 4.33. Omar Daal was 8-12 and 2.88, Jeff Suppan went 6-9 and 6.68, and Willie Blair rounded out the rotation with a 4.15 mark and a 5.34 ERA.

In the bullpen, Greg Olsen led the staff with 60 appearances and 30 saves to go along with his 3-4 record and 3.01 ERA. Clint Sadowsky was 3-6, at 5.68 in 45 games; and Alan Embree pitched in 35 games with a 3-2 record and a 4.11 ERA.

Colangelo opened up the doors to the vault before the 1999 season. The ploy worked, as the Diamondbacks went on to win thirty-five more games than they had in 1998, and the team captured the National League West Division with a 100-62 record, becoming the fastest expansion team to win a division title, in just its second year. The San Francisco Giants finished a distant second with an 86-76 record, fourteen games behind Arizona.

Before the '99 season, Arizona signed a number of free-agent players, including pitchers Randy Johnson and Greg Swindell. All Johnson did was cop the Cy Young Award with his 17-9 record with a 2.48 ERA, leading the league in complete games (12) and strikeouts (364). He joined Pedro Martinez and Gaylord Perry as the only three pitchers to earn Cy Young honors in both leagues.

Johnson was joined on the staff by Omar Daal, who went 16-9 with a 3.65 ERA; Andy Benes, 13-12 and 4.81; and Todd Stottlemyre, 6-3 and 4.09.

In the bullpen, Gregg Olson appeared in 32 games, with a 9-4 record and a 3.71 ERA with 14 saves. Matt Mantei led the staff with 22 saves, which he garnered in just 30 games, with an 0-1 record and 2.79 ERA. And newly acquired Swindell might not have won the Cy Young Award, but he appeared in 34 games with a 4-0 record, posting a 2.51 ERA and 1 save.

But Arizona players could hit the baseball as well. Luiz Gonzalez led the regulars with a .336 average, with 26 home runs and 111 RBIs. Matt Williams had a spectacular season, as his .303 average with 35 homers and a team-high 142 RBIs will attest. Shortstop Jay Bell hit .289 with a team-high and career-high 38 homers and 112 RBIs, and Steve Finley contributed a .264 campaign, with 34 round trippers and 103 RBIs.

The team ran out of gas in the National League division series, however, losing three games to one against the New York Mets.

After a fantastic sophomore season, hopes were high as we entered a new century. But the Diamondbacks fell back in 2000, finishing in third place with an 85-77 record, twelve games behind the division champion Giants and one game behind the Los Angeles Dodgers, who placed second.

They continued to smack the ball around, with Luis Gonzalez hitting at a .311 clip, with 31 home runs and 114 RBIS. Steve Finley had another fine season, hitting .280 with 35 homers and 96 RBIS. Jay Bell had a .267 campaign, with 18 round trippers and 68 RBIS while first baseman Greg Colbrunn hit .313, with 15 homers and 57 RBIS. Craig Counsell was a force off the bench hitting .316, with 2 home runs and 11 RBIS.

On the pitching mound, Randy Johnson was once again borderline untouchable. He went 19-7 with a 2.64 ERA fanning 347 hitters in 248.2 innings pitched, with 8 complete games. Brian Anderson was 11-7, with a 4.05 ERA; Armando Reynoso was 11-12 at 5.27; and Todd Stottlemyre went 9-6 and 4.91. Lefty holdover Omar Daal was 2-10 and 7.22 in 20 games.

In the bullpen, Matt Mantei led the staff, with 17 saves to go along with his 1-1 record and 4.57 ERA in 47 games. Greg Swindell led the staff with 64 appearances and went 2-6 and 3.20. And newcomer Byung-Hyun Kim was 6-6 and 4.46, with 14 saves in 61 games.

But the key day of the season was July 26, 2000, when the Diamondbacks engineered a whopper of a trade, acquiring a right-handed pitcher to complement the overpowering Randy Johnson in the rotation. Arizona acquired the disgruntled Curt Schilling from the Phillies in exchange for Omar Daal, Nelson Figueroa, Travis Lee, and Vicente Padilla.

Schilling would soon make this four-for-one-deal a steal for Arizona. He finished the 2000 season going 5-6 with a 3.69 ERA in 13 starts, 4 of which he completed. This top of the rotation tandem was poised to do some remarkable stuff in 2001, but Buck Showalter would not be around to reap the rewards. As a result of the disappointing third-place finish, he was fired, even though he had a 250-236 record in the new franchise's first three years.

New manager Bob Brenly inherited the best lefty-righty combination in the game in Johnson and Schilling. This latter-day Koufax and Drysdale pair was accountable for forty-three wins as the Diamondbacks rebounded with a 92-70 season, good enough for first place in the National League West Division. They finished two games ahead of the San Francisco Giants.

Schilling went 22-6 with a 2.98 ERA and 293 strikeouts, while Johnson was 21-6 with a 2.49 ERA and 372 strikeouts. Brian Anderson was 4-9 and 5.20, and Miguel Batista finished 11-8 in 48 games as a spot starter and reliever.

In the bullpen, Byung-Hyun Kim led the team in appearances with 78 and saves with 19, to go along with a 5-6 record and a 2.94 ERA. Greg Swindell was 2-6 in 64 games with a 4.53 ERA.

Luis Gonzalez had a monster year, hitting .325 with 57 home runs and 142 RBIs. Reggie Sanders hit .263 with 33 homers and 90 RBIs. Free-agent signee first baseman Mark Grace had a solid year, hitting .298 with 15 round trippers and 78 RBIs, while Matt Williams was his steady self, hitting .275 with 16 home runs and 65 RBIs. And Arizona continued to get timely hitting from the likes of Craig Counsell, .275 with 4 home runs and 38 RBIs; David Dellucci, .276 with 10 home runs and 40 RBIs; and Erubiel Durazo, .269 with 12 home runs and 38 RBIs.

After walking off with West Division honors, the Diamondbacks took care of St. Louis in the National League division series in five games, then beat Atlanta in five games in the National League championship series. They then faced off against the New York Yankees, America's darling since the tragedy of September 11 of that year.

What followed was one of the most exciting Fall Classics in modern history, accentuated by walk-off home runs and enough stomach-churning excitement to last a season. The Diamondbacks won the seventh and deciding game when Gonzalez had a walk-off, bloop single against the game's premier relief pitcher, Mariano Rivera, with a drawn-in infield. Just four years in their existence, the Arizona Diamondbacks were World Series champions.

Arizona won the National League West Division crown again in 2002, but they were swept by the St. Louis Cardinals in the playoffs. The team slumped in ensuing years, and Colangelo sold his interest in the team in 2005. Amid criticism that he spent too much too soon, he made the following comments to Hal Bodley in an interview with *USA Today*.

I understand where some people felt I wasn't doing it appropriately. The only analogy I can use is that Tampa Bay [the other '98 expansion team] went one direction and where did they end up [six last-place finishes and low attendance]? . . . We went another direction to establish a fan base because our investment was much larger than Tampa Bay's. And we put so much money into our own stadium [$130 million]. After the first year and the decrease in season tickets, I was convinced we had to build a fan base. . . . We bought three division titles, a World Series and established a fan base.

I believe what we did will last a long, long time. . . . Right or wrong, a number of teams today are in the $50 million payroll range and competitive—Oakland, Minnesota, Texas are examples. Our goal was to get returns from our farm system. We built into our cash-flow that we would be paying out the deferments and that our payroll could drop to $50 million for a few years. . . . A few things hurt us. . . . The economy was bad, and I was hoping for more national money [from baseball's central fund] coming in.

The Diamondbacks have had just one player who has been elected to the Hall of Fame, Roberto Alomar. But the likes of Randy Johnson, Curt Schilling and Luis Gonzalez are sure to get plenty of attention from Cooperstown voters.

Some key members of the team include Johnson, Schilling, Gonzalez, Matt Williams, Steve Finley, Tony Womack, and Jose Valverde.

Tampa Bay Devil Rays

The St. Petersburg area had its fair share of flirtation with Major League Baseball. In addition to hosting spring training baseball in the Grapefruit League, the area had been in serious discussions over the years with numerous existing franchises about the possibility of relocating to this desirable area. During the 1980s and 1990s, talks were held with the Minnesota Twins, San Francisco Giants, Chicago White Sox, Texas Rangers, and Seattle Mariners, all of whom chose to remain in their current locations.

The flirtation with San Francisco turned serious in 1992, when Giants owner Bob Lurie agreed to sell his team to a group of investors based in the Tampa Bay area who would have moved the team to St. Petersburg. But Major League Baseball refused to ratify the idea under pressure from officials in San Francisco.

It should be noted that even though "Tampa Bay" is the official name for not only the Devil Rays (now the Rays), as well as the Tampa Bay Lightning of the National Hockey League and the Tampa Bay Storm of the Arena Football League, there is no such city as Tampa Bay. Rather, that name represents a geographic area consisting of cities that surround the body of water known as Tampa Bay, including St. Petersburg, Tampa, Clearwater, and Bradenton.

Vince Naimoli, whose investment group was basically left at the altar in its efforts to bring the San Francisco Giants to Tampa Bay, was awarded a new franchise on March 9, 1995, by Major League Baseball. Along with Arizona, they would begin play in 1998.

Under manager Larry Rothschild, the Devil Rays finished their inaugural season in last place in the American League East Division, with a 63-99 record, fifty-one games behind the division champion New York Yankees and sixteen games behind fourth-place Baltimore. The team actually got off to a promising start with an 11-8 record after nineteen games. But the typical first-year curse of a lack of depth and a talent level that just didn't match up with other teams soon took over.

That's not to say that Tampa Bay didn't have its share of talented players. Quinton McCracken led the regulars with a .292 average, adding 7 home runs and 59 RBIs. At first base, "Crime Dog" Fred McGriff had a solid season with a .284 average, leading the team in home runs with 19 and RBIs with 81. Bobby Smith hit .276 at third base, with 11 homers and 55 RBIs. Randy Winn led the team in steals with 26 to go along with his .278 average, and veteran hit machine Wade Boggs hit .280, with 7 round trippers and 52 RBIs.

On the mound, Rolando Arrojo led the staff with a 14-12 record and a 3.56 ERA. He was joined in the rotation by Tony Saunders, who went 6-15 and 4.12; Wilson Alvarez, who was 6-14 and 4.73; Julio Santana, who went 5-6 and 4.23; and Dennis Springer, who had a 3-11 mark and a 5.45 ERA.

In the bullpen, Roberto Hernandez led the way, getting into 67 games with a 2-6 record, a 4.04 ERA, and a team-high 26 saves. Jim Mecir led the staff with 68 appearances and sported a 7-2 and 3.11 record. Esteban Yan was in 64 games with a 5-4 and 3.86 record, while Albie Lopez was 7-4 and 2.60 in 54 games.

In the team's second year, Tampa Bay showed a six-game improvement, with a 69-93 record. They still finished in last place in the American League East Division, twenty-nine games behind the champion New York Yankees and nine games behind fourth-place Baltimore.

During the off-season, Tampa Bay made some noise by signing free agents Julio Franco and Jose Canseco. While Franco did not work out for the team, the always controversial Canseco paid immediate dividends for the Devil Rays by hitting .279 while smacking a team-high 34 home runs with 95 RBIs. Fred McGriff hit .310, best of the regulars, with 32 homers and a team-high 104 RBIs. Wade Boggs hit .301, while Kevin Stocker improved to .299. And Bubba Trammell hit .290 with 14 homers and 39 RBIs.

On the pitcher's mound, Wilson Alvarez led the team with a 9-9 record with a 4.22 ERA. He was joined in the starting rotation by Ryan Rupe, who went 8-9 and 4.55, Rolando Arrojo, who was 7-12 and 5.18, and veteran right-hander Bobby Witt, who had a 7.15, 5.84 mark.

Roberto Hernandez led the staff with 72 appearances and 43 saves to go along with his 2-3 record, with a 3.07ERA. Norm Charlton, one of the infamous Nasty Boys of Cincinnati Reds lore, got into 42 games with a 2-3, 4.44 record; and Rick White appeared in 63 games with a 5-3, 4.08 record.

That team also featured a human-interest story that was eventually made into a movie, *The Rookie*, starring Dennis Quaid. The film was based on the true story of pitcher Jim Morris, who completed a long journey to make it to the Major Leagues and pitch for the Devil Rays. A high school teacher and baseball coach at the age of thirty-five, Morris had seemingly seen his big league dream die years before due to arm miseries. But after his Reagan County Owls baseball team won their district championship, Morris kept a promise he made to his players and went to a try out for the team. Much to the surprise of everyone, including himself, the lefty threw consistently at 98 MPH at the tryout and was offered a Minor League contract.

He pitched well at Double-A Orlando and then was also effective at Triple-A Durham before having his contract purchased by the big club. Morris made his Major League debut on September 18, 1999, pitching for the Devil Rays in his home state of Texas and striking out the Rangers' Royce Clayton. In 5 games for Tampa Bay that season, Morris went 0-0 with a 5.79 ERA. He appeared in 16 games in 2000 before arm injuries reoccurred, ending his career after 21 games in the Show.

It was a long struggle for the Tampa Bay franchise to reach a level of success. The team finished in last place for the first six years of its existence and nine of its first ten. But that eleventh season was pure magic.

The Devil Rays changed their name to the Tampa Bay Rays for the 2007 season. And a steady influx of talented young players took shape in 2008. The team enjoyed its first winning season, with a 97-65 mark, capturing the American League East Division title, two games better than the Boston Red Sox.

Catcher Dioner Navarro led the regulars with a .295 average, adding 7 home runs and 54 RBIs. Carlos Pena led the team in both home runs with 31 and RBIs with 102, along with a .247 average. Young star Evan Longoria hit a solid .272, with 27 homers and 85 RBIs. Speedy B. J. Upton led the team with 44 stolen bases, hitting .273, with 9 round trippers and 67 RBIs. Carl Crawford also hit .273, with 8 home runs and 57 RBIs.

The pitching staff was anchored by a pair of fourteen-game winners, James Shields (14-8, 3.56 ERA) and Edwin Jackson (14-11, 4.42 ERA). They were joined in the rotation by Andy Sonnanstine, who went 13-9 and 4.38, Scott Kazmir, who was 12-8 at 3.49, and Matt Garza, who had an 11-9, 3.70 season.

In the bullpen, Troy Percival led the staff with 28 saves and a 2-1 record, with a 4.53 ERA in 50 games. Dan Wheeler appeared in a team-high 70 games, sporting a 5-6 and 3.12 record with 13 saves. And southpaw Trevor Miller was 2-0 and 4.15 in 68 games.

In the playoffs, the Rays defeated the White Sox in four games in the American League division series and then upset Boston in seven games to capture the American League pennant. But the magic ended in the Fall Classic, as Tampa Bay fell to the Philadelphia Phillies in five games.

The Rays franchise has fared better in recent years, winning the division once again in 2010. The only member of the Baseball Hall of Fame to play for the Rays has been Wade Boggs. But the franchise has had numerous impact players on its roster throughout the years. They include the likes of Longoria, Upton, Pena, Crawford, McGriff, Aaron Ledesma, Aubrey Huff, Rafael Soriano, David Price, Ben Zobrist, and Randy Winn.

For now, expansion in baseball seems to have reached its peak. There have been flirtations with Puerto Rico and Buffalo and Sacramento, but any further expansion seems a long way off.

But considering how slowly baseball normally moves, a review of all that has happened in the last generation is truly amazing. Clearly, there was a lot more involved in expansion than meets the eye.

10 Expanding on Expansion

What a difference a generation or two can make. Back in 1954 there was no Internet, no social networking, no cell phones, no text messaging, no GPS technology, no microwave ovens. Back at that time in our history, the first kidney transplant was performed; Boeing unveiled the 707 aircraft; the first nuclear-powered submarine, the Nautilus, was launched; the United States Supreme Court ruled that segregation was unconstitutional; the Army-McCarthy Hearings were held; the Geneva Accords ended the Vietnam War (albeit temporarily); and five Puerto Rican nationalists fired gunshots from the gallery of the House of Representatives, wounding five congressmen.

In Major League Baseball, the New York Giants swept the Cleveland Indians to win the World Series. Yogi Berra of the New York Yankees and Willie Mays of the New York Giants won Most Valuable Player honors for their leagues, and Yanks pitcher Bob Grim and St. Louis Cardinals outfielder Wally Moon won Rookie of the Year Awards. While there was no such thing as a Cy Young Award in those days, as that award would not be presented until 1956, Bob Lemon of Cleveland and Johnny Antonelli of the New York Giants were named the *Sporting News* Pitchers of the Year.

The landscape of the game had begun to change. While there were still eight teams in both the National and American Leagues, some shifts had occurred. Since 1903, all sixteen teams had been sited in ten cities located primarily in the mid-Atlantic section of the United States. New York had three teams, while Boston, Chicago, Philadelphia, and St. Louis each had two. St. Louis was the city furthest west and furthest south in baseball, and a trip from that city to Boston by train could take nearly twenty-four hours.

But there were issues concerning fan support for the cities with two teams, and as a result, the Boston Braves became the Milwaukee Braves in 1953. The following season, the St. Louis Browns moved east and became the Baltimore Orioles. And following yet another last-place finish in the American League in 1954, the Philadelphia Athletics moved to Kansas City.

But even with these moves, as the 1950s began to ebb, Major League Baseball still consisted of sixteen teams in thirteen cities, with Kansas City being the farthest point west.

As these changes were occurring in the world and America's Game saw some franchise adjustments, few people ever thought that any drastic changes would occur in New York City, home to the Yankees in the American League and the Dodgers and Giants in the National League. After all, it was New York. But a combination of factors began to click into place like tumblers in a lock that opened up a Pandora's box that ushered in a whole new face of the game.

Crosstown rivals, the Dodgers and Giants acted in concert to relocate to the West Coast for the 1958 season, leaving New York with just one team. The move hurt and angered fans and power brokers in New York, which then led to efforts by Mayor Robert Wagner's hired gun, William Shea, to convince another team to relocate there.

Thanks to inroads made by an offshoot of that effort, the proposed Continental League and the never-ending, ever-present threat of antitrust lawsuits against Major League Baseball, expansion was the only answer. But even that process was flawed from its original concept.

While Branch Rickey suggested that filling a number of teams to play in their own division, à la the American Football League, might be the best way to tackle the idea of expansion, teams were allowed into Major League Baseball at different times for different reasons. All of the Continental League cities were to be accepted into the Major Leagues. They included New York, Houston, Toronto, Denver, Minneapolis–St. Paul, Dallas, Miami, Atlanta, and Buffalo. While all of those cities except Buffalo eventually gained access to the MLB Country Club, the process took much longer than it was originally envisioned. Those never-ending legal considerations and concerns caused by franchise shifts saw to that.

Just a quick review of the origins of many of today's teams shows just how the geography of the game has changes. Atlanta had its roots in Boston and later Milwaukee. San Francisco began in Troy and later New York City. The Dodgers originated in Brooklyn. Philadelphia began in Worcester. The latest Washington franchise began in Montreal. And Milwaukee was reborn upon the death of the Seattle Pilots. While certain teams like the Reds, Cubs, Pirates, and Cardinals have never moved, some of these changes in locale put MLB clearly behind the eight ball, tying its hands relative to more than one expansion.

Be that as it may, baseball was expanding into new areas. When the Colt .45s were born in Houston, they represented the first franchise in the South since the Louisville Colonels folded in 1899. (In cultural terms, Louisville is not completely southern, and the city was a Union stronghold in the Civil War; in fact, historically St. Louis has strong ties to the South and was fairly divided during the war.) When the Braves moved to Atlanta, MLB entered the Deep South.

When a team moves to a different city, they take front office personnel, players, and bats and balls with them. But when a new franchise enters the fray, it must be stocked with players. And it was the expansion draft that was the primary vehicle for supplying these new franchises with on-field talent. All those involved will admit that it is an imperfect process.

Existing teams are able to protect some players from the new teams, leaving some of their less-effective players ripe for the picking. Every team, existing or expansion, had a plan or strategy. Some have worked better than others.

"In 1961 the American League expanded into Los Angeles and Washington," said Peter Golenbock.

Each existing team was allowed to protect the forty players on its Major League roster. Anyone else could be drafted. As a result, a handful of outstanding youngsters were made available to the new teams, including pitcher Dean Chance, infielder Jim Fregosi, and catcher Bob Rodgers.

Having seen what their American League counterparts lost, the National League owners decided to make sure that didn't happen to them. Instead of making their best prospects available, the National League owners gave themselves the flexibility to reshuffle their forty-man rosters before the Mets and Houston Colt .45s made their picks. Instead of allowing their best prospects to be plucked, they replaced them with players in their system either too old or not talented enough.

But no matter how it works out, whether discussing an existing franchise trying to lose the least or a new team looking for that diamond in the rough, an expansion draft takes considerable preparation.

"We just had a lot of people out there looking at the talent," said Tal Smith, president of baseball operations for the Houston Astros, who was involved with that initial player draft for the Colt .45s.

Paul Richards had a lot of contacts in the game and was able to draw on that as well as his own knowledge. We had some great baseball people, like Bobby Bragan, Grady Hatton, and Paul Florence, who were all key evaluators. Bobby Mattick was with us too.

So we had the evaluations from our people and we had a rating system, and Richards went from there. Our philosophy was to get the best available talent as well as getting talent we thought was marketable. For instance, our first pick was Eddie Bresseud, who was quickly traded along with Bobby Shantz and Sam Jones. Some of the guys we chose were guys you were going to build the franchise around, but others you picked to get them to somebody else who had players you could acquire to help build your franchise.

We wound up with the likes of Bob Aspromonte, Bob Lillis, Roman Mejias, Ken Johnson, Hal Smith, Al Spangler, Turk Farrell, and Jim Umbricht, who did a great job for us before passing away with cancer. We got some good service out of all these guys.

The strategy was to take the most valuable player on the board. It becomes a chess game, and we rehearsed and had mock drafts. We had good evaluations and good information and made the best of what we could. The Mets pick[ed] a lot of guys who were at the tail end of their careers.

An additional consideration is that especially in today's game, the way a team is built has less to do with pure talent and more to do with the bottom line. A new team can draft for the future, concentrating on inexperienced players rather than selecting more experience or higher-paid talent, and hope that some of the young players they choose will grow with the team and still be part of it when they become good. Or, if ownership is willing to pay the price, moves can be made to draft more-expensive players who are already at their peak and acquire additional players who will have a more immediate impact. It's left to front office personnel to carry out the wishes of ownership in this regard. With arbitration and free agency as a part of the mix now, even an expansion team can quickly become a contending team unlike in the early days of expansion.

Pat Gillick has experienced the perspective of building both an existing team and a new team. His experience lends a realistic view of the challenges involved in the process. You don't just scout and evaluate players. A good organization also does its due diligence on the new teams as well, attempting to lure them into taking players that you are willing to lose.

"As an existing club, you know the players that are your core," Gillick said.

Those ten or twelve are no brainers. You just protect those guys. It gets dicey between the thirteenth and twentieth players. An expansion club might get a good player from that group. So you try to size up which way the expansion club is headed. Arizona was a team looking for more experience, whereas a Tampa Bay was looking toward the future. When you have two clubs coming into the league with different ideas of what they want to accomplish, it's a little bit difficult.

What we'd try to do was stick out a player who we felt was overpaid that a team looking to win sooner would take. You wouldn't be upset because you thought the guy was overpaid. So from the thirteenth pick on, we'd keep what we felt were overpriced players available.

Of course, if you are an expansion team, you are trying to get the best talent. But that is dictated by ownership as to which way you go, either try to win right away or build toward the future. In Toronto, we were owned by a brewery, a public company. They took a long-term approach to it and had paid a lot for the franchise and did not wish to show a loss on their books that would affect the bottom line on the brewery. So they were very conservative and took a long-term approach, deciding not to blow our money right away. So the ownership said to build the slow way and get there at the end.

Other guys like Wayne Huizinga and Jerry Colangelo wanted to spend money right now and have instant success. And Arizona and Miami both won a World Series.

An interesting realization is that while the last few expansions have seen new teams have literally years to prepare, in the early days an organization had to get its ducks in a row in a matter of days. When the the Los Angeles Angels franchise was awarded to Gene Autry, he had only eight days to prepare for the draft.

In that first expansion a truly new team, the Los Angeles Angels, come into existence. But because of political pressure, Washington DC was granted an expansion team at the same time, the new version of the Senators to replace the old version of the Senators, who were allowed to move to Minnesota following the 1960 season. The old Senators had moved after a long history of failure both on the field and at the turnstiles, which was to be a classic example of history repeating itself. Baseball fans react to and support a good product, something that has long been missing in the nation's capital.

"One thing about Washington that has hasn't happened is that I don't know if they've ever been given a very good product," said Pat Gillick. "I'm not sure the caliber of product has ever been very good, interesting, or competitive. People keep telling me that Washington is a gold mine that hasn't been treated well. I keep hearing a lot about potential, but I'd like to see them give fans a good product."

While that struggle continues to this day with the Nationals, other true expansion cities have thrived. In 1962 New York got a new National League team in the Mets, and one of the Continental League cities, Houston, got the Colt .45s, later to be known as the Astros.

Successful or not, a multitude of good baseball people get involved in the expansion process. And just as Smith and his personnel helped make the original Colt .45s a reality on draft day, just seven years later the shoe was on the other foot, forcing them to try to keep their best players when the National League expanded again.

"I was very involved with that process as well," he said.

Paul Richards had left, and I was director of player personnel. We had ten or twelve people evaluate everyone in our system, and we developed a ranking of our players. You hate to lose a Nate Colbert, but we felt that we had better talent available at that position. I thought that Ivan Murrell was a five-tool player, and he got some big league time but fell short of our expectations. Colbert had some good years with San Diego.

We had another alternative when we signed John Mayberry [in the team's second season]. Then you make a decision as to what is going to hurt you the least and you go with that. It gets right down to assessments and evaluations. I'd have our staff rate pitchers, one through twelve, or one through twenty. Then the ratings are averaged out. We didn't have spreadsheets in those days, we did it manually.

The aforementioned Seattle Pilots had one inglorious season in the American League in 1969, and they were joined by the Kansas City Royals, who came into existence largely because that fine city lost the Athletics to Oakland in 1968. They were accompanied by two new National League teams that year, the Montreal Expos and the San Diego Padres. The Seattle franchise moved to Milwaukee in 1970 to become the Brewers, which of course resulted in legal issues.

In 1972 the new lackluster expansion team in Washington, the new Senators, quit on that city and moved to Arlington, Texas, to become the Rangers.

The great Canadian experiment went well in Montreal, at first opening the door for another North-of-the-Border team in the next expansion, the Toronto Blue Jays, who joined the Junior Circuit along with the Seattle Mariners in 1977. Pressure from Seattle, as the former home of the Pilots, and a new stadium made that addition a necessity.

Both leagues stayed intact until 1993, when the Florida Marlins and the Colorado Rockies joined the National League. The final expansion to date occurred in 1998, when each league added a new team, the Arizona Diamondbacks to the National League and the Tampa Bay Devil Rays to the American League. That was also the year that the Milwaukee franchise once again became a National League team so that both leagues would have even numbers.

The baseball landscape has changed quite dramatically since the mid-1950s. It has truly become a national game that has even spread its wings into Canada. No one can deny that it's been quite a ride since that first expansion of 1961.

"Expansion certainly expanded horizons geographically," said Tal Smith. "Obviously the Dodgers and Giants move in 1958 started that. Expansion then brought baseball to the Southwest, to the upper Midwest, and to Canada. So we really expanded geographically from what had been an east of the Mississippi game to a game that covered the United States plus Canada. Going from sixteen to thirty clubs made it twice as big as far as the number of players and so on."

To this day, Walter O'Malley is vilified in New York and revered in Los Angeles and San Francisco for his decision to move the Dodgers to Los Angeles in 1958 and for his influence on Horace Stoneham, who brought the New York Giants out west with him. The addition of the Giants to that move was of paramount importance because of travel concerns. At that time in Major League Baseball, the closest team to Los Angeles would have been the St. Louis Cardinals, who were 1,600 miles away. The move by both the Dodgers and the Giants made West Coast trips much more economically feasible for other teams. But those hard feelings remain about that move all these years later, and many people still contend that the move of the Dodgers could have been and should have been avoided.

"Eventually, a solution would have arisen in Brooklyn," said Bob McGee in *The Greatest Ballpark Ever*.

If you look at the Brooklyn Sports Center Authority's effort to build a new stadium for the Dodgers, the issue really became the availability to carry the bonds. If you follow the money it becomes clear that O'Malley wanted the land to be given to him and said that he'd build the stadium with his own money. He wanted the piece of land to be given to him which is basically what happened in Los Angeles when he traded tiny Wrigley Field for Chavez Ravine and the land that was being taken by eminent domain. It was a monumental give away at the largess of the taxpayers to one man and one family that was unprecedented in the history of sport. To the day it represents the most egregious kind of corporate greed.

And he did not give up the lease he held on Ebbets Field until after such time that the ballot measure passed. There was a Los Angeles Dodgers office that existed in Brooklyn until 1960. The keys were handed over to the developer who put the bids on the site in early 1960. The fellow who manned the office for the Dodgers had to drive in from Long Island for the publicity shot on a cold winter morning.

While the loss of the two New York teams certainly represented a cold and bitter winter morning, it was the technological advances that were occurring around the world that made expansion to the West and Midwest a reality.

"Expansion was inevitable," said former Dodger pitcher Carl Erskine. "The jet plane caused it. Without that we'd still be traveling on a train with St. Louis being the western-most baseball city. When the jet plane became a reality, expansion was now a reality. Thanks to that, Denver, Kansas City, and all points west were saying, 'Hey, we should get a team.' That was the centerpiece of expansion."

The advent of jet travel was a welcome change for players, who often had white-knuckle junkets on older, propeller-driven planes. Not all of the transitions were smooth ones.

"The method of travel for baseball teams changed from trains and busses to airplanes," said former Colt .45s pitcher Bob Bruce.

It was still pretty tough. In the Minor Leagues, you'd fly in DC-3s, and the cars below on the highway were going faster than we were. We flew through everything. It was a good plane, but wow. We'd land on that flat-top mountain in Charleston, West Virginia, at five in the morning through heavy fog. You flew Purdue Airlines, and they were training pilots. It always seemed like we had some young kid out there landing the plane we were flying in.

They have expanded again and again. I just think it gave a lot of good ballplayers an opportunity to play and compete. It gave guys that were outfielders behind guys like Willie Mays and Willie McCovey a chance to play. A friend of mine, Mel Corbo, got stuck behind guys at first base with the Dodgers, and he hit nothing but line drives all the time in Double-A and Triple-A. Norm Larker got a chance to play every day. If you got stuck behind a Jim Bunning or a Harvey Kuenn you'd never get a chance.

Not only has expansion been good for the players, but it has also meant Major League Baseball for fans all across the country. If you moved from a city that had a team to a place without one, you might have seen your last game. Thanks to expansion, live professional baseball has been a reality for countless fans.

"It's been good for a lot of people," said Peter Golenbock.

Take the Rays for instance. I never thought I'd ever see Major League Baseball again living in St. Petersburg. Tropicana Field is ten minutes from our house. You now have the Marlins, the Rangers, the Rockies, and the Diamondbacks. These were areas with no Major League Baseball for a long time. Since the St. Louis Cardinals were the farthest west team, people in Oklahoma, Arizona, and New Mexico had to root for the Cards and would drive four or five hundred miles to see a game. Now they don't have to do that. A lot more people have an opportunity to see Major League Baseball today as a result of expansion.

Baseball has long been a game of sheep following the innovative shepherds who come up with new concepts or ideas. Just look how quickly every Major League team imitated Tony La Russa's use of Dennis Eckersley as a one-inning closer. Consider the specialization in every bullpen now with closers, set-up men, long men, and the left-handed specialist. It seems hard to believe that not so long ago the likes of Goose Gossage and many others pitched as many as two or three innings to close out a game. But if one team has success thanks to a new innovation, others will quickly follow suit.

The Giants have had success in San Francisco, for the most part, and the Dodgers have been a stunning success story in Los Angeles on and off the field. That is until recently, when the fiasco concerning the divorce settlement between owner Frank McCourt and his ex-wife Jamie McCourt left the once-proud franchise at a point where they were struggling to make payroll. One wonders how Brooklyn fans feel about that. Could this entire situation be a latter-day payback for the team's move out of Brooklyn so many years before?

"The McCourts and a cosmic payback?" asked Bob McGee.

There is no schadenfreude for me in this misfortune. He bore no ill will to the borough of my birth. I would rather see [Jamie McCourt's attorney] David Boies take on baseball's antitrust exemption and overturn it, turning the notion of territorial rights for franchises into history's dustbin, placing the first stone paving the way for the time when Major League Baseball might again be played in the borough where Charles Ebbets is buried, with no franchise trumpeting territorial rights standing in the way.

The Angels are now calling themselves the Los Angeles Angels of Anaheim; just up the road there are the Brooklyn Dodgers of Los Angeles. And in 2011, the Dodgers even occasionally started wearing uniforms with "Brooklyn" across their chests.

It's a sacrilege, of course, that Peter O'Malley waited for writers like Dick Young, Red Smith, and Jack Mann to die before hiring a PR firm to attempt to sanitize Walter F. O'Malley's image among generations that did not know him in order to make it somehow palatable to get him into the Hall of Fame. It's a sacrilege that he made five-figure contributions to the Hall of Fame for years and years to grease the skids to facilitate that blot. How is it that you could have Branch Rickey, who called what O'Malley did "a crime against three million people" in the same supposedly sacrosanct room as Walter F. O'Malley? No rationale could justify the two extremes.

Why, the Yankees under Dan Topping and Del Webb won ten world's championships and several more pennants to boot. Are they in the Hall? No. Why? Because no one remains to pay for them.

Major League Baseball's drive to expand no doubt was influenced by the success of the National Football League and the upstart American Football League, which had teams spread across the country. There might have been concerns over the fact that many pro football teams piggybacked on the success of college programs. It was a risky move, but baseball was truly America's Pastime and that certainly aided the decision to expand. And the country's love of the game proved to be a positive force that made this great experiment a success.

"When baseball expanded, I think the country was ready for that," said Professor John P. Rossi.

I think that playing football nationally and the success they had showed that you could play all around the country and that you could have fans in cities all across the country. When expansion came in the early 1960s, it seemed logical. The cities made a lot of sense, especially in the National League with New York. The idea of Houston also made sense. The American League I think made a mess of things and had to placate the Senators in Washington. They put a team in Los Angeles against the Dodgers, who had already established themselves. The American League muffed again putting a team in Seattle and then had to move it after one season. The National League putting teams in Montreal and San Diego made more sense.

If you figure when baseball was established, the population of the country was 75 million for sixteen teams. Now we have thirty teams with 300 million people. It sustains the number of fans. In 1900 and 1901 the sport had no rivals. But now you have thirty teams, but you also have football and basketball as major competition and hockey as a minor competition. To some extent, thirty teams is probably too high a number. The realistic number would be twenty-four or twenty-five teams. But from an economic point of view, how can you expect to take out four teams, and what teams? The union will never give that up. The talent has been diluted, but that could be from dilution of other sports. Baseball was the only real sport for fifty years. Jim Thorpe was a great football player, but he played baseball because you could make a living at it.

Rossi also discussed the advent of radio and television broadcasting of games. For years many club owners would not allow games to be broadcast on TV for fear that it would keep fans out of the stands and listening and watching at home. Once again, one of the leading proponents of baseball broadcasting was the always innovative Branch Rickey.

"One of the great benefits is that when baseball started facing serious problems after the war, one of the big transitions was from radio to TV," Rossi said.

Branch Rickey said baseball on the radio whets the appetites of fans. But on TV it satiates their appetites. Pro baseball dealt with the problem of broadcasting. They solved the radio issue in the 1930s. Three New York teams agreed not to allow the radio broadcasts of their home games. But then in 1939, Larry McPhail stopped that and brought Red Barber from Cincinnati to broadcast the Dodgers' games. Baseball discovered that radio does draw fans.

They felt that TV was killing them and that people would not go to the games if they were televised, which was nonsense. TV attracts fans as much or more than radio. I attribute this to Lew Fonseca, who somehow got the ear of the American League president, Will Harridge. He became the expert of broadcasting baseball and film.

Baseball took time welcoming new ideas, whereas football commissioner Bert Bell knew he was competing with baseball and was much more open-minded, as was Pete Rozelle, where football really adopted TV.

Through all the trials and tribulations, baseball grew exponentially sometimes in spite of itself. There are those who insist that the caliber of play has suffered. But that might not necessarily be the case.

While there certainly are more teams than there were a generation ago, creating jobs for about six hundred additional players at the Major

League level at any particular time, the very presence of new teams in different regions may have increased the talent pool by capturing the interest of young players who might not have gotten involved in baseball were it not for expansion. But that is a debate that could go on into infinity.

"Well I think expansion has given more opportunities to players," said Pat Gillick. "It could be that the level of play and the caliber of player is not where it was when you had sixteen teams in the league, or like when you had six teams in hockey. But it's allowed fans and people from coast-to-coast the chance to see better-caliber entertainment. And a better level of play. At one time you never had any teams west of St. Louis, or Chicago, until O'Malley and Stoneham went to California. Now we have eight or nine teams out there now. I think it's been positive for the game."

Looking at the talent level in the game and trying to differentiate pre- and post-expansion eras is exceedingly difficult. There are a lot more players in the game now, but it could be argued that the talent pool is bigger because of expansion. The advent of the amateur draft has also given teams a fairer way of accessing young talent.

Pitcher Larry Colton was just beginning his professional career when expansion became a topic throughout baseball. He has mixed views of the concept.

"I always thought that it was diluting the talent, but as a player it gave another option," he said.

There was no draft yet; you could sign with any team. There were only sixteen teams then, half of what you have now.

I was talking with Bob Skinner, who had been my manager at San Diego when I played there in the Pacific Coast League. He and I were talking about the difference between baseball when I played it and now. The players are bigger and faster and stronger today. The major difference is in the depth of pitching. When there were 10 guys on a pitching staff, you had 160 in the big leagues. Now you have over 300.

You've basically moved a whole new league of pitchers. You can only throw the ball so hard. It's the depth of pitching that has diluted the game and is the most noticeable.

In pitching today, you have so much specialization. Back then, when I played in the '60s, anyone in the bullpen was shit. There were no pitch counts and all that stuff. Back in 1967 I pitched four hundred innings and led the PCL in innings pitched. Then, I went to the Instructional League and pitched sixty or seventy innings and then pitched a hundred innings in winter ball. I could barely lift my arm in spring training. Pitchers are treated differently today.

The depth of quality pitching is also a concern for former San Diego pitcher Steve Arlin, who agrees with Colton's assessment. "I think that expansion has not been all that great for the game," he said. "It has so diluted the game that it has changed it in a massive way. You have at least five or six pitchers on every team that don't belong in the Major Leagues. The talent is so diluted in the Major Leagues that it's a different game. You have the game in more cities, which is great for the fans. But in some places, it's just not making it. San Diego has not drawn all that well."

Filling rosters with quality hurlers has always been a challenge, one that has been made more difficult with twice as many teams in Major League Baseball now than in the pre-expansion years. And in many ways, it could be argued that pitchers today are all the same. They all have the same type of wind-up, they pitch the same way, and nearly every reliever feels the need to enter a game and pitch from the stretch even with no one on base. Pitchers of today have become similar to the baseball parks of the 1970s—all very much alike.

"Expansion has depleted pitching in baseball," said former Angel Eli Grba.

In my day they still had quite a few Minor League teams. As a result, teams could sign a lot more players. The Dodgers always had good pitchers. It was like anyone who could throw they'd sign.

In those days you had to learn your craft more. You started out in D Ball, then you'd advance to C Ball. I jumped from C Ball to Triple-A, going from San Jose to Triple-A in San Francisco. If you're in Double-A these days and have a good year, they are rushing kids to the big leagues.

Look closely at how they wind up and deliver the ball today. Fifty percent of them are cloned and doing the same thing. They don't use a big motion. There is no effort to deceive the hitter or hide the ball. It's like here's the ball, see it and hit it. Some of them have the worst breaking stuff I've ever seen. Of course, when they lowered the mound that didn't help much either. It's like you're throwing uphill. But that being said, some guys will win no matter what.

But no matter what the complaints might be and how some aspects of the game might not measure up to some part of previous eras, baseball has made the game healthier than it has ever been. Some franchises might face challenges, and big market teams have an edge because of their financial health over small market teams. But at the end of the day, baseball is in great shape.

"I think expansion has had its plusses and minuses," said Philadelphia Phillies exec Bill Giles. "You had fewer good pitchers simply because you needed more. Now, there are more good pitchers than position players. Initially pitching was thin, and it created more run scoring. But all things considered, I think expansion has been great. Attendance has never been better than it's been. My dad [Warren Giles] was league president during the time of the first expansions. He felt it was a good idea and wanted to have baseball in all corners of the continent so that people would have greater access to the game."

Baseball has always been America's Game, the National Pastime. But thanks to the concept and reality of expansion, the National Pastime is now actually a national game. From sea to shining sea, millions of fans flock to see their favorite teams play. That concept would have been music to the ears of an innovator like Branch Rickey.

The cities are chosen, the franchises are developed, and the teams are assembled. Then it is time for the newbies of the game to compete against the old guard. It's not always pretty, but it is always interesting. One of the effects of expansion deals with statistics and records. While some of the newer expansion franchises have enjoyed more success earlier than the older new teams, the opportunity to feed on weaker teams can alter the history of a franchise. Existing teams that are bottom feeders, taking no prisoners when playing an expansion team, can find themselves moving up in the standings.

11 | Bottom Feeding

Taking Advantage of the
New Kids in Town

Expansion in baseball has had a number of effects on the game. It has made baseball a national sport by bringing it to cities and regions all across the country. The support of the game and the love of the game, warts and all, has never been higher. It has afforded an opportunity to play in the Major Leagues to thousands of players who would not have had that shot had baseball not expanded. And it has also given existing teams a chance to feast on new teams that in many cases are not able to compete on a fair level. Had baseball followed the American Football League model of adding a new league whose teams played amongst themselves, the new teams might have enjoyed much more success much quicker, as opposed to playing under the house rules of the old guard.

As a result there are teams that have dramatically increased their win totals and placement in the standings in years when expansion teams were introduced into the Major Leagues. In addition to that, individual players have also entered the record books with their performances in those same years. For instance, Roger Maris, of the New

York Yankees, broke Babe Ruth's single-season home run record when he blasted his sixty-first round tripper on the final day of the 1961 season. Regardless of the controversy over whether or not an asterisk should have been placed next to the record because he had 162 games rather than the 154 that Ruth had, Maris broke the record. And nine of his sixty-one homers came against the Washington Senators.

The following year in 1962, Maury Wills of the Los Angeles Dodgers set a new stolen base record when he swiped 104 bags during the course of the season. But the speedy shortstop had extraordinary success against the two National League expansion teams, stealing a combined 27 bases against the New York Mets and Houston Colt .45s.

There are only two times since World War II that two National League teams won at least 102 games. One occurred in 1993, when the Atlanta Braves went 104-58 and the San Francisco Giants were 103-59 in the National League West Division. The only other time it happened in the postwar era was in 1962 when the Giants went 103-62 and the Los Angeles Dodgers were 102-63. What's the connection? Both years also marked the first year of play for two new National League clubs.

In 1977, an expansion year in the American League, sweet-singing Rod Carew hit a lofty .388 for Minnesota. That marked the highest batting average in baseball since 1957, when the Splendid Splinter, Ted Williams, hit an identical .388 for the Boston Red Sox.

Considering the comments made previously about the dilution of pitching and pitching depth in the expansion era, it's not surprising that offense goes up in an expansion year. Certainly some league-wide statistics were affected by the fact that there was a new team or two playing in the league, adding to the stats. But the increase in offensive production never fails, indicating that while good pitching usually stops good hitting, there is less good pitching when baseball expands. Suffice to say that it's good to be a starting position player or DH when a new team is accepted into the league.

Another old sports axiom is that you need to beat the teams you're better than. While managers and coaches all know the perils of looking past a particular opponent, a contending team should be a club that is just playing out the string a lot more often than not. That does not always happen, however, since as we all know the games are not played on paper.

The perfect place for a good team to move up in the standings and magnify its win total is when playing against an expansion team. No matter how good they draft, or how much money they have to buy better players, a first-year team is a fabulous foil to pad your win column against.

In 1961, when the Angels and Senators became members of the American League, other teams approached them like sharks sensing blood in the water. Los Angeles finished the season 70-91, while the Senators went 61-100. That's a combined 131-191. A lot of teams had field days against the new teams.

The Detroit Tigers went 14-4 against the Angels and 13-5 against Washington, for a league best 27-9 record against the two new teams. They saw their record improve from 71-87 in 1960 to 101-61 in 1961, good enough to jump from sixth to second place.

The Baltimore Orioles were 14-4 against Washington and 10-8 over the Angels, for a total of 24-12 versus the new teams. Their record improved from 89-65 in 1960 to 95-67 the following year.

The New York Yankees won the American League pennant both seasons. But even they saw an appreciable increase in victories, which they needed to keep Detroit and Baltimore at bay. The Bronx Bombers were 12-6 against Los Angeles and 11-7 versus Washington, for a combined 23-13 record. They finished the 1960 campaign with a 97-57 record, which was handily bettered in 1961, when New York went 109-53.

Even a pedestrian fan knows that this was also the season that Babe Ruth's single-season home run record of 60 was to fall. Both Roger Maris and Mickey Mantle, the M&M boys, spent much of the summer tearing up the league. Maris ultimately broke the record on the final day of the season, hitting his 61st homer. He was followed by

Mantle with 54, Harmon Killebrew and Jim Gentile each with 46, and Rocky Colovito with 45. The previous season, the home run king was Mantle with 40, followed by Maris with 39, Jim Lemon with 38, Colovito with 35, and Killebrew with 31.

League wide, hitters raised their collective batting average from .255 in 1960 to .256 the following year. But home run production increased from 1,086 to 1,534, runs jumped from 5,414 to 7,342, and pitchers' earned run averages went from 3.87 to 4.02.

The same thing happened the following year, 1962, when the Houston Colt .45s and the New York Mets became card-carrying members of the National League. The Colt .45s were 64-96, while New York was a league-worst 40-120. National League opponents handled the two new teams at a 216-104 mark.

In 1962 the Philadelphia Phillies feasted on the new teams, going 17-1 against Houston and 14-4 against the Mets, for a total of 31-5. While they had been a less-than-mediocre 47-107 in 1961, the Phillies improved to 81-80 in 1962.

Pittsburgh took care of the Mets 16-2 and Houston 13-5, for a total of 29-7. The team improved from a 75-79 mark in 1961 to 93-68 the following year.

The Dodgers were 16-2 versus the Mets and 12-6 against Houston, for a 28-8 total. They saw their record improve from 89-65 in 1961 to 102-63 in 1962.

The San Francisco Giants ultimately won a three-game playoff series against the Dodgers to win the pennant and get to the World Series. They handled the Mets 14-4 and went 11-7 against the Colt .45s for a 25-11 record. They went from a third-place finish in 1961 with an 85-69 record to a 103-62 campaign the following year. The only negative for the Giants was falling to the Yankees in a seven-game Fall Classic.

Orlando Cepeda led the league in home runs in 1961 with 46, followed by Willie Mays with 40, Frank Robinson with 37, and Dick Stuart and Joe Adcock, each with 35. During the season after the Mets and Colt .45s came on the scene, 1963, Mays won the home run crown with 49 dingers. He was followed by Hank Aaron with 45, Robinson with 39, Ernie Banks with 37, and Cepeda with 35.

League wide, offensive production was on the rise. While batting averages were a wash, with National League hitters at .261 after having a .262 average the previous year, more power was evident as home runs increased from 1,196 to 1,449, and runs increased from 5,600 to 7,278. Pitchers' ERAS actually went down from 4.03 in 1961 to 3.94 in 1962.

Baseball expanded again following the 1968 season, with the Kansas City Royals and Seattle Pilots entering the American League while the San Diego Padres and Montreal Expos came into the National League. The game had expanded by a third since the beginning of the decade, and 1969 marked the first year of realignment with two divisions in each league and the introduction of the league championship series. Following the "Year of the Pitcher" in 1968, the strike zone was shrunk and the pitcher's mound lowered.

Kansas City went 69-93 while the Pilots were 64-98 in 1969 for a combined 133-191 against the American League. The Oakland Athletics were 13-5 against Seattle and 10-8 versus Kansas City for a 23-13 mark against the new teams. Their record went from 82-80 in 1968 to 88-74 in 1969, good enough for second place in the division.

Minnesota had similar success, with a 12-6 mark against Seattle and a 10-8 record versus the Royals for a 22-14 total. After finishing 1968 with a 79-83 record, the Twins jumped to a 97-65 campaign in 1969, good enough for the American League West title.

The Baltimore Orioles were 11-1 against Kansas City and 9-3 with the Pilots for a 20-4 mark. They went from a second-place finish in 1968 with a 91-71 record to an American League East title the following season and a 109-53 record.

Offensive production rose considerably due to the new strike zone, the lowered pitcher's mound, and two new teams to rough up. In 1968 Frank Howard led the American League in home runs with 44, followed by Willie Horton with 36, Ken Harrelson with 35, and Reggie Jackson with 29. Those figures jumped in 1969 as league leader Harmon Killebrew smacked 49 home runs, Frank Howard hit 48, Jackson 47, Carl Yastrzemski 40, and Rico Petrocelli 40.

Around baseball, offense was on the rise after a pitching-dominated trend had reached its apex in 1968. That year, American League batters hit an anemic .230 with 1,104 home runs and 5,532 runs. In 1969 hitters improved their average to .246, slugging 1,649 round-trippers and scoring 7,960 runs. Pitchers' ERAs rose from 2.98 in 1968 to 3.62 in 1969.

In the National League, the Padres and Expos each had a challenging season. Both teams posted records of 52-110, for a combined record of 104-220. Needless to say, National League hitters enjoyed the ride.

The New York Mets were 11-1 against San Diego and 13-5 against Montreal, for a 24-6 record against expansion teams. From a ninth-place finish in 1968 with a 73-89 record, the Mets rebounded in 1969 with a 100-62 mark, good enough to win the National League East title. San Francisco was 11-1 against Montreal and 12-6 versus the Padres, for a record of 23-7 against the two new teams. The Giants were 88-74 in 1968 but improved to 90-72 the following year. Neither season garnered them a playoff berth.

The Atlanta Braves went 13-5 against San Diego and 8-4 versus the Expos, for a 21-9 record. They went from a respectable 81-81 in 1968 to a spectacular 93-69 in 1969, good enough to capture National League West honors.

The Chicago Cubs had their fans expecting nothing but the best in 1969, but sadly such optimism was not to be rewarded. Chicago went 11-1 against San Diego and 10-8 versus Montreal, for a 21-9 record. They went from an 84-78 record in 1968 to a 92-70 log in 1969. The Cubs built a nine-and-a-half-game lead in the National League East Division near the end of August, but they lost ten of eleven games during a disastrous stretch that saw them overtaken by the Mets, finishing in second place.

There was an upswing in power in the National League as Willie McCovey slammed 45 home runs, followed by Aaron with 44, Lee May with 38, Tony Perez with 37, and the Toy Cannon, Jimmy Wynn, with 33. That was a significant increase over 1968, which saw McCovey lead the league with 36 homers, followed by Dick Allen with 33, Ernie Banks with 32, Billy Williams with 30, and Aaron with 29.

National League hitters as a whole had a much better season in 1969 as well. They hit .250 with 1,470 home runs and scored 7,890 runs. A year prior, they hit just .243 with 891 homers and 5,577 runs. Pitchers had a 2.43 ERA in 1968, followed by a 3.59 ERA in 1969.

It wasn't until 1977 the baseball expanded again, this time adding a second team in Canada, the Toronto Blue Jays, and giving Seattle another try with the Mariners. The Junior Circuit now had fourteen teams, while their National League counterparts remained at twelve.

And as usual, some teams just had a seemingly unfair advantage over their new expansion team neighbors, although it was not quite as pronounced as it had been in previous expansions. The Boston Red Sox were 10-1 against Seattle and 13-2 versus Toronto, for a 23-3 record. While they remained in third place in the American League East, as they had been in 1976 with an 83-79 record, the 1977 version of the Bosox went 97-64.

A former expansion team in their own right, the Kansas City Royals went 11-4 against Seattle and 8-2 versus Toronto, for a 19-6 record. American League West title winners in 1976 with a 90-72 record, the 1977 squad also won the division crown with a 102-60 record. Sadly for the Royals, they squandered a late-game lead in the American League championship series against the New York Yankees, who prevailed and eventually defeated the Dodgers in the Fall Classic.

The Chicago White Sox were 10-5 against Seattle and had an 8-3 advantage over Toronto for an 18-8 record. They went 64-97 in 1976 but improved to a 90-72 record in 1977.

Baltimore also played well against the two new teams, sporting a 10-5 record against Toronto and a 7-3 mark versus Seattle en route to a 17-8 record. While they remained in second place, the 1977 Orioles were 97-64, an impressive improvement over the 1976 team that had finished 88-74.

There was a power spike in 1977, with Jim Rice leading the league with 39 dingers, followed by Graig Nettles and Bobby Bonds, each with 37, George Scott with 33, and Reggie Jackson with 32. That was a big increase over the previous season, in which Nettles led the league with 32, followed by Jackson and Sal Bando, each with 27.

League wide, hitters went from a .256 average in 1976 to .266 in 1977. Home runs increased from 1,122 to 2,013, and runs soared from 7,753 to 10,247. Earned run averages went from 3.52 to 4.06.

By the time baseball expanded again in 1993, offense had become such a force that many of baseball conspiracy theorists were charging that Major League Baseball was using a juiced ball. Certainly the two new National League teams, the Colorado Rockies and the Florida Marlins, brought some offense to the league, as well as the continuation of the first-year improvements by expansion teams. That is evidenced by the fact that for the first time in an expansion year, neither of the new teams finished in last place. Colorado finished in sixth place with a 67-95 in the National League West, six games ahead of the San Diego Padres. In the East, Florida went 64-98, five games ahead of the New York Mets.

While both teams were pretty good as far as expansion teams are concerned, existing clubs still had their way with them. At the top of that list was Atlanta, which went 13-0 against Colorado and 7-5 versus the Marlins, for a 20-5 record against the new teams. The Braves won the National League East Division crown with a 104-58 record, which was an improvement over their first-place finish the year before, in which they went 98-64.

One of the biggest benefactors of expansion that year were the Philadelphia Phillies. Cellar dwellers in 1992 with a 70-92 record, the Phillies went from worst to first, winning the National League East honors with a 97-65 record. They were 9-3 against Colorado and 9-4 against the Marlins for a mark of 18-7. While there were other good things happening for the team that year, the success against these two teams certainly helped.

Another team that did well against the expansion teams was the Giants. They went 10-3 against Colorado and 8-4 versus Florida for an 18-7 record. In the standings, San Francisco jumped from a 72-90, fifth-place finish in 1992 to a 103-59 second-place finish in 1993.

The Montreal Expos also played well and maintained their second-place status in the standings. They went 9-3 against Colorado and 8-5 versus the Marlins for a 17-8 record. They had been 87-75 in 1992 and improved to 94-68 in 1993.

Fred McGriff led the league in home runs in 1992 with 35. He was followed by Barry Bonds with 34, Gary Sheffield with 23, and Dave Hollins and Darren Daulton, both tied with 27. But a year later, Bonds led the league with 46 round trippers, followed by David Justice with 40, Matt Williams with 38, McGriff with 37, and Ron Gant with 36.

Offensive stats league wide improved dramatically in 1993. Batting averages rose from .252 the previous year to .264. Home runs increased from 1,262 to 1,956, and runs went from 7,539 to 10,190. Pitchers' ERAs rose from 3.50 in 1992 to 4.40 in 1993. Sadly over the years to come, juicing charges went from the baseball to the baseball players.

Five years after the National League added teams thirteen and fourteen, both leagues added an additional team. The National League welcomed the Arizona Diamondbacks and the American League the Tampa Bay Devil Rays. The Milwaukee Brewers also switched to the National League.

With the advent of interleague play and the ability to build strong teams faster, the days of numerous existing teams taking great advantage of the expansion teams lessened. Arizona finished the year with a 65-97 record, while Tampa Bay was 63-99.

Of course this is not to say that some teams didn't beat up on the new guys. The New York Yankees were 11-1 against Tampa Bay. That helped them improve their second-place 96-66 season from 1997 into a first-place 114-48 record in 1998.

Boston went 9-3 against the Devil Rays and also saw their record improve from 78-84 in 1997 to 92-70 the following season.

And Kansas City went 8-3 against Tampa Bay, improving to a 72-89 record from a 67-94 the year prior.

In the National League, San Diego had a 9-3 record against Arizona. The Padres improved from a fourth-place finish in 1997 and a record of 76-86 to a first-place record of 98-64 the following year.

The Atlanta Braves fared well against Arizona, going 8-1. They lost all three interleague games to Tampa but were still 8-4 against the new teams. They went from a 101-61 season in 1997 to a 106-56 mark the following year.

National League offense improved. While batting average went down from .263 in 1997 to .262 in 1998, all the other numbers were up. Home runs increased from 2,163 to 2,565. Runs went up from 10,440 to 11,932. And earned run average increased from 4.20 to 4.23.

This was also the year that the Mark and Sammy Power Tour captivated the country. Mark McGwire and Sammy Sosa had a season-long effort to break the single-season home run mark of 61 set by Roger Maris in baseball's first expansion year. By the end of the season, McGwire had smashed 70 homers, followed by Sosa with 66, Mo Vaughn with 50, Vinny Castilla with 46, and Andres Galarraga with 44. These power numbers were a huge jump from 1997, when Larry Walker led the league with a mere 49 home runs, followed by Jeff Bagwell with 43 and Galarraga with 41.

While news of baseball's steroid and performance-enhancing drug scandals had not yet been taken seriously, McGwire openly displayed bottles of a legal, over-the-counter supplement, Androstenedione. It was the tip of the iceberg. While diluted pitching staffs thanks to expansion have always resulted in more offense and higher home run totals, pharmaceuticals represented a completely unacceptable means of padding statistics. And many of the players who had such bolstered home run numbers have come under scrutiny because of the Mitchell Report, which brought to light many instances of players using performance-enhancing drugs.

In the American League in 1998, the power surge was not nearly as pronounced as in the Senior Circuit, but some names would be bandied about concerning allegations. In 1998 Ken Griffey Jr., an old-time warrior who has never been accused of anything other than playing like a Hall of Famer, led the league with 56 home runs, followed by Albert Belle with 49, Jose Canseco with 46, and Manny Ramirez and Juan Gonzalez, both tied with 45.

The previous year, Griffey had also led the league with 56 home runs, followed by Tino Martinez with 44, Gonzales with 42, and Jim Thome and Jay Buhner, who tied with 40.

Home runs increased from 2,477 in 1997 to 2,499 in 1998. Batting averages remained constant at .271, and runs increased from 11,164 to 11,385. And pitchers' ERAs went from 4.56 to 4.65. Clearly, artificial enhancements were not as widespread in the American League at this time. But that dark and dastardly part of the game was gaining momentum and would not be stopped for years.

While the subject of performance-enhancing drugs has to be considered with any discussion of the game in the last decade, it is not a major part of the discussion of how offensive production has always spiked when new teams enter the leagues. Pitching is affected, particularly the depth on a pitching staff. While some feel that the lessening of talent is only felt at the back of the rotation and the back of the staff, others are certain that as many as half of the pitchers on most big league staffs are not what would have been considered Major League pitchers a generation ago.

There are other theories as well. While a high tide raises all boats, a low tide has the opposite effect. Asher B. Chancey wrote on June 28, 2008, an interesting article on BaseballEvolution.com titled "Expansion Dilutes Hitting?" His article is in response to theories by respected baseball man Bill James:

> I'm working on a theory that has resulted from dwelling for too long on Bill James' insistence that expansion does not dilute pitching any more than it does hitting.

If this is true (and it makes logical sense, but I've always thought the empirical evidence seems to say otherwise), then there must be some other explanation for the performances of Roger Maris and Mickey Mantle in 1961, Harmon Killebrew and Willie McCovey in 1969, George Foster in 1977, and Mark McGwire and Sammy Sosa in 1998. It simply can't be denied that there have been many noteworthy individual season accomplishments in expansion years which happened to coincide with expansion.

But maybe this is the key—maybe expansion dilutes hitting and pitching equally, so the leagues as a whole don't improve significantly on offense, because the dilution of hitting and pitching is balanced. But the individual hitters improve, because the pitchers they are facing have been diluted. Thus, while the National League as a whole would not expect too many more runs per game in 1977 than in 1976 (which for the record they did do, since scoring jumped from 3.98 in 1976 to 4.40 in 1977), because the bad hitters brought in expansion counter-balance the bad pitchers. George Foster individually could be expected to hit more home runs that the year before because of the decline of the overall pitching talent he is facing.

But then Chancey takes control of the discussion by logically considering how pitching should have been affected if this thought of equal dilution were true. "It occurs to me," he wrote, "that expansion must impact the caliber of play in every facet, meaning diluted pitching, diluted hitting and diluted fielding. Two of these things favor increased run production, one of these things favors decreased run production. Maybe this explains the thing Bill James is trying to deny. But do you know what that means? It means the same would be true for the pitchers. While pitching would not improve as a whole, individual pitchers would improve because they were facing a diluted pool of hitters. But that did not happen."

While it certainly had nothing to do the expansions of 1961, 1962, and 1969, another reason for more offensive firepower in the game was the advent of the designated hitter, which came into being in the American League in 1973. What the DH does is allow American League teams to have nine hitters in a lineup, as opposed to the National League, which has eight plus the pitcher, who is most often a weak hitter.

During All-Star games and World Series games held in the American League city, it's almost like the Junior Circuit is the existing team and the National League is the expansion team. Within the first five years of the DH rule, the American League surpassed the National League in categories such as runs batted in, slugging percentage, and base hits.

The American League All-Stars have been victorious thirteen times in the past seventeen, with three losses and one tie. Coupled with new expansion teams, American League teams now play a different game than their National League counterparts. And at the end of the day there are quantities of less qualified pitchers throwing to nine hitters in a lineup rather than eight plus the pitcher.

While the DH has added much offense to the American League, along with expansion and the dilution of pitching depth, not all baseball people have come around to appreciate the designated hitter.

Baseball broadcaster extraordinaire Bob Costas states in a column for *USA Today*, "The loss of strategy and the over-emphasis on power at the expense of some of the game's subtleties is simply too great a price to pay for the advantages of the DH."

As Dean Christopher J. Smith concluded in his paper "Baseball's Designated Hitter: History of and Concerns Regarding the DH Position in Baseball," "Well, in the era which the game was deemed 'America's sport,' there was no designated hitter, not to mention the game's greatest hitter, Babe Ruth, entered the league as a pitcher. Who said pitchers couldn't hit?"

In a game where good pitchers seem to be more and more difficult to find to fill out Major League pitching staffs, the question since the advent of expansion might well be, "Who said pitchers can pitch?"

12 | The Characters of Expansion Who Have Brightened the Game

It's not just the game of baseball that has captured the hearts and minds of millions and millions of fans over the years. The symmetry of the game, the orderliness, the strategy, the simplicity that is often based in complexity, and the wonderful pace of the game are undeniable. Baseball represents a rebirth every year among Grapefruits and Cactuses in spring training. While much of the country is still immersed in frigid temperatures and snow, the rites of spring always represent a fresh start. Heating up early in the season, with the dog days of summer often separating the men from the boys and finally reaching a loud crescendo in the fall as the return of a chill in the air often is like a crisp smack in the face to the hopes of some teams that just aren't quite there yet.

These are all just some of the marvelous things that make baseball the greatest sport ever created. It's a generational game that is handed down from parents to children time and again and can often act as a bridge to help bring people back together. Hey, who can't bury the sword long enough or look past an issue for a few hours to enjoy a ball game together?

Another part of the undeniable charm of the game is that we can relate to the players on the field. No, not the spoiled multimillionaires who act out, get arrested, beat their wives, smack their girlfriend's father around, speed, drink too much, abuse drugs, or abuse the game through the use of performance-enhancing drugs and supplements. At the end of the day, they are a small minority, a blemish on an otherwise beautiful face.

We can relate to the players because we've done what they do. We've felt that knot in our stomach while pitching in a game against another school, or a neighborhood friend in a tight situation that a big leaguer feels in a similar situation on a far different playing field. Who hasn't said a secret little prayer that we will not swing at that stinking off-speed pitch that ends up out of the strike zone? It's the same way in the Major Leagues. You know better but just can't help yourself. And while there are times you actually dare the hitter to hit the ball to you, there are also times when you hope it will be hit anywhere but at you, whether on a sandlot field or a big league field of dreams.

So we can relate to the players on the field because we've all been there. At some point in our lives, we've been able to do exactly what they do, just not nearly as well or consistently. Hey, even a horrible golfer can get off a half dozen shots during a round of golf that are just perfect. But it's all about consistency. You can put a lesser player out at second base who might surprise everyone including himself by making a great play, diving, rolling, and throwing a base runner out by half a step. But it's the ability make routine play after routing play that makes you a pro.

A lot of people go about their lives and perform their jobs and tasks in a satisfactory manner. They don't cause any problems and don't draw any attention to themselves. It's the same with baseball. Most guys are just happy to be in the Major Leagues and just trying to stay beneath the radar, or in the truest Satchel Paige tradition, not turn around for fear that other players could be catching up to them.

But then there are the other kind of people. No matter how profi-

cient they may or may not be at what they do, you know that they are
there. Make no mistake. They are louder, funnier, and sometimes more
annoying than the rest of the office combined. And it's the same way
with a sports team.

Baseball has always had its characters. There was Babe Ruth, Dizzy
Dean, Yogi Berra, Satch, Jim Bouton, Dennis "Oil Can" Boyd, Bill
"Spaceman" Lee, Bob Uecker, Jay Johnstone, Larry Andersen, Mark
"The Bird" Fidrych, and the old master, Casey Stengel.

So much has happened to America's Game since it expanded for
the first time back in 1961. Since we're a society of that appreciates
characters, here is a compilation of some of the true characters of the
expansion era. While some of them were around before expansion,
such as Richie Ashburn and Casey Stengel, they continued to make
their mark as the game grew. Some of the characters of expansion are
household baseball names, but many are not.

Bo Belinsky

Bo Belinsky was ahead of his time. Being the trend-setter was an honor,
but perhaps if he had seen how someone else did it, Bo might have
had a longer, more successful career. But make no mistake, Robert
"Bo" Belinsky was a playboy athlete in the truest sense. He was also a
left-handed pitcher in the truest sense, possessing good stuff and a
screwball, which was difficult to hit. Had he followed the likes of a
Joe Namath who combined carousing and athletic achievement well,
Belinsky might be more of a household name. But to those who knew
him, he was a legend.

He accumulated a 28-51 record with a 4.10 ERA in the 1960s, pitching for the Los Angeles Angels (1962–64), the Philadelphia Phillies
(1965–66), the Houston Astros (1967), the Pittsburgh Pirates (1969),
and the Cincinnati Reds (1970). But while he won just twenty-eight
big league games, he may have led the game in other conquests, dating the likes of Hollywood starlets Ann-Margaret, Mamie Van Doren,
Tina Louise, and Connie Stevens. He was married to a *Playboy* Play-

mate in Jo Collins and an heiress, Janie Weyerhaeusen. As his teammates would say, Bo showed up late reeking of bitch and booze.

Looking more like a Latin lover than a kid born in New York and
raised in Trenton, New Jersey, by a Polish American Catholic father
and a Jewish American mother. He was a streetwise kid in Trenton,
where he also became a pool hustler. But baseball was his ticket to the
big time.

"I remember when he brought Mamie Van Doren to spring training," said Stan Hochman. "Mamie was just spectacular, and Bo told
us she was there as his physical conditioning coach. He was not the
greatest pitcher, but he was a charming guy."

As a rookie with the Angels, he won his first five games in 1962.
But it was his fourth victory, on May 5, 1962, to set him apart. Belinsky tossed a no-hit, no-run game against the Baltimore Orioles, the
team that let him go to the Angels. He threw the gem at Dodger Stadium, and it was the first no-hitter thrown at the venue and the first
in Angels history.

"Bo was in the Orioles organization, and I met him in winter ball,"
said his teammate and good friend Dean Chance. "He was a good
left-handed pitcher who could turn the ball over like a change-up
screw ball. If anybody was fit for Hollywood it was him. They should
have his name on the Walk of Fame."

Belinsky's no-hitter was the first of eight thrown by Jewish pitchers from 1962 to 1971. Sandy Koufax threw four, Ken Holtzman threw
two, and Joe Horlen threw one.

"If I'd known I was gonna pitch a no-hitter," Belinsky said after the
game, "I would have gotten a haircut."

Ironically, just a little more than a month later, he was on the losing end in the first no-hitter thrown against the Angels by Boston's Earl
Wilson, on June 26 at Fenway Park. Wilson also homered in that game.

After a 7-1 start, Belinsky finished the season with a 10-11 record
with a 3.56 ERA. He was as wild on the field as he was off, leading the
American League with 122 walks.

But Bo was the toast of the town. And the stories are limitless and never get old.

According to Pat Jordan's account in "Authentic: Pat Jordan Recalls Bo Belinsky: A Modern-Day Athlete from A Bygone Era," Bo had climbed out of the hotel room where the Angels were staying after bed check and partied with actress Ann-Margaret until 5 a.m. When his taxi pulled up to the hotel, he discovered that the building was on fire. All of his teammates and the manager were on the sidewalk in their pajamas. Bo was sent to the Minor Leagues the next day.

He was able to continue building his image there as well. It's often said that pitchers can cause their managers to have a heart attack, in the figurative sense. But Belinsky and two other wild and crazy left-handed pitchers, Steve Dalkowski and Steve Barber, actually gave one of their managers a coronary in the Minor Leagues.

It must have seemed that nearly every night the poor skipper would get a call from the local police chief asking him to come down to the jail and bail out one or more of his trio of hard-throwing and hard-living southpaws. One night they had an idea. So at 3 a.m., impersonating the police chief, they told the manager that they had a baseball player on a slab in the morgue. Upon hearing the news, their manager had a heart attack. Thankfully, he survived.

Bo was just 2-9 for the Angels in 1963, then 9-8 the following season. On December 3, 1964, he was dealt to the Phillies in exchange for pitcher Rudy May and first baseman Costen Shockley. He was able to win four games for the '65 Phillies and three for the '67 Astros before finishing up with the Reds for three games in 1970.

Following his career, Belinsky's life took a different turn. He overcame alcoholism to become a counselor and spokesman for the alcohol abuse program he entered in Hawaii. Later, as an auto agency representative living in Las Vegas, he was clean, sober and a born-again Christian.

He even intervened with one of his former Angels teammates, pitcher Eli Grba, who was trying to overcome alcoholism. Belinsky drove to Grba's Yorba Linda home in 1980 and took charge.

"Bo and I had never been that close, like best friends or anything," Grba said. "He was too Hollywood. But he came and took me to an Alcoholics Anonymous meeting. I was really nervous but Bo just told me, 'Don't worry Eli. They're all drunks just like you and me.'"

Happily, Grba has been sober ever since.

After battling bladder cancer Bo Belinsky passed away of a heart attack at the age of sixty-four on November 23, 2001. He was a wild man who never lived up to his potential as a ball player, but no one can ever say he didn't grow into a remarkable person.

Rick Bosetti

This speedy, right-handed-hitting outfielder from Redding, California, made his Major League debut in 1976 with the Philadelphia Phillies. He was later sent to St. Louis in a trade with the Cardinals and eventually wound of patrolling center field for the Toronto Blue Jays starting in 1978. He led all American League outfielders in putouts that year, and then in 1979 led the league in games played and topped the list of outfielder putouts and assists.

While he was an above-average fielder, he was not an impact player at the plate, but he hit a respectable .259 for the 1978 season in Toronto and .260 in 1979. A broken arm early in the 1980 season cost him playing time, and he was never a regular performer again during his seven-year career. But that's not to say that the likable Bosetti didn't leave his mark on the game.

While still in the Phillies' Minor League system, Bosetti took part in an age-old tradition that resulted in one of his buddies having an atrocious Major League debut.

Bosetti and some of his Triple-A teammates found out that one of the team's pitchers was being called up to the Major Leagues. As has always been the case since the early days of the game, teammates treated their Major League–bound friend to a night of heavy drinking and partying before he left in the morning to begin his big league career.

They didn't let the tradition down, and party they did. Their teammate was absolutely snookered and feeling the awful effects of his last night in the Minors as he flew to meet his big league team. In spite of how bad he felt, the pitcher realized that he wouldn't be used that night. So he could regain his health. But the baseball gods interfered.

The game got out of hand, and the opposition had built a big lead early on. It was decided that it was a great no-pressure situation to give a young guy his first appearance in the Majors, forcing this twenty-year-old to attempt to gather himself and enter the game. The pitcher will not be identified to protect his youthful exuberance, but his line for that first appearance is as follows:

⅓ IP   4 H   6 R   6 ER   2 W   I K   162.00 ERA

Years later Bosetti still chuckled at his involvement in the situation. It should also be mentioned that the young pitcher rebounded from this inglorious debut and had a very successful Major League career. But that is not the only example of Rick Bosetti leaving his mark on the game.

While preparing for a Triple-A game in the outfield at Oklahoma City, he needed to relieve himself. Fans had not yet arrived at the park, and a teammate suggested just peeing in the outfield rather than trek all the way back to the clubhouse. It seemed like a good idea at the time, and Bosetti did just that.

He continued this unique tradition in the Minor Leagues, and at the start of his Major League career. Bosetti began to break in every big league park and made each uniquely his. He was able to urinate in every American League outfield. He also left his mark on numerous National League parks, but as he appeared in just thirteen games with the 1976 Phillies and forty-one games with the 1977 Cardinals, he was unable to complete a sweep of all big league parks. His National League "stats" might be akin to winning the batting title but not having enough at-bats to qualify.

"All the publicity started when Rick Cerone mentioned me in a magazine article about flakes of the game," Bosetti said. "It got blown all out of proportion, and people would watch to see if they could catch me. I never did it during a game. Hey, I was twenty-four years old and it was all fun."

Following his playing career, Bosetti got involved in the technology field. He is now the coach of the Simpson University Red Hawks baseball team and was elected to the Redding, California, City Council in 2006. He has also served as mayor.

There is no information available as to whether he has continued his hobby of marking municipal meetings.

Jim Bouton

There are plenty of New York Yankees fans as well as American League fans of the early to mid-1960s who remember Jim Bouton as the crew-cut, hard-throwing right-hander. His wind up and delivery were so violent that after nearly every pitch he threw, his ball cap flew off of his head. He was hardcore, so much so that his intensity on the pitching mound earned him the nickname, "Bulldog."

After breaking in with the Yankees with a 7-7 mark in 1962, he followed with a 21-7 season in 1963 and an 18-13 mark in 1964. But arm injuries befell him, and between 1965 and 1968 he was 9-24. The sore-armed hurler returned to the Minor Leagues and learned a new pitch that was to revitalize his career, the knuckleball.

Had the Seattle Pilots not purchased Bouton's contract on October 21, 1968, from the Yankees, that one wretched season in Seattle certainly would have not gained the notoriety it has over the years. Bouton was writing a book titled *Ball Four*, which would chronicle the 1969 baseball season. But unlike other books about America's Pastime, this was a tell-all book that gave a great description about how athletes play the game and prepare for the game. But it also named names and dealt with subjects such as womanizing, voyeurism, drinking, partying, drug use, and other aspects of the game that had never been published in such a way before.

In addition to his diary-like entrees, Bouton's discussions about the years he spent with the Yankees was particularly harmful to relationships he had with former teammates such as Mickey Mantle, from whom he was estranged for many years after publication of the book. A number of former teammates and coaches ostracized him for the book, and he was largely ignored by the game for a number of years.

But at the same time it gave fans a view of just how much fun baseball players have and also an idea of just how human players are.

"That book changed things in that nothing was sacred anymore," said Stan Hochman. "He'd talk about peeping toms, orgies, drunkenness. There was nothing really terrible about what he wrote; it's just that it was very revealing. He violated that rule about things staying in the clubhouse. But it was very well written and I was impressed with it."

So were millions of fans who took a more active interest in the game thanks to his book. It was just plain, good, old fun in the same vein as the movie *Animal House*.

His season in Seattle was not bad on the field. Bouton appeared in 57 games for the Pilots and was 2-1 with a 3.91 ERA in 92 innings pitched. His late-season trade to Houston saw him join the Astros and appear in 16 more games, going 0-2 with a 4.11 ERA.

In 1970 Bouton was not as effective as his 4-6 record and 5.40 ERA, a career high, would indicate. Nearly a year after being acquired by Houston, he was released by the Astros on August 12, 1970. While his career seemed over, nearly a decade later, Jim Bouton had a surprise for everyone—a comeback.

At the age of thirty-nine in 1978, he decided to scratch the big league itch one more time. His quest to return to the game had actually happened three years earlier, when he pitched for the Class A Portland Mavericks and had a 5-1 record. A foiled TV series followed in 1976, but 1977 saw him back on the mound, sharing time between a stint in the Chicago White Sox system, the Mexican League, and a return engagement with Portland.

Impressed with Bouton's desire and never shying away from a publicity stunt, Atlanta Braves owner Ted Turner signed Bouton to a contract in 1978, and after a successful stint with the Braves' Double-A affiliate in Savannah, Jim Bouton returned to the Major Leagues in September of that year. He posted a 1-3 record in 5 starts with a 4.97 ERA.

As his big league career finally ended, old No. 56 continued to play semipro baseball in Northern New Jersey with the Teaneck Merchants.

Bouton is one of the inventors of "Big League Chew," a bubble gum product that resembles chewing tobacco. And he has continued to write, making updates to his most famous and infamous work, *Ball Four*. In addition, he penned *I'm Glad You Didn't Take It Personally*, *I Managed Good but Boy Did They Play Bad*, and *Foul Ball*.

Richie Ashburn

Here was a guy who was involved in many aspects of the game of baseball and did them all at a Hall of Fame level. As the spark plug of the 1950 National League champion Philadelphia Phillies, affectionately known as the Whiz Kids, "Whitey" Ashburn began a lifelong love affair with the city of Philadelphia.

He was an All-Star performer in center field who saw some pretty good players at his position overshadow him during his career. Willie Mays, Duke Snider, and Mickey Mantle, all power hitters, also probably delayed Ashburn's induction into the Baseball Hall of Fame, since he was a pesky singles hitter who always hit .300.

Following his playing career he became an announcer for the Phillies and later a columnist for the *Philadelphia Bulletin* and the *Philadelphia Daily News*. Always willing to share his different way of looking at life and looking at baseball, Richie Ashburn was the toast of the town.

"Right down the middle for a ball," he would comment when an umpire missed an obvious strike. When a player would take a called third strike, fans would often imitate his cry of, "Froze 'em, Harry!"

His Mets teammate in 1962, pitcher Jay Hook, relates an interesting story about Ashburn, who had begun his career as a catcher. "Whitey" knew the game and he knew that he knew the game.

"I was pitching a game that we won," said Hook. "I had pitched well and Richie comes up to me after the game and says, 'How'd you like the game I called?' He had spoken to Chris Cannizzaro, our catcher, and told him that he wanted to call the pitches in the game. So Richie and Chris worked out a set of signals from center field to the catcher. Turns out that he called every pitch of the game from center field. It really went well. I wish he'd have kept calling them."

There was also another interesting, albeit painful story that happened during that 120-loss season of 1962. Ashburn was a speedy, dependable outfielder. The Mets had a young shortstop, Elio Chacon, who was from Venezuela, who made twenty-two errors that season and kept getting in Ashburn's way. It seemed as if every time a ball was hit to left-center field, Ashburn would yell, "I got it! I got it!" But the 160-pound Chacon, who was also trying to catch the ball, would run into him, often causing the ball to fall in for a hit.

Finally, they figured out the problem. Chacon didn't speak any English and therefore didn't realize that Ashburn was calling him off the ball.

Ever the innovator and never too old to learn something new, the thirty-five-year-old Ashburn learned how to say "I got it" in Spanish—"Yo la tengo." Now that they had solved the language barrier, Ashburn assumed that nothing else could go wrong.

The next time a ball was hit between Chacon and him, Ashburn yelled, "Yo la tengo! Yo la tengo!" To his delight and relief, he saw Chacon back off. He relaxed, settled under the ball, and was ready to make the catch. But then he was run over by 200-pound left fielder Frank Thomas, who spoke no Spanish.

Ashburn was known for his disdain of pitchers. He didn't trust them and considered them cheaters and much worse, as is evidenced by the following quote from *Richie Ashburn Remembered*, by Fran Zimniuch: "After 15 years of facing [pitchers], you don't really get over them," he said. "They're devious. They're the only players in the game allowed to cheat. They throw illegal pitches, and they sneak foreign substances on the ball. They can inflict pain whenever they wish. And they're the only ones on the diamond who have high ground. That's symbolic. You know what they tell you in war—'Take the high ground first.'"

Many of his sayings are still used with regularity in Philadelphia, such as, "He looks a little runnerish," describing a base runner who is about to attempt a stolen base. "Boys, the game looks a whole lot easier from up here," he'd say of the broadcasting booth.

That Ashburn wit and sense of humor had rookie announcer Tim McCarver in shock and at a loss for words during a game in 1980. Injured Phillies pitcher Larry Christenson had gone home to Washington shortly after the eruption of Mount St. Helens and brought back some volcanic ash for his friends to see. While on the air working with Ashburn, McCarver began discussing the descriptive properties of the ash and how the ash taken from where the explosion had taken place was fine, like dust, while the ash from the other side was coarser.

McCarver turned to Ashburn for his response. Without batting an eye, Ashburn stated, "I think if you've seen one piece of ash, you've seen them all."

While he had a disarming personality and was completely entertaining whether in the broadcasting booth or just chatting with fans on the street, Richie Ashburn was a total professional on the baseball field.

"He was the most competitive player I ever played with," said his late teammate with the Mets, Rod Kanehl. "When he put his uniform on, he was all business. Even with the Mets in 1962, his last year, he just went out there every day and ran every ball out. He even hit .300."

Casey Stengel

"The Old Professor," as he was known, spent decades in the game. As a rather nondescript player, Casey hit .284 from 1912 to 1925 for Brooklyn, Pittsburgh, the Philadelphia Phillies, and the Boston Braves. But it was as a manager that he made his ultimate mark on the game.

He managed the Brooklyn Dodgers from 1934 to 1936, the Boston Braves from 1938 to 1943, the New York Yankees from 1949 to 1960, and the Amazin' New York Mets from 1962 to 1965. With a career record of 1,905-1,842 in 3,761 games, his managerial ability was plain to see. But his years with the Yankees saw him win ten pennants and seven World Series (1949, 1950, 1951, 1952, 1953, 1956, and 1958). His tenure in pinstripes ended with a record of 1,149-696 in his twelve years as skipper.

But Stengel, while certainly respected by baseball people for his contributions to the game, has become a legendary character for the way in which he did it. Suffice to say that Casey Stengel had a unique way of looking at things.

"Being with a woman all night never hurt no professional baseball player," he said. "It's staying up all night looking for a woman that does him in."

A left-hander, he had a good perspective of what southpaws are all about.

"Left-handers have more enthusiasm for life," he said. "They sleep on the wrong side of the bed and their head gets more stagnant on that side."

Obviously as a successful manager who won seven World Series titles, the man was a great judge of talent. What follows is a comment that Stengel made about a pair of twenty-year-old rookies, Ed Kranepool and Greg Goossen, with the New York Mets in 1965. It is oft quoted and for good reason.

"You see that fellow over there," he said, referring to Kranepool. "He's twenty years old and in ten years, he has a chance to be a star. Now, that other fellow over there," referring to Goossen, "he's twenty too. In ten years, he has a chance to be thirty."

Stengel's predictions were not far off. While he was never a star, Kranepool has a solid eighteen-year Major League career. And ten years later, Greg Goossen turned thirty.

Casey had such an impact on the game that his language and sayings even have a name, Stengelese, which is used to describe his vocabulary and implausible double talk.

Garnering an understanding of what he was truly saying took time and experience. Some of his sayings included: butcher boy (a chopped ground ball); embalmed (sleeping); green pea (a rookie); plumber (a good fielder); road apple (a bum); whiskey slick (a playboy); he could squeeze your ear brows off (a tough player); and hold the gun (I want to change pitchers). Hard to believe that people would walk away from a chat with Stengel wondering what he was talking about.

"Casey was the right guy at the right time for the Mets," said former Mets pitcher Jay Hook.

> We were a below-average team, but he had the New York market, and what he did was realize that his customers were the writers of New York. Through them he stimulated an interest in baseball and in the New York Mets. After a game, Casey would tell the writers to grab a beer and come into his office. He made the jobs of the writers easier because he gave them material to write about.
>
> He was also very conscious of the fans, the end customers. He was trying to make the job of the writer easier so that more fans got interested in the New York Mets. What you learned is to be really sensitive to your customer base.

He was also genuinely funny. He once told his players to line up alphabetically, according to their height. And then there was the time while still with the Yankees, when he approached outfielder Bob Cerv.

"Nobody knows this yet," Stengel said. "But one of us has just been traded to Kansas City."

Reporters loved him and quoted him regularly, if not always accurately.

"A lot of the New York guys loved to invent things that Stengel may or may not have said," said Stan Hochman. "He was just a funny old codger with an interesting way of speaking. It wasn't so much doubletalk, but you had to really pay attention to what he was saying.

He called the New York writers 'my writers,' and he made sure that they were informed and never scooped. He was a celebrity."

He was a showman and a comic and a great ambassador for the game. It was his personality that made the Mets lovable losers during his tenure at Shea Stadium. He knew the game inside and out and lived the game throughout his entire life. But make no mistake—Casey Stengel was first and foremost an excellent manager. He played a hunch every now and then that didn't work out, but he is a member of the Baseball Hall of Fame, and that's not because he was a comic and showman. He was an incredible baseball man.

"If we're going to win the pennant," he once said, "then we've got to start thinking we're not as good as we think we are."

13 Baseball's Brave New World

Where We've Been and What the Future Holds

America's Game is certainly a different game than the baseball that your typical Baby Boomer grew up with. It's even different than what a person who discovered the game in the 1970s saw. The truth be known, it is a different sport than we saw at the turn of the century and new millennium. Much like life and society, baseball is in a constant state of change and transition.

In spite of it all, baseball is still a remarkably popular sport with more lives than a cat. It has survived the gambling scandals that reached their peak when the 1919 Chicago White Sox Scandal threw the World Series, forever earning the moniker of Black Sox. It survived the dead ball era, the tragic death of Ray Chapman, World War II when so many of its star players went off to serve their country, the insurgency from the Mexican League, the move of the Dodgers and Giants to California, the threat from the Continental League, Curt Flood, arbitration, the reserve clause, Messersmith and McNally, free agency, a ridiculous strike that canceled the World Series, and most recently, baseball's drug era. Our game is like a tipsy old actress who occasionally shows up at an event three sheets to the wind, acts out every now and then, but still has the hearts of her fans and will forever.

Of all the instances of baseball reflecting societal issues, it seems that none has been more flagrant than civil rights. Baseball and society were both long overdue in treating everyone equally and fairly. Hatred, racism, bigotry, and greed will always be a part of our lives, on and off baseball fields. But it's clear that while the game of baseball has failed as much as society as a whole, that it was America's Pastime that helped pave the way for the civil rights movement.

"Our country is floundering," said Justice George Nicholson, Court of Appeals, Third Appellate District, State of California, and a lifelong baseball fan.

> It has been for decades. In an attempt to outlaw discrimination, we have passed laws and regulations intruding into every aspect of American life, public and private. Even so, those laws do not motivate all our people, of all races, creeds and colors, to become family.
>
> The more the legal definition of discrimination has grown, the more discrimination is seen. There is even dispute on the seminal event that signaled the demise of Jim Crow. Seeking to specify any particular event in human history, especially a particular event in transformative human history may be difficult. Even so, we humans persist in trying to pinpoint such events. The challenge is to do so dispassionately, with integrity and humility.
>
> Timing is sometimes described as everything in baseball and human history. And timing can be of immense help in pinpointing a seminal event, in baseball and in life. Some people assert the role of Branch Rickey in bringing Jackie Robinson to the Brooklyn Dodgers in 1947 and thus, breaking baseball's color barrier was the key pivotal point in baseball and in the nation.
>
> Mr. Rickey was arguing with no one when he simply observed, "Baseball is the proving grounds for civil rights."

Clearly baseball was as guilty as society as a whole when it came to equal rights and for its unwillingness to allow black players into Major League Baseball. For years so many great players toiled in the Negro Leagues in relative obscurity. But the bold move by Branch Rickey, against the wishes of most of Major League Baseball to integrate the game, set an unstoppable force into motion in the country. Branch Rickey and Jackie Robinson were the original odd couple who changed baseball and very likely changed the complexion of an entire nation.

"Though it took him almost a half century to do so, Branch Rickey, solitarily, conceived and crafted a series of events as complex as a symphony, and harmoniously conducted a vast orchestra of people, stationed strategically in more than a dozen quite different cities," said Justice Nicholson. "He filled the previously discordant notes in the Declaration of Independence and the Gettysburg Address, 'All men are created equal,' and gave them resilience and resonance."

Baseball resisted with all its heart and soul and yet, baseball led the way with a purposefulness that would result in life altering effects on the game and on society. Baseball showed that people like Jackie Robinson were the same as everyone else. His skin may have been darker, but the passion with which he played the game of baseball and the undeniable restraint he showed in the face of adversity saw him win over Brooklyn fans and baseball fans across the nation. But his example also made it much easier for the civil rights movement, which was right on his heels. The game has its faults, but it also has its glorious moments in the sun, between the white lines and socially. And Jackie Robinson and Branch Rickey may have provided baseball's best day.

At the end of the day, baseball is truly America's Game, and the country will forgive it time and again. The game, those who play it, and some of the people who own the teams can anger you, frustrate you, and make you want to smack them upside the head and say, "Snap out of it," like Cher said to Nicholas Cage in the wonderful movie *Moonstruck*. But much like one of your children who always seems to get that one last chance, over and over again, so does America's Pastime. And while it never ceases to frustrate you on some level, it also never stops you from falling head over heels in love with it time and again each and every season.

No matter how long you've been a fan and followed your favorite team or teams, there is always the chance that today's game will result in you seeing something happening that you've never seen before, whether this is your first year as a fan or your fiftieth. You just never know what the game has in store just around the next corner.

Baseball can't match the single-day ratings and interest of Super Bowl Sunday. But America's Pastime is a marathon, while despite talk of a longer football regular season, that sport is more of a sprint. Baseball teams have changed cities, changed divisions, and even changed leagues. The game has been ripped by drug scandals, collusion, and countless other challenges, but it still continues to grow and change. And after all of these years of simultaneously embracing and resisting change in so many ways, there could be more changes on the way.

It could be argued that the designated hitter is an issue that needs to be addressed. Because of the way an American League roster has evolved due to the DH, there has been a competitive imbalance when the leagues meet up in interleague play. American League teams have dominated in the World Series as well as the All-Star games. The time may have come for baseball to unify in this case. The DH should either be abolished, or expanded to both leagues.

Watching a pitcher hit can be as painful for fans as it can be for the pitcher. But at the same time, most pitchers like to hit. They practice and take great pride in helping themselves in a game. A good pitcher is also a baseball player who can throw, field his position, hit, and run the bases. While there is much specialization in today's game of baseball, the basic abilities to do those things are what make up a ball player. But how will this play out?

"I hate that they have two sets of rules," said Stan Hochman. "I hope that sooner or later they agree on the rules."

He is not alone. But because of the tremendous power that the players' union wields, it seems inconceivable that the designated hitter would be abolished. That would result in DH types losing their jobs. If a player isn't capable of fielding a position, he can't play. There simply seems no way that the players will ever give up a single roster spot, be it for the good of the game or not.

So it could be that in the relatively near future both leagues will employ the DH. While it would add offense to the game and bring back more parity between the leagues, this move would represent the biggest change to the game on the field since the early days of the game when hitters were able to pick the location that they'd like pitchers to throw to. Purists would scoff at the idea, but a game with two completely different rules in each league simply does not work anymore.

"I'd like to see the game go back to where it was without the DH," said Bill Stoneman. "I think the National League had the better game and that's coming from me, who was a general manager in the American League. I like the strategy in the National League. A manager has to make a choice in tough situations. If you're down a run getting later in the game, do you pinch hit for a guy pitching a great game? I just like the game better without the DH."

Baseball tried to fix waning interest in its midsummer classic, the All-Star Game, by awarding the winning team with the home-field advantage in the World Series. So now instead of just trying to get as many players into the game as possible and keeping guys from getting hurt, now All-Star skippers have the added weight of their entire league's postseason on their shoulders.

While the game has become more important come World Series time, the truth is that the Home Run Hitting Contest the night before is a much more popular event. Television ratings have fallen as well. Clearly, giving a false sense of importance to the All-Star classic has not worked.

"I really worry about the All-Star Game deciding home-field advantage in the World Series," said Stan Hochman. "I'd rather see them decide home field on the best record. That could make it a little tougher for them travel-wise, as you wouldn't know for sure where the World Series was going to be played until a few days before, but that would be a better system. Or, you could just go back to alternating years. I think that interleague play has diluted the impact of the World Series because you've seen them before."

One thing that does work is postseason play, and there has been talk that the playoffs could be expanded. At this rate, the World Series could begin on Christmas Eve. Those who support the idea of a larger playoff pool of teams also seem to realize that the regular season might have to include fewer games, perhaps 144 rather than the current 162.

But that would create havoc with the numbers of baseball, the statistics that make it possible for fans of all ages and experience to enjoy the endless debate that such comparisons enable. Changing the number of regular season games would reinstitute the great debate of 1961 when Roger Maris broke Babe Ruth's single-season home run record but had an additional eight games to do so. Cutting the number of regular season games seems inconceivable on many fronts. It would also mean less revenue for teams who were not going to the playoffs, many of whom need that money to try to compete more on the field.

Another thought is to make earlier playoff rounds best of five, or maybe even best of three, with the thought that it would enable an additional pair of wild card teams. While that concept might work on paper, the thought of a division champion getting beat in a short series would not go over well. So there is obviously much work still to do on the subject of realignment and expanding the playoffs.

No one will ever fully know just how much steroids and performance-enhancing drugs have influenced the baseball record books in the past fifteen years. Changing the number of games played during the regular season would make it next to impossible to substantiate numerical discussions and comparisons. Is the specter of a larger postseason invitation list worth the effort? And is it correct to "dummy down" the playoffs even more with additional wild card teams? Anything can happen in a short series, and a team that has been at the top of its game and division through 162 games probably doesn't deserve staring an early playoff exit in the eye if a seemingly inferior team wins two out of three games to move on to the next level.

Part of this complicated picture is also that currently the National League has sixteen teams while the American League has fourteen. Having an equal number of teams in each league would lead to an easier path to the postseason. Would the National League consider closing, or constricting a pair of franchises? Never gonna happen. A reasonable answer to that question might be when Hell freezes over. The last time that issue was raised, Montreal moved to Washington by way of San Juan, and the Twins ultimately stayed in Minnesota.

Moving one team to the Junior Circuit would raise havoc with scheduling. Having an odd number of teams would make interleague play necessary all season long. Baseball purists are still suffering from heart palpitations over the limited interleague scheduling that we see in use now. That won't work. But there is a possible answer that could solve many of the issues lurking out there. Expansion.

While realignment has been the topic of many discussions within the game, coupling that with an expansion of two teams, bringing the total number of Major League teams to thirty-two, might be the answer. Despite the economy and the difficult times in society, baseball has prospered, with league-wide attendance in the 73 million range in 2010. Each league could have two eight-team divisions, with each having a wild card entry.

There are still some issues out there with existing franchises. Washington has still not proven it can support and sustain a team. Florida got a new stadium in 2012, but fan support there has been spotty. Oakland and Tampa Bay have both expressed frustration with their facilities. And for every team with even a modicum of unhappiness with its current situation, there are numerous cities out there trying to make them a Don Corleone offer that they simply can't refuse.

If an existing team would relocate to a different city, it would once again cause history to repeat itself with threats of antitrust legislation that would once again hold the game hostage and force any proposed expansion to include areas that have not worked in the past. Wait long enough and there's a pretty good chance that they will need to replace the Nationals in Washington.

While it is one of the loveliest cities in North America, Montreal would always be on a list of possible cities to expand to, even though the Expos franchise failed. Another Canadian prospect could be Vancouver.

Las Vegas has money and an interest in sports. But a big part of that interest is gambling, which could scare baseball away. The weather conditions there would also necessitate an enclosed stadium. Portland has been considered before and might be a safe bet. Other possibilities include Sacramento, San Antonio, Orlando, Nashville, Memphis, New Orleans, or possibly even Brooklyn. Talk about coming full circle.

But the thought of expansion has to be weighed against the reality of the new game of baseball. The financials have changed drastically over the last twenty years.

"I'd be surprised if baseball expanded," said Bill Stoneman.

Montreal? No way. Before you expand you have to first turn the system into one like they have in football or hockey. How do you field a club? What market could succeed? The revenues you'd need to be successful would be staggering.

For a league to work credibly and have fans that really look at what you are trying to do to be credible, your team has to have a shot. When you have teams that should be at the top and aren't and others that are surprised when they get to the top does not work for me. I am not a socialist or a communist at all, but for a league to work, every team has to have a shot. To me, adding a market that might be a helluva market, in a general sense, that still can't stand in with the Bostons, the Chicagos, the Philadelphias, the New Yorks and Los Angeleses, the answer is no.

If you could figure out a way to give everyone a shot, that would be great. It can't just be the team with the deepest pocket, but the guys who operate their franchise better should be rewarded. The National Football League is a whole lot closer to that. The National Hockey League has got it. In their last labor agreement, they wound up getting more from the players than they were asked to give. The NHL has the best parity of any sport. That's great, and that will help them moving forward.

I just don't see expanding as the answer. Hopefully, we'll get over the performance-enhancing drug stuff. We need to find a system that works even better than what we have now. It's not perfect, but better than what we had before.

Could baseball be ready to be an international sport with teams in areas other than North America? Some have bandied about the idea of a Japanese team, or possibly even a Japanese division. The success of the World Baseball Classic and the ever-increasing number of countries represented has shown that America's Pastime has interest far beyond our borders.

In January 2010 it was reported by *Nikkan Sports*, a Japanese daily sports newspaper, that the U.S. and Japanese baseball champions could meet in a global World Series. Nippon Professional Baseball commissioner Ryozo Kato said that he and Major League Baseball commissioner Bud Selig agreed that the winners of the two countries' professional leagues should meet.

When he took office in 2008, Kato said that one of his goals was an international series between baseball's two biggest nations. Selig reportedly told Kato that he would like to see the global World Series plan realized before his scheduled retirement in 2014.

Major League Baseball officials have been meeting with their counterparts from Nippon Professional Baseball, according to *Business Week*. Any global World Series could be affected by cold weather, Major League Baseball free agency, and competition from other sports.

"When you really get into the details of it, it's a difficult thing to see happening," said Jim Small, Major League Baseball's vice president for Asia. "But we will continue to do it. Not all those things are insurmountable, but they co create some issues."

Imagine: a true World Series. It boggles the mind. However, you get the feeling that one mind it would have fascinated would have been that of Branch Rickey.

Baseball has taken its fans on a panoramic journey since those days a generation ago that found New Yorkers reeling over the loss of both its National League clubs. Would anyone have thought back in 1958 that baseball in 2012 would be the game it is now, played in so many cities across North America? There is a good chance that the next fifty years might very well be as surprising as the last fifty have been.

It will be a great ride for those who will be around to enjoy it.

Play Ball!

Sources

Published Sources

Alito, Samuel, Jr. "The Origin of the Baseball Antitrust Exemption." *Baseball Research Journal* 38, no. 2 (Fall 2009): 86–93.

Angell, Roger. *Once More around the Park: A Baseball Reader*. New York: Ballantine Books, 1991.

Blake, Mike. *Baseball Chronicles: An Oral History of Baseball through the Decades*. Cincinnati: Betterway Books, 1994.

Bouton, Jim. *Ball Four, Plus Ball Five: An Update, 1970–1980*. New York: Stein and Day, 1981.

Chancey, Albert B. "Expansion Dilutes Hitting?" BasaeballEvolution.com, June 28, 2008, http://baseballevolution.com/asher/expansion.html.

D'Antonio, Michael. *Forever Blue: The True Story of Walter O'Malley, Baseball's Most Controversial Owner, and the Dodgers of Brooklyn and Los Angeles*. New York: Riverhead Books, 2009.

Drysdale, Don, with Bob Verdi. *Once a Bum, Always a Dodger: My Life in Baseball from Brooklyn to Los Angeles*. New York: St. Martin's Press, 1990.

Golenbock, Peter. *Amazin': The Miraculous History of New York's Most Beloved Baseball Team*. New York: St. Martin's Press, 2002.

Jordan, Pat. "Authentic: Pat Jordan Recalls Bo Belinsky: A Modern-Day Athlete from a Bygone Era." Deadspin, March 23, 2011, http://deadspin .com/5784828/pat-jordan-recalls-bo-belinsky-a-modern+day-athlete-from-a-bygone-era.

Kates, Maxwell. "A Brief History of the Washington Stars." In *The National Pastime. Monumental Baseball: The National Pastime in the National Capital Region*, edited by Bob Brown. Cleveland: Society for American Baseball Research, 2009.

Leventhal, Josh. *Take Me Out to the Ballpark: An Illustrated Tour of Baseball Parks Past and Present*. New York: Workman Publishing Company, 2000.

McGee, Bob. *The Greatest Ballpark Ever: Ebbets Field and the Story of the Brooklyn Dodgers*. New Brunswick NJ: Rivergate Books, 2005.

McNeil, William F. *The Dodgers Encyclopedia*. 2nd ed. Champagne IL: Sports Publishing, 2003.

Palmer, Pete, with Gary Gillette. *The 2005 ESPN Baseball Encyclopedia*. New York: Sterling Publishing, 2005.

Rader, Benjamin G. *Baseball: A History of America's Game*. Urbana: University of Illinois Press, 1992.

Reisner, Alex. "Baseball Geography and Transportation." *Baseball Research Journal* 35 (2007): 46–47.

Rosenbaum, Dave. *If They Don't Win It's a Shame: The Year the Marlins Bought the World Series*. Tampa: McGregor Publishing, 1998.

Shapiro, Michael. *Bottom of the Ninth: Branch Rickey, Casey Stengel, and the Daring Scheme to Save Baseball from Itself*. New York: Times Books / Henry Holt and Company, 2009.

———. *The Last Good Season: Brooklyn, the Dodgers, and Their Final Pennant Race Together*. New York: Doubleday, 2003.

Smith, Curt. *Pull Up a Chair: The Vin Scully Story*. Washington DC: Potomac Books, Inc., 2009.

Smith, Dean Christopher J. "Baseball's Designated Hitter: History of and Concerns Regarding the DH Position in Baseball." Baseball @ suite101, June 30, 2007, http://www.suite101.com/article/no-dh-a27479.

Snyder, Brad. *A Well-Paid Slave: Curt Flood's Fight for Free Agency in Professional Sports*. New York: Plume, 2007.

Thorn, John, and Pete Palmer. *Total Baseball: The Ultimate Encyclopedia of Baseball (Third Edition)*. New York: Harper-Perennial, 1989.

Vescey, George. *Baseball: A History of America's Favorite Game*. New York: Modern Library Books, 2006.

Zimmer, Don, with Bill Madden. *The Zen of Zim: Baseballs, Beanballs and Bosses*. New York: St. Martin's Paperbacks, 2004.

Zimniuch, Fran. *Fireman: The Evolution of the Closer in Baseball*. Chicago: Triumph Books, 2010.

———. *Going, Going, Gone! The Art of the Trade in Major League Baseball*. Lanham MD: Taylor Trade Publishing, 2008.

———. *Phillies: Where Have You Gone?* Champagne IL: Sports Publishing LLC, 2004.

———. *Richie Ashburn Remembered*. Champagne IL: Sports Publishing LLC, 2005.

———. *Shortened Seasons: The Untimely Deaths of Major League Baseball's Stars and Journeymen*. Lanham MD: Taylor Trade Publishing, 2007.

Interviews

Steve Arlin

Rick Bosetti

Jerrold Casway

Larry Colton

Bill Giles

Peter Golenbock

Stan Hochman

Ken Johnson

Tim McCarver

George Nicholson

John P. Rossi

Bill Stoneman

Dick Beverage

Bob Bruce

Dean Chance

Carl Erskine

Pat Gillick

Eli Grba

Jay Hook

Rod Kanehl

Bob McGee

Branch Rickey III

Tal Smith

Brad Snyder